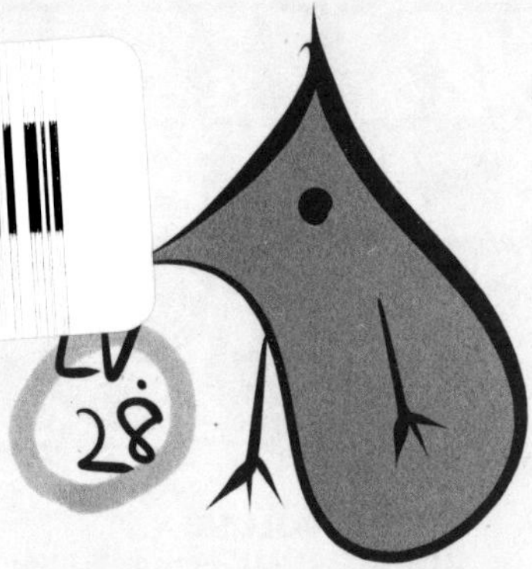
LV. 28

Hirofumi Neda

It's already volume 4. I guess I have to admit that anyone who's made it this far likes *Smash!!* To those of you who have put yourself in that category, I love ya lots!! Knowing that there are people out there who enjoy the series makes me that much more eager to keep creating it!!

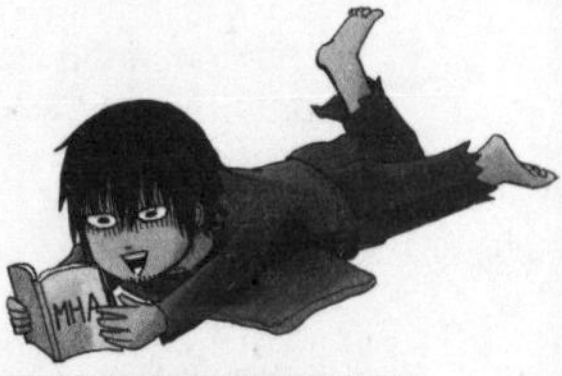
MHA

HIROFUMI NEDA began his professional career as a manga artist in 2007, winning the Akatsuka Prize Honorable Mention for his short story "Mom Is a Spy." After publishing several other short stories, he began working as an art assistant to Kohei Horikoshi on *Oumagadoki Zoo* and later on *My Hero Academia*.

KOHEI HORIKOSHI was born in Aichi, Japan, in 1986. He received a Tezuka Award Honorable Mention in 2006, and after publishing several short stories in *Akamaru Jump*, his first serialized work in *Weekly Shonen Jump* was *Oumagadoki Zoo* in 2010. *My Hero Academia* is his third series in *Weekly Shonen Jump*.

MY HERO ACADEMIA SMASH!!

VOLUME 4
SHONEN JUMP Manga Edition

STORY & ART BY HIROFUMI NEDA
ORIGINAL CONCEPT BY KOHEI HORIKOSHI

Translation/Caleb Cook
Touch-Up Art & Lettering/John Hunt
Designer/Julian [JR] Robinson
Editor/Hope Donovan

BOKU NO HERO ACADEMIA SMASH!!
© 2015 by Kohei Horikoshi, Hirofumi Neda
All rights reserved.
First published in Japan in 2015 by SHUEISHA Inc., Tokyo.
English translation rights arranged by SHUEISHA Inc.

The stories, characters and incidents mentioned in this publication
are entirely fictional.

Printed in the U.S.A.

Published by VIZ Media, LLC
P.O. Box 77010
San Francisco, CA 94107

10 9 8 7 6 5 4 3 2 1
First printing, May 2020

viz.com

shonenjump.com

PARENTAL ADVISORY
MY HERO ACADEMIA: SMASH!! is rated
T for Teen and is recommended for ages
13 and up. This volume contains fantasy
violence and crude/sexual humor.

MY HERO ACADEMIA SMASH!!

4

STORY & ART BY
HIROFUMI NEDA
ORIGINAL CONCEPT BY KOHEI HORIKOSHI

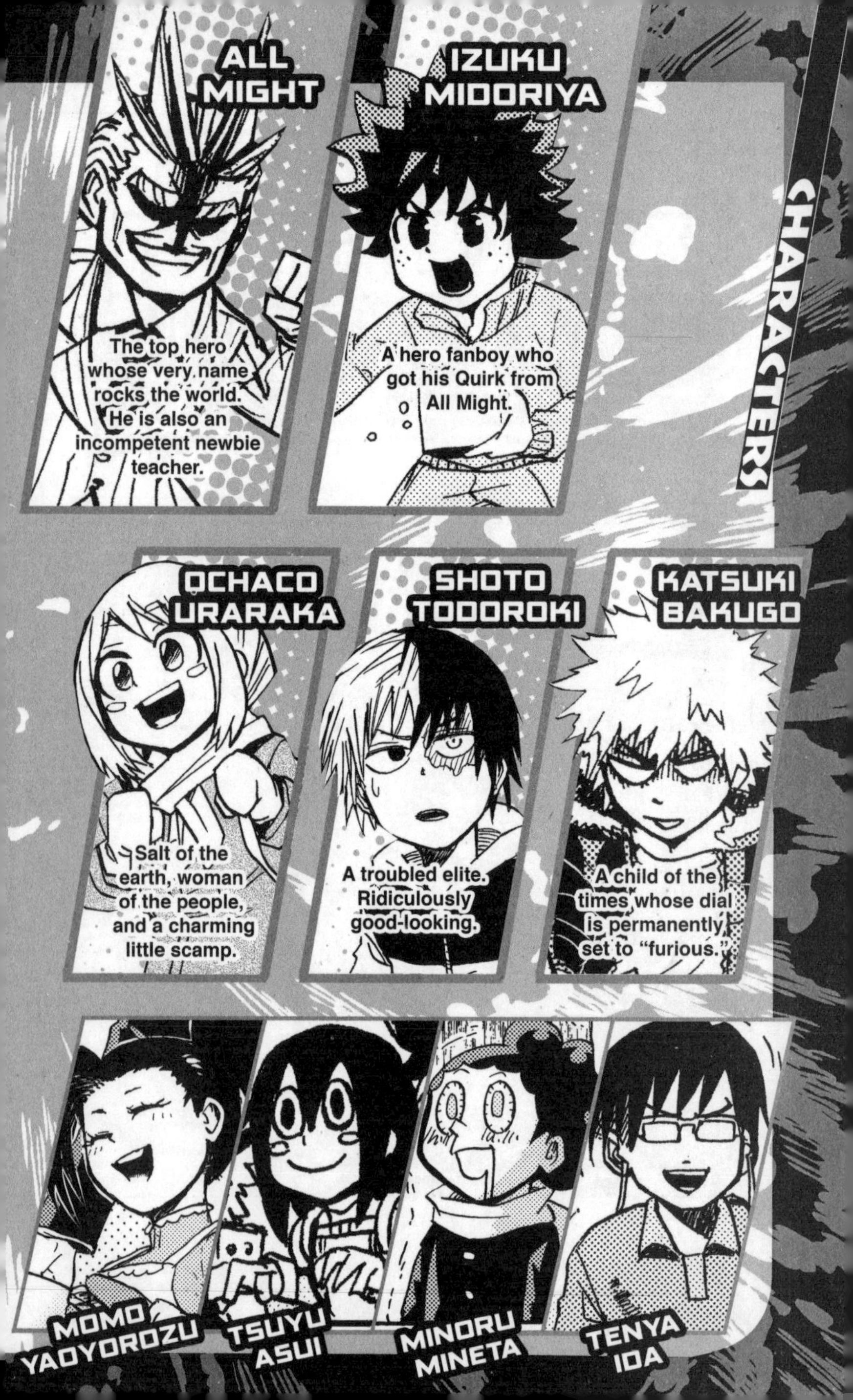
CHARACTERS
IZUKU MIDORIYA
A hero fanboy who got his Quirk from All Might.
ALL MIGHT
The top hero whose very name rocks the world. He is also an incompetent newbie teacher.
KATSUKI BAKUGO
A child of the times whose dial is permanently set to "furious."
SHOTO TODOROKI
A troubled elite. Ridiculously good-looking.
OCHACO URARAKA
Salt of the earth, woman of the people, and a charming little scamp.
TENYA IDA
MINORU MINETA
TSUYU ASUI
MOMO YAOYOROZU

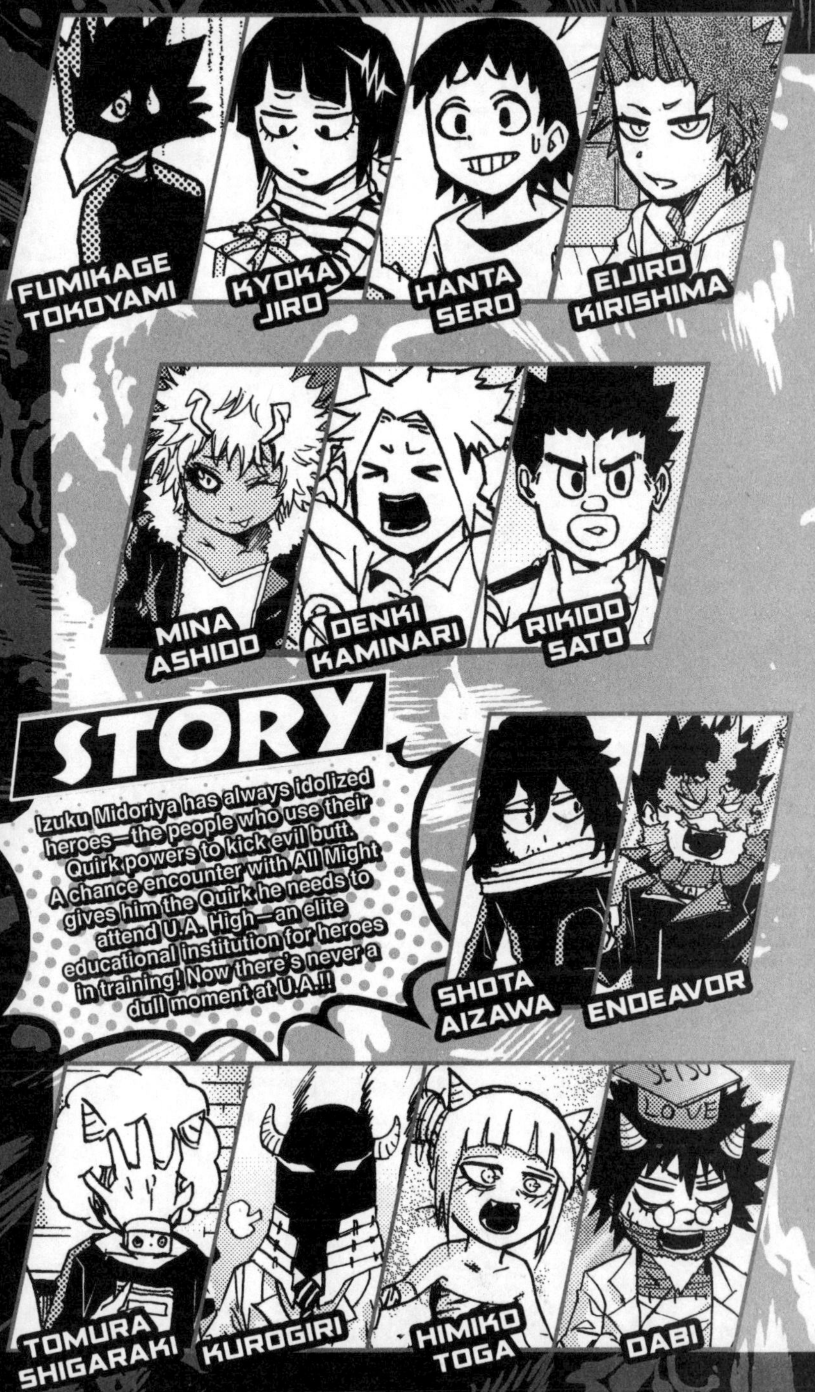
EIJIRO KIRISHIMA
HANTA SERO
KYOKA JIRO
FUMIKAGE TOKOYAMI
RIKIDO SATO
DENKI KAMINARI
MINA ASHIDO
ENDEAVOR
SHOTA AIZAWA
STORY
Izuku Midoriya has always idolized heroes—the people who use their Quirk powers to kick evil butt. A chance encounter with All Might gives him the Quirk he needs to attend U.A. High—an elite educational institution for heroes in training! Now there's never a dull moment at U.A.!!
DABI
SETSU LOVE
HIMIKO TOGA
KUROGIRI
TOMURA SHIGARAKI

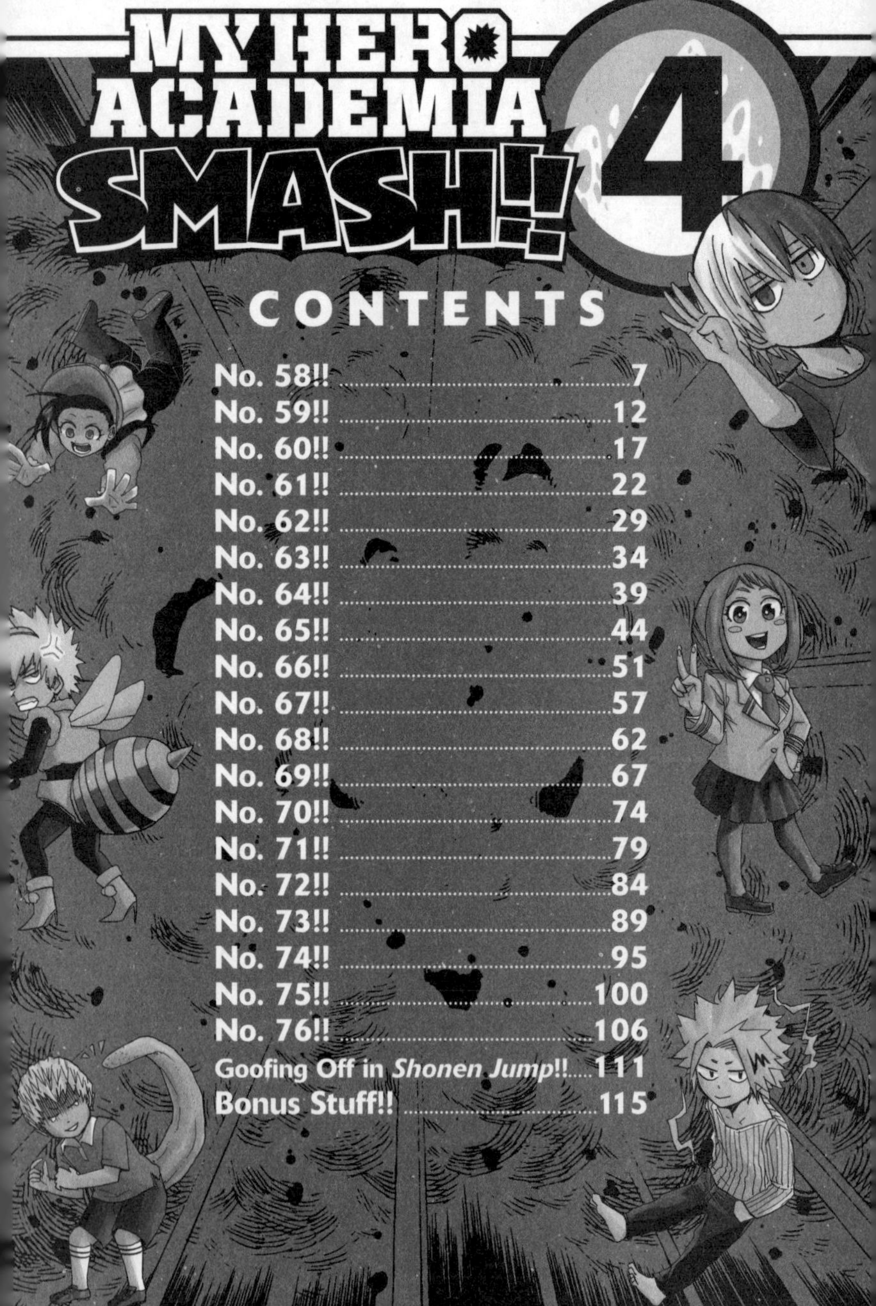

MY HERO ACADEMIA SMASH!! 4

CONTENTS

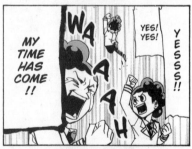

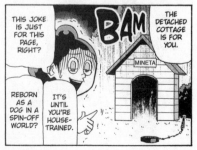

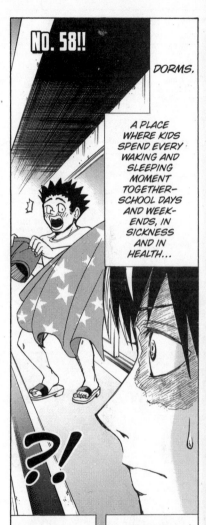

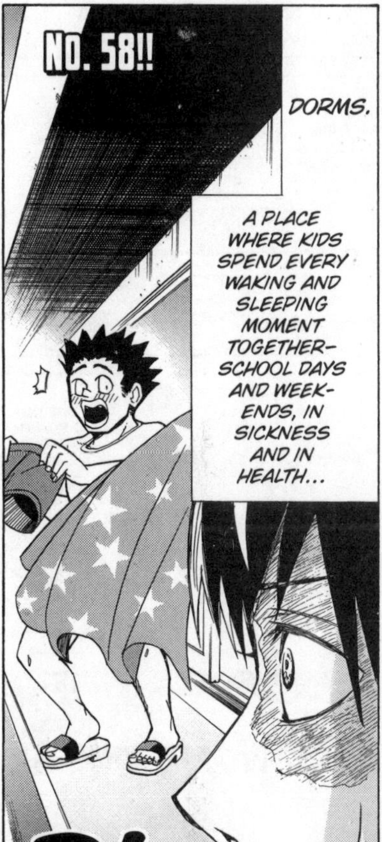
NO. 58!!
DORMS.
A PLACE WHERE KIDS SPEND EVERY WAKING AND SLEEPING MOMENT TOGETHER-SCHOOL DAYS AND WEEK-ENDS, IN SICKNESS AND IN HEALTH...
?!
WHETHER THEY LIKE IT OR NOT, THE PROTAGONISTS OF OUR STORY ARE NOW GETTING THE FULL BOARDING SCHOOL EXPERIENCE.
YES, EVEN THE ELITES OF THE HERO COURSE HAVE TO CONTEND WITH THIS DRASTIC CHANGE IN LIFESTYLE.

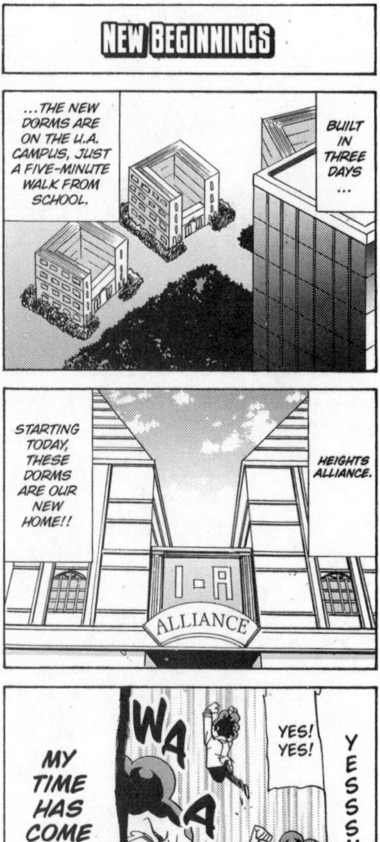
NEW BEGINNINGS
BUILT IN THREE DAYS ...
...THE NEW DORMS ARE ON THE U.A. CAMPUS, JUST A FIVE-MINUTE WALK FROM SCHOOL.
HEIGHTS ALLIANCE.
STARTING TODAY, THESE DORMS ARE OUR NEW HOME!!
1-A
ALLIANCE
YESSS!!
YES! YES!
WAAAAH
MY TIME HAS COME !!
THE DETACHED COTTAGE IS FOR YOU.
BAM
THIS JOKE IS JUST FOR THIS PAGE, RIGHT?
MINETA
IT'S UNTIL YOU'RE HOUSE-TRAINED.
REBORN AS A DOG IN A SPIN-OFF WORLD?

FI-DO OR DIE TRYING

SPEND THE REST OF TODAY GETTING ALL MOVED IN.

OKAY!!

THESE ARE YOUR ROOM ASSIGNMENTS.

3 F			
KODA		JIRO	
KAMINARI			
IDA			
OJIRO		HAGAKURE	

2 F			
		MIDORIYA	
AOYAMA			
TOKOYAMI			

5 F			
		YAOYOROZU	
SATO			
TODOROKI			
SERO		ASUI	

4 F			
SHOJI		URARAKA	
KIRISHIMA			
BAKUGO			
		ASHIDO	

MINETA

ALL OF US LIVING IN THE SAME BUILDING?

FROM TODAY FORWARD, HUH... THINGS COULD GET WEIRD.

HUH. SO KAMINARI'S ABOVE ME, AND AOYAMA'S NEXT DOOR.

CREAK

SECOND FLOOR

FROM TODAY FORWARD?

I'M OUT HERE?

WOMP WOMP

MINETA

DETACHED COTTAGE

NAH! WE'VE GOT FAITH IN YOU!

FAITH? THEN LEMME INSIDE!

FWIP

ARGH!

THIS ISN'T RIGHT! I MIGHT AS WELL MOVE BACK HOME!

LAP OF LUXURY

THERE ARE FOUR BOYS' ROOMS AND FOUR GIRLS' ROOMS ON EACH FLOOR, FROM THE SECOND TO FIFTH.

THE FIRST FLOOR IS A COMMON AREA.

YOU'VE GOT AIR CONDITIONERS, TOILETS, REFRIGERATORS AND CLOSETS.

ENJOY THE LUXURIES.

ONE STUDENT PER ROOM.

THE SCHOOL WILL COVER ALL OF THAT.

ONE LESS THING FOR YOU TO THINK ABOUT.

DO YOU WANT CASH OR CHECK? WILL AN I.O.U. DO?

SHAKA

W-WHAT ABOUT UTILITY BILLS, SENSEI?

SHAKA

OH MY GOD!!

I CAN ONLY IMAGINE THE LIFE SHE'S LED.

How wonderful

GLOMP

HOW COLD ARE WE ALLOWED TO SET THE A.C.?

UM... AS COLD AS YOU WANT.

Do Not Tumble Dry

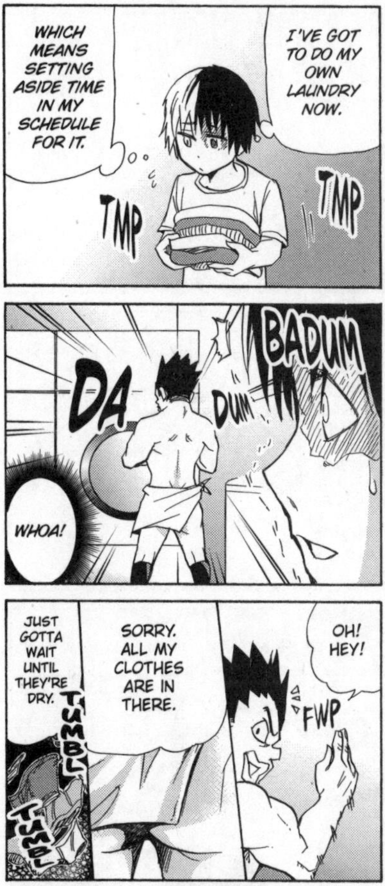
I'VE GOT TO DO MY OWN LAUNDRY NOW.
WHICH MEANS SETTING ASIDE TIME IN MY SCHEDULE FOR IT.
TMP
TMP
BADUM
DA
DUM
WHOA!
OH! HEY!
FWP
SORRY. ALL MY CLOTHES ARE IN THERE.
JUST GOTTA WAIT UNTIL THEY'RE DRY.
TUMBL
TUMBL
HMM? THIS MACHINE'S FREE NOW.
SHUFFLE
THE SUN'S OUT, SO I'LL LINE DRY THESE.
NO ROOM IN MY SCHED-ULE FOR THAT.

The (Dis)honest Woodcutter

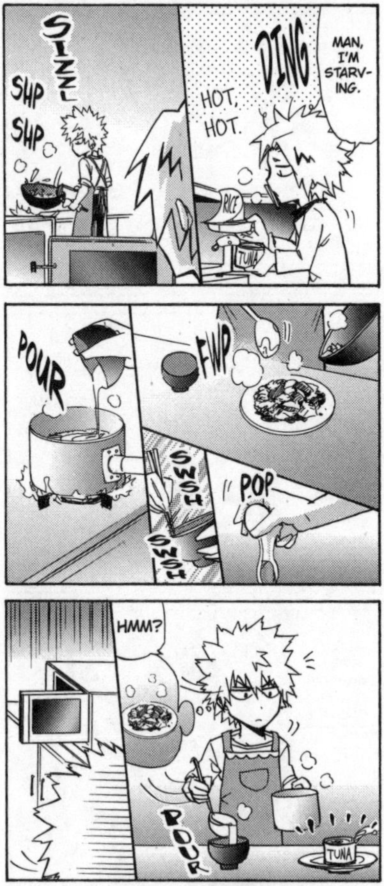
MAN, I'M STARV-ING.
DING
HOT, HOT.
RICE
TUNA
SIZZL
SHP
SHP
FWP
POUR
POP
SWSH
SWSH
HMM?
POUR
TUNA
DIDJA FORGET YOUR CAN, KAMINARI?
BAM
JOLT
H-HUH? MUST'VE TAKEN THE WRONG PLATE.
HA HA HA... DON'T KILL ME!!

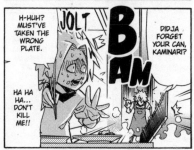

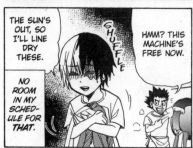

Heated Debate

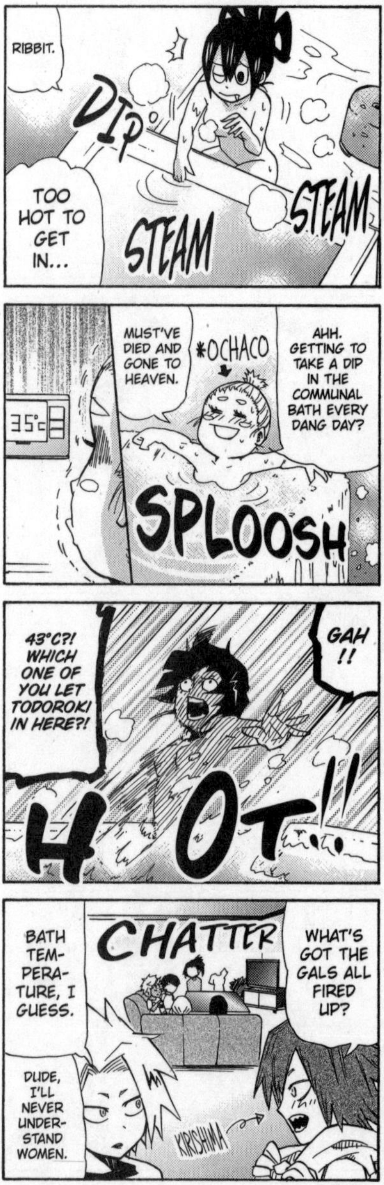
RIBBIT.
DIP
STEAM
STEAM
TOO HOT TO GET IN...
AHH. GETTING TO TAKE A DIP IN THE COMMUNAL BATH EVERY DANG DAY?
*OCHACO
MUST'VE DIED AND GONE TO HEAVEN.
35°C
SPLOOSH
GAH!!
43°C?! WHICH ONE OF YOU LET TODOROKI IN HERE?!
HOT!!
WHAT'S GOT THE GALS ALL FIRED UP?
CHATTER
BATH TEMPERATURE, I GUESS.
KIRISHIMA
DUDE, I'LL NEVER UNDERSTAND WOMEN.

As the Ochacrow Flies

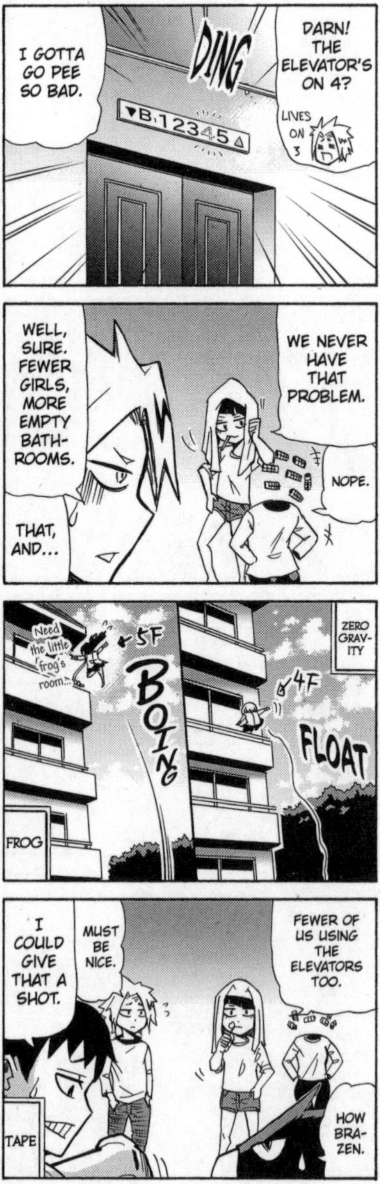
DARN! THE ELEVATOR'S ON 4?
LIVES ON 3
DING
▼B 1 2 3 4 5 ▲
I GOTTA GO PEE SO BAD.
WE NEVER HAVE THAT PROBLEM.
NOPE.
WELL, SURE. FEWER GIRLS, MORE EMPTY BATHROOMS.
THAT, AND...
ZERO GRAVITY
4F
FLOAT
5F
Need the little frog's room...
BOING
FROG
FEWER OF US USING THE ELEVATORS TOO.
HOW BRAZEN.
MUST BE NICE.
I COULD GIVE THAT A SHOT.
TAPE

DIFFERENT NOTES FOR DIFFERENT FOLKS

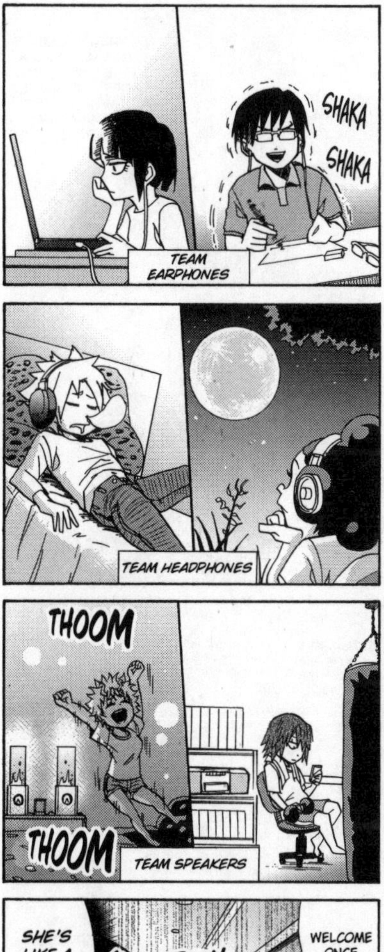
SHAKA
SHAKA
TEAM EARPHONES
TEAM HEADPHONES
THOOM
THOOM
TEAM SPEAKERS
WELCOME ONCE AGAIN, LADIES.
BOW
SPLORT
SHE'S LIKE A MEDIEVAL COUNTESS!!
TEAM LIVE MUSIC

WHERE THE HEART IS

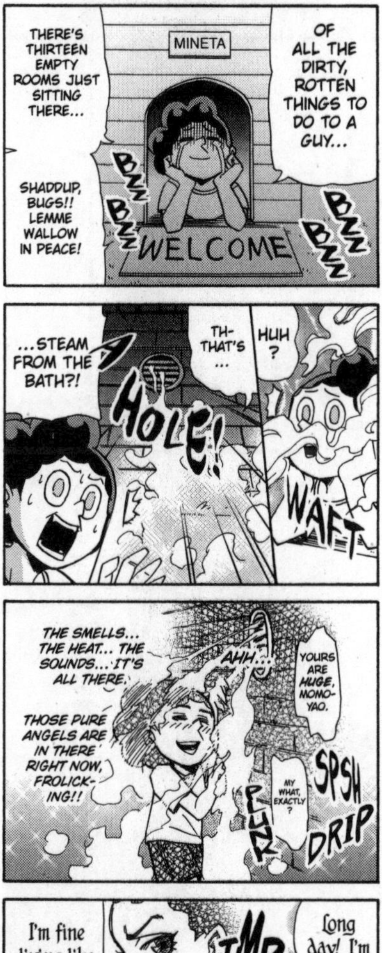
OF ALL THE DIRTY, ROTTEN THINGS TO DO TO A GUY...
MINETA
THERE'S THIRTEEN EMPTY ROOMS JUST SITTING THERE...
BZZ BZZ
SHADDUP, BUGS!! LEMME WALLOW IN PEACE!
WELCOME
BZZ BZZ
HUH?
TH-THAT'S...
...STEAM FROM THE BATH?!
A HOLE!
WAFT
YOURS ARE HUGE, MOMO-YAO.
AHH...
THE SMELLS... THE HEAT... THE SOUNDS... IT'S ALL THERE.
THOSE PURE ANGELS ARE IN THERE RIGHT NOW, FROLICKING!!
SPSH
MY WHAT, EXACTLY?
PLUNK
DRIP
Long day! I'm off to bed!
TMP
I'm fine living like a dog!
SPARKLE
WHY DON'TCHA TRY PETITIONING AIZAWA SENSEI AGAIN?
WAIT, WHY?

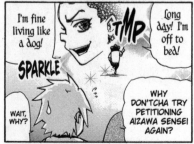

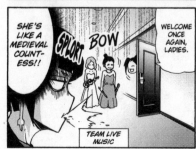

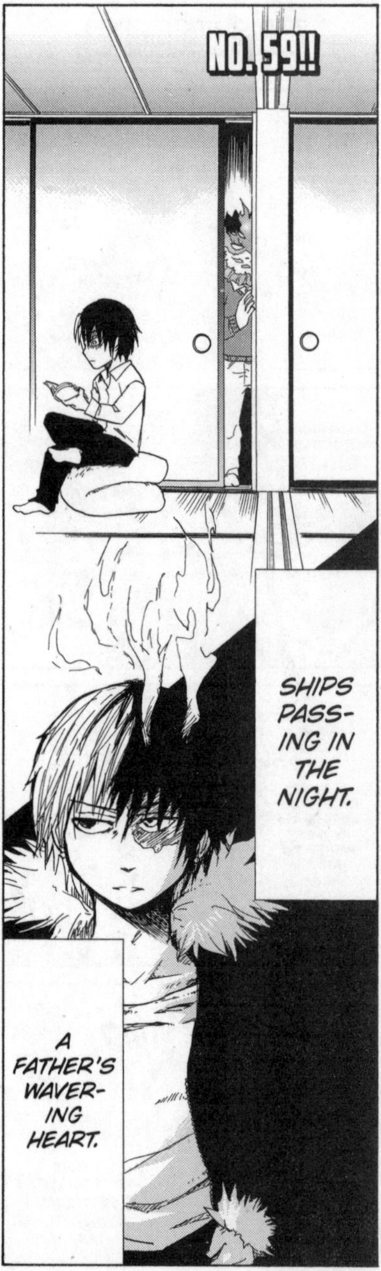
No. 59!!
SHIPS PASSING IN THE NIGHT.
A FATHER'S WAVERING HEART.

PRO'S QUID PRO QUO

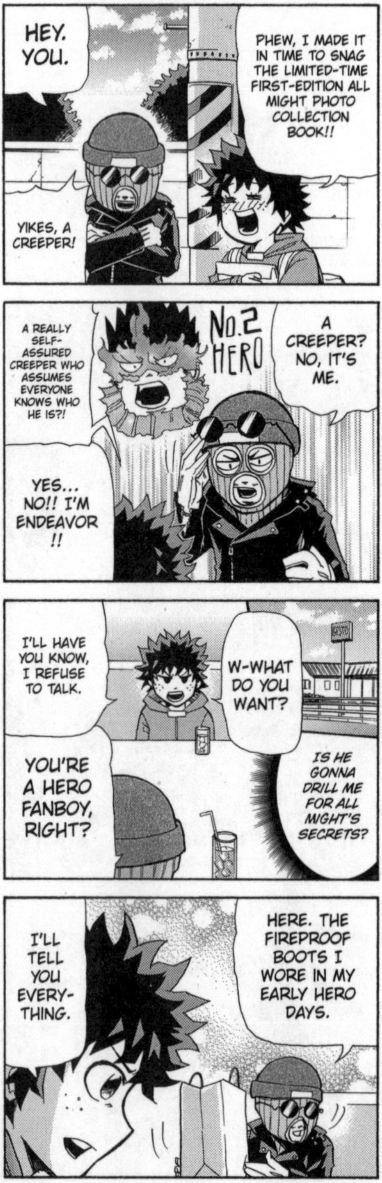
PHEW, I MADE IT IN TIME TO SNAG THE LIMITED-TIME FIRST-EDITION ALL MIGHT PHOTO COLLECTION BOOK!!
HEY. YOU.
YIKES, A CREEPER!
A CREEPER? NO, IT'S ME.
No.2 HERO
A REALLY SELF-ASSURED CREEPER WHO ASSUMES EVERYONE KNOWS WHO HE IS?!
YES... NO!! I'M ENDEAVOR!!
W-WHAT DO YOU WANT?
I'LL HAVE YOU KNOW, I REFUSE TO TALK.
IS HE GONNA DRILL ME FOR ALL MIGHT'S SECRETS?
YOU'RE A HERO FANBOY, RIGHT?
HERE. THE FIREPROOF BOOTS I WORE IN MY EARLY HERO DAYS.
I'LL TELL YOU EVERYTHING.

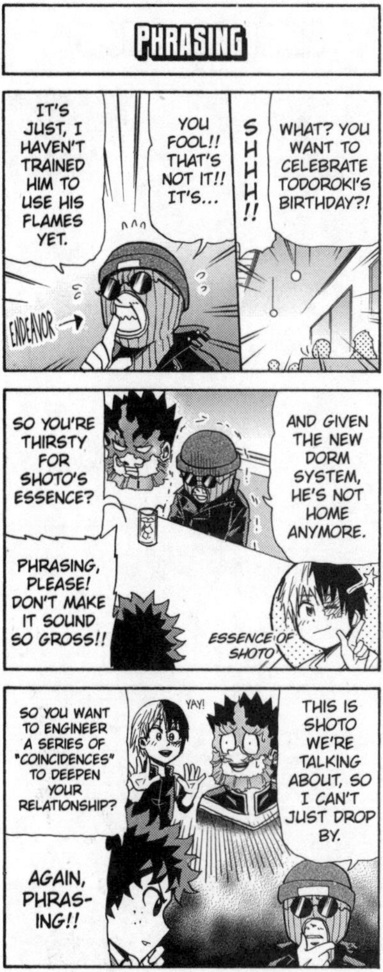
PHRASING
WHAT? YOU WANT TO CELEBRATE TODOROKI'S BIRTHDAY?!
SHHH!!
YOU FOOL!! THAT'S NOT IT!! IT'S...
IT'S JUST, I HAVEN'T TRAINED HIM TO USE HIS FLAMES YET.
ENDEAVOR →
AND GIVEN THE NEW DORM SYSTEM, HE'S NOT HOME ANYMORE.
SO YOU'RE THIRSTY FOR SHOTO'S ESSENCE?
ESSENCE OF SHOTO
PHRASING, PLEASE! DON'T MAKE IT SOUND SO GROSS!!
THIS IS SHOTO WE'RE TALKING ABOUT, SO I CAN'T JUST DROP BY.
YAY!
SO YOU WANT TO ENGINEER A SERIES OF "COINCIDENCES" TO DEEPEN YOUR RELATIONSHIP?
AGAIN, PHRASING!!
UNDERSTOOD. I'LL FIGURE OUT A WAY TO IGNITE SOME PASSION IN THE FRIGID RELATIONSHIP BETWEEN YOU AND YOUR SON.
I swear it on these boots.
HAVE YOU EVER EXPERIENCED A THIRD-DEGREE BURN, BOY?!
FWOOM
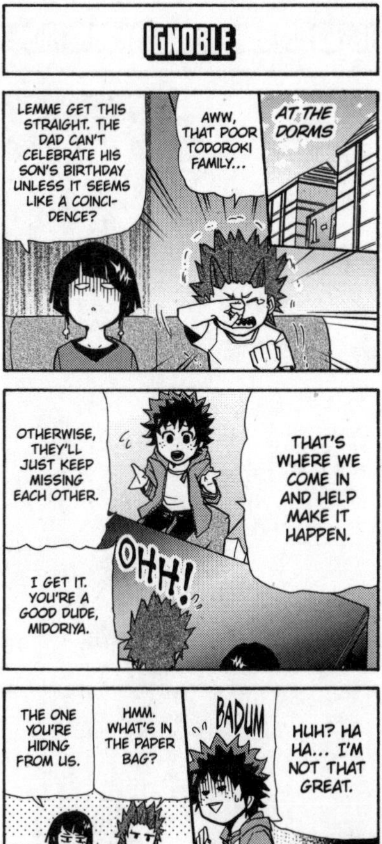
IGNOBLE
AT THE DORMS
AWW, THAT POOR TODOROKI FAMILY...
LEMME GET THIS STRAIGHT. THE DAD CAN'T CELEBRATE HIS SON'S BIRTHDAY UNLESS IT SEEMS LIKE A COINCIDENCE?
THAT'S WHERE WE COME IN AND HELP MAKE IT HAPPEN.
OTHERWISE, THEY'LL JUST KEEP MISSING EACH OTHER.
OHH!
I GET IT. YOU'RE A GOOD DUDE, MIDORIYA.
HUH? HA HA... I'M NOT THAT GREAT.
BADUM
HMM. WHAT'S IN THE PAPER BAG?
THE ONE YOU'RE HIDING FROM US.
HIDE
THIS? NOTHING. I SWEAR.
JOLT
YOU TOTALLY GOT PAID OFF!!
GLOOM
I ADMIT IT. I AM SCUM.
WHATEVER. WE STILL WANNA HELP TODOROKI.

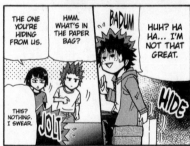

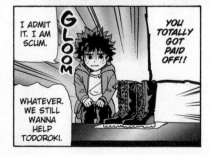

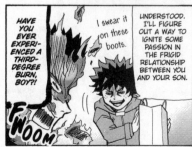

If You See Something, Say Something

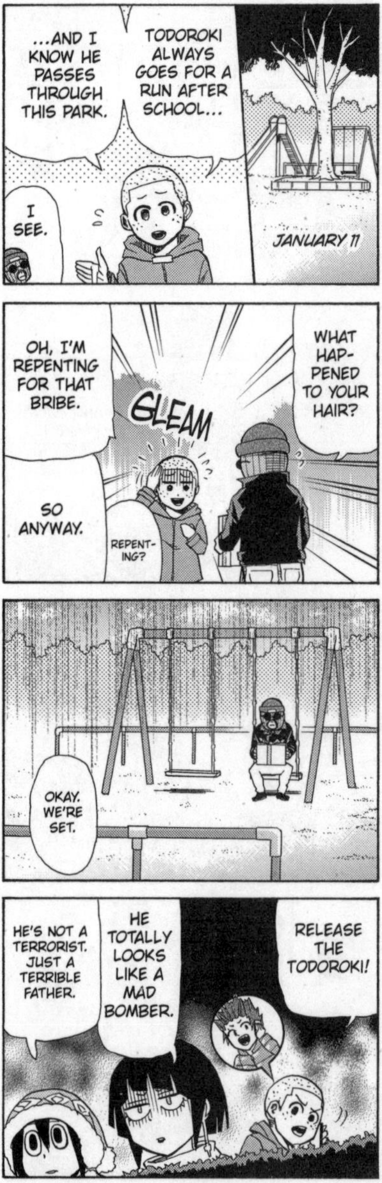
JANUARY 11
TODOROKI ALWAYS GOES FOR A RUN AFTER SCHOOL...
...AND I KNOW HE PASSES THROUGH THIS PARK.
I SEE.
WHAT HAPPENED TO YOUR HAIR?
GLEAM
OH, I'M REPENTING FOR THAT BRIBE.
REPENTING?
SO ANYWAY.
OKAY. WE'RE SET.
RELEASE THE TODOROKI!
HE TOTALLY LOOKS LIKE A MAD BOMBER.
HE'S NOT A TERRORIST. JUST A TERRIBLE FATHER.

Coming Home to Roost

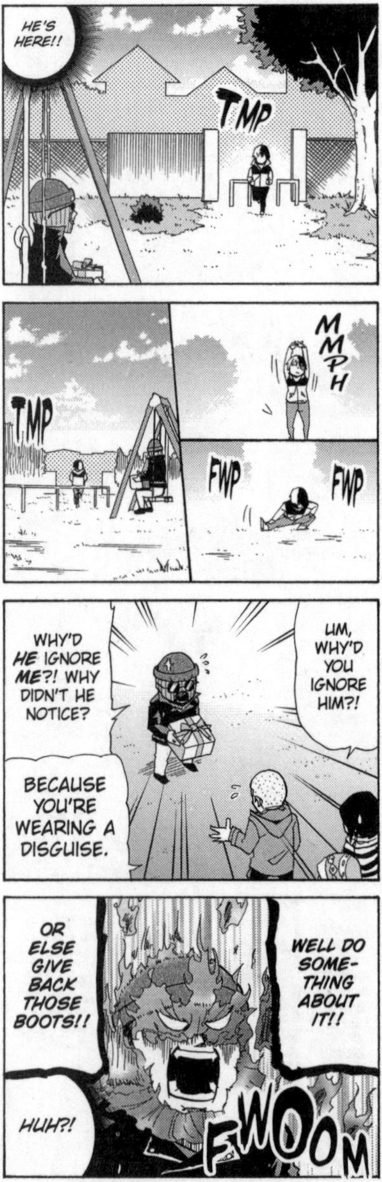
TMP
HE'S HERE!!
MMPH
FWP
FWP
TMP
UM, WHY'D YOU IGNORE HIM?!
WHY'D HE IGNORE ME?! WHY DIDN'T HE NOTICE?
BECAUSE YOU'RE WEARING A DISGUISE.
WELL DO SOMETHING ABOUT IT!!
OR ELSE GIVE BACK THOSE BOOTS!!
FWOOM
HUH?!

PLAN B

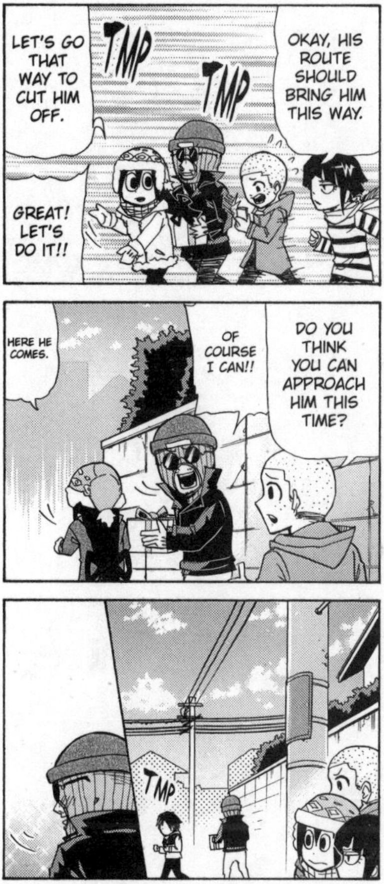
OKAY, HIS ROUTE SHOULD BRING HIM THIS WAY.
LET'S GO THAT WAY TO CUT HIM OFF.
TMP
TMP
GREAT! LET'S DO IT!!
DO YOU THINK YOU CAN APPROACH HIM THIS TIME?
OF COURSE I CAN!!
HERE HE COMES.
TMP
WHAT SUPERIOR JOGGING FORM.
BEAM
WHO CARES ABOUT THAT? TALK TO YOUR FREAKING SON!!

OPPORTUNITY UP IN FLAMES

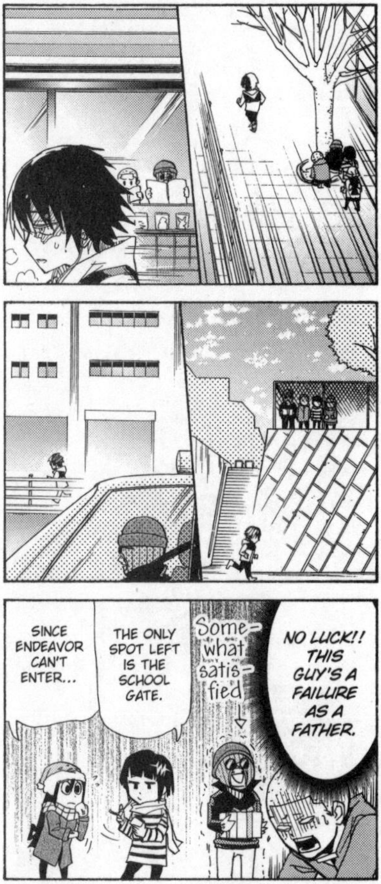
NO LUCK!! THIS GUY'S A FAILURE AS A FATHER.
Somewhat satisfied
THE ONLY SPOT LEFT IS THE SCHOOL GATE.
SINCE ENDEAVOR CAN'T ENTER...
DIDJA HEAR THAT? THIS IS YOUR FINAL CHANCE!
G-GOT IT!!
WORST CASE, WE'LL DOGPILE TODOROKI AND HOLD HIM DOWN FOR YOU!!
FINE! YOU DON'T GOTTA MAKE ME FEEL BAD ABOUT IT!!

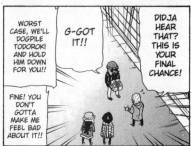

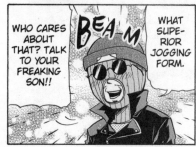

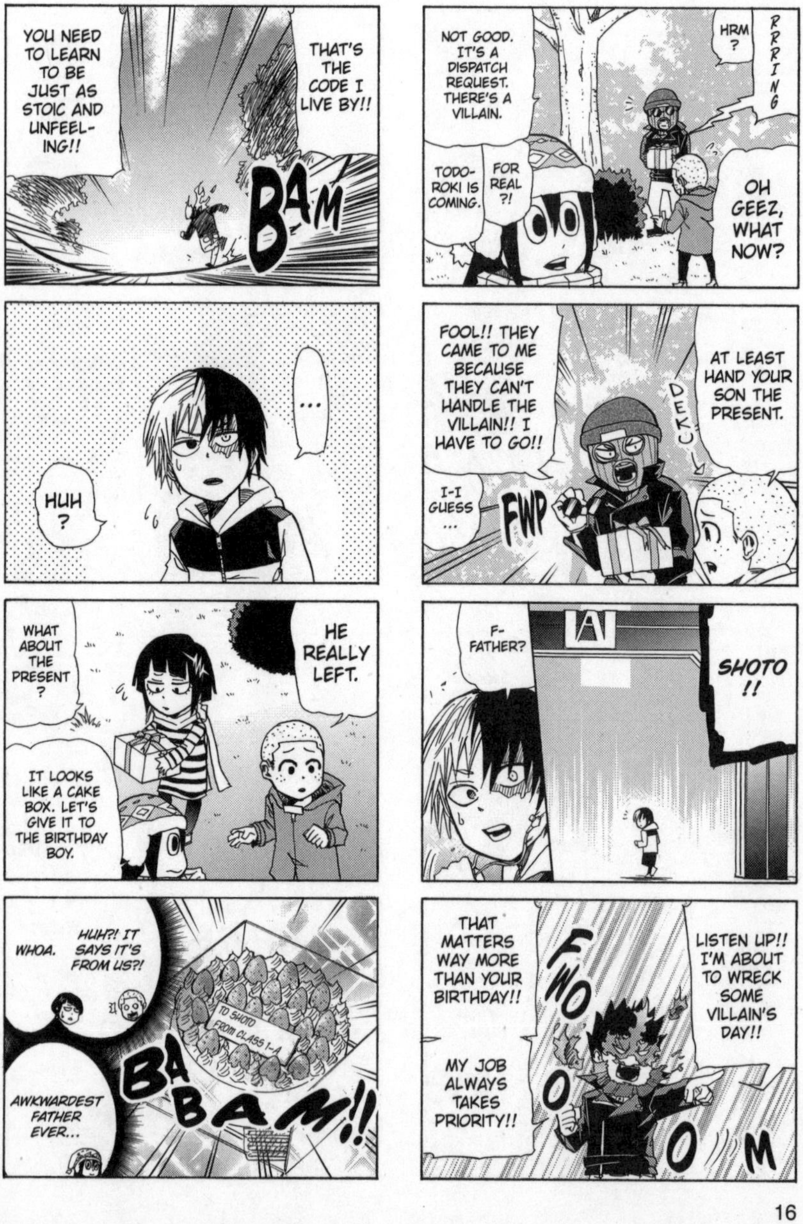

RRRING
HRM ?
NOT GOOD. IT'S A DISPATCH REQUEST. THERE'S A VILLAIN.
OH GEEZ, WHAT NOW?
FOR REAL ?!
TODO-ROKI IS COMING.
THAT'S THE CODE I LIVE BY!!
YOU NEED TO LEARN TO BE JUST AS STOIC AND UNFEEL-ING!!
BAM
AT LEAST HAND YOUR SON THE PRESENT.
FOOL!! THEY CAME TO ME BECAUSE THEY CAN'T HANDLE THE VILLAIN!! I HAVE TO GO!!
DEKU
FWP
I-I GUESS ...
...
HUH ?
SHOTO !!
F- FATHER?
HE REALLY LEFT.
WHAT ABOUT THE PRESENT ?
IT LOOKS LIKE A CAKE BOX. LET'S GIVE IT TO THE BIRTHDAY BOY.
LISTEN UP!! I'M ABOUT TO WRECK SOME VILLAIN'S DAY!!
FWOOOOM
THAT MATTERS WAY MORE THAN YOUR BIRTHDAY!!
MY JOB ALWAYS TAKES PRIORITY!!
HUH?! IT SAYS IT'S FROM US?!
WHOA.
TO SHOTO FROM CLASS 1-A
BABAM!!
AWKWARDEST FATHER EVER...

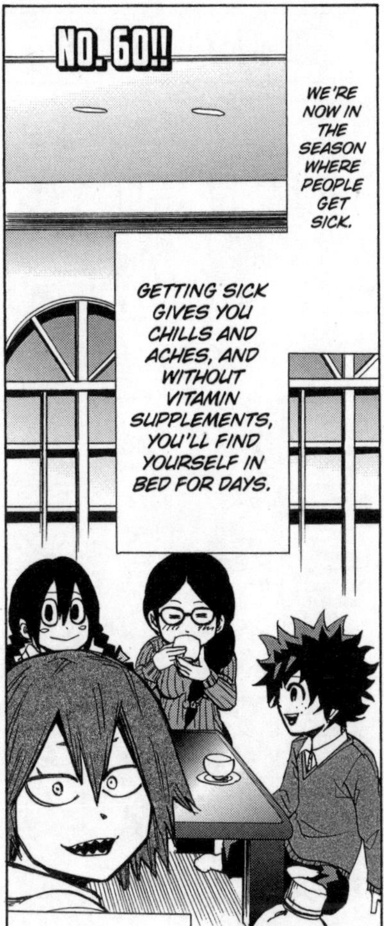
NO. 60!!
WE'RE NOW IN THE SEASON WHERE PEOPLE GET SICK.
GETTING SICK GIVES YOU CHILLS AND ACHES, AND WITHOUT VITAMIN SUPPLEMENTS, YOU'LL FIND YOURSELF IN BED FOR DAYS.
BUT YOU'LL BE FINE, CUZ WE'RE HERE FOR YOU.

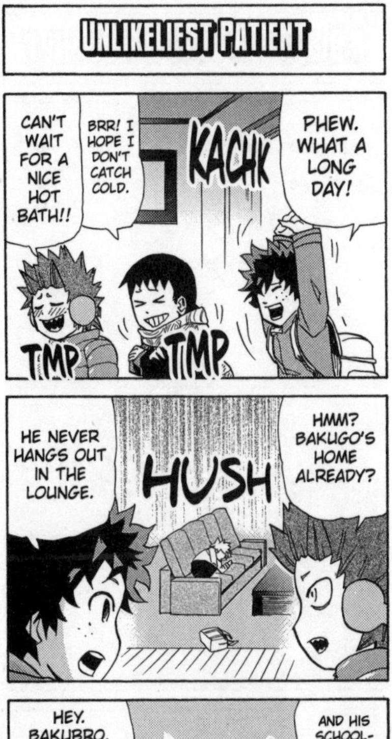
UNLIKELIEST PATIENT
PHEW. WHAT A LONG DAY!
KACHK
BRR! I HOPE I DON'T CATCH COLD.
CAN'T WAIT FOR A NICE HOT BATH!!
TMP
TMP
HMM? BAKUGO'S HOME ALREADY?
HUSH
HE NEVER HANGS OUT IN THE LOUNGE.
AND HIS SCHOOL-BAG'S JUST SITTING HERE?
HUP
HEY. BAKUBRO. YOU'RE GONNA GET SICK LYING OUT HERE.
HUH?
B-BAKUGO?!
SHAKA
SPEAK TO ME, DUDE!!
SHAKA
SHAKA

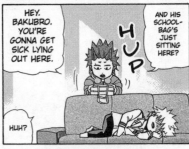

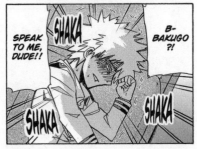

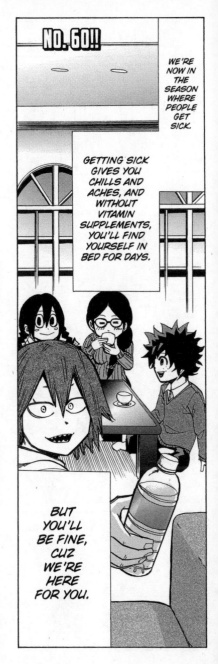

A Dish Best Served Fever Hot

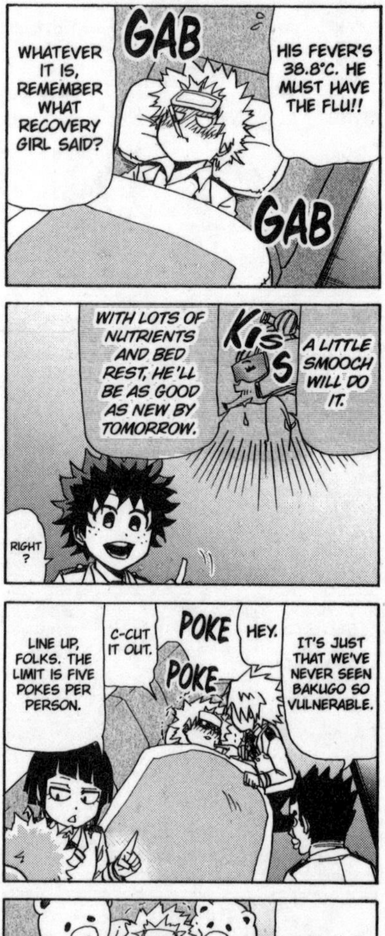
HIS FEVER'S 38.8°C. HE MUST HAVE THE FLU!!
GAB
WHATEVER IT IS, REMEMBER WHAT RECOVERY GIRL SAID?
GAB
A LITTLE SMOOCH WILL DO IT.
KISS
WITH LOTS OF NUTRIENTS AND BED REST, HE'LL BE AS GOOD AS NEW BY TOMORROW.
RIGHT?
IT'S JUST THAT WE'VE NEVER SEEN BAKUGO SO VULNERABLE.
HEY.
POKE
C-CUT IT OUT.
LINE UP, FOLKS. THE LIMIT IS FIVE POKES PER PERSON.
POKE
THIS IS A ONCE-IN-A-LIFETIME PIC.
FLASH
LI'L BAKUGO
FLASH
YOU'LL PAY... YOU'LL ALL PAY.

Two Birds, One Hot Pot

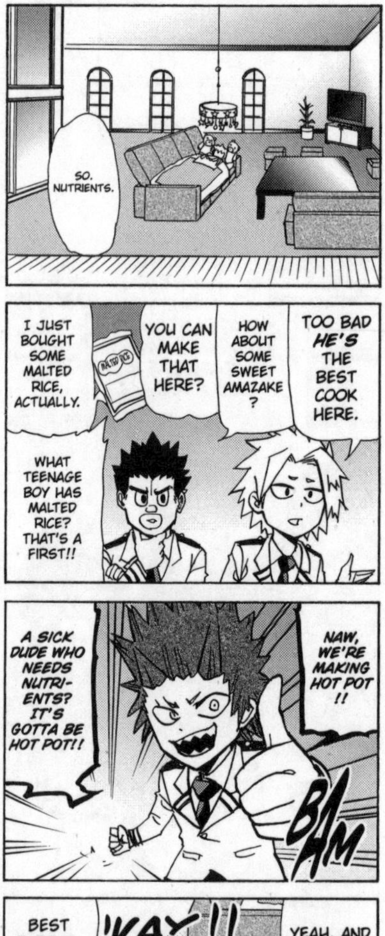
SO. NUTRIENTS.
TOO BAD HE'S THE BEST COOK HERE.
HOW ABOUT SOME SWEET AMAZAKE?
YOU CAN MAKE THAT HERE?
I JUST BOUGHT SOME MALTED RICE, ACTUALLY.
MALTED RICE
WHAT TEENAGE BOY HAS MALTED RICE? THAT'S A FIRST!!
NAW, WE'RE MAKING HOT POT!!
A SICK DUDE WHO NEEDS NUTRI-ENTS? IT'S GOTTA BE HOT POT!!
BAM
YEAH. AND THEN SOME RICE GRUEL...
'KAY!!
BEST PART IS, IT'LL BE OUR DINNER TOO!
WOO!
YEAH!!
FWP

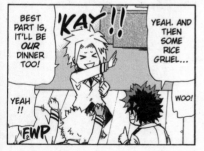

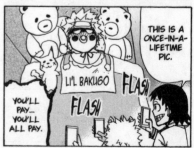

POTLUCK

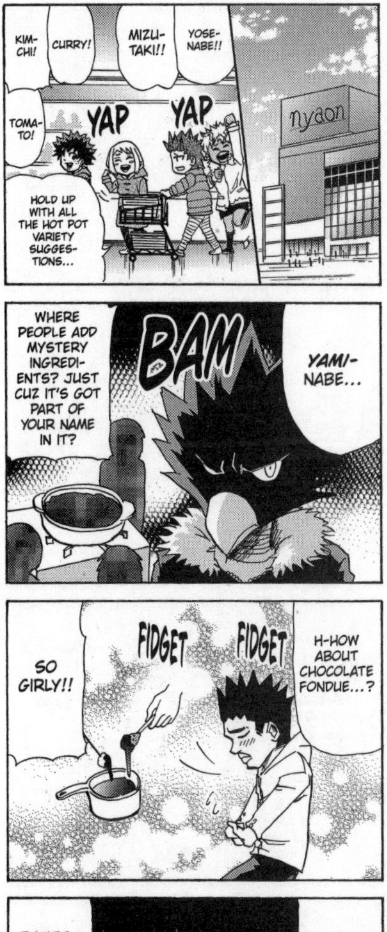
YOSE-NABE!!
MIZU-TAKI!!
CURRY!
KIM-CHI!
YAP
YAP
nyaon
TOMA-TO!
HOLD UP WITH ALL THE HOT POT VARIETY SUGGES-TIONS...
YAMI-NABE...
BAM
WHERE PEOPLE ADD MYSTERY INGREDI-ENTS? JUST CUZ IT'S GOT PART OF YOUR NAME IN IT?
H-HOW ABOUT CHOCOLATE FONDUE...?
FIDGET
FIDGET
SO GIRLY!!
SHABU-SHABU...
PANT
PANTS-LESS SHABU-SHABU...
PANT
YIKES!! IS THAT EVEN A THING PEOPLE DO?!

APPROPRIATING FUNDS

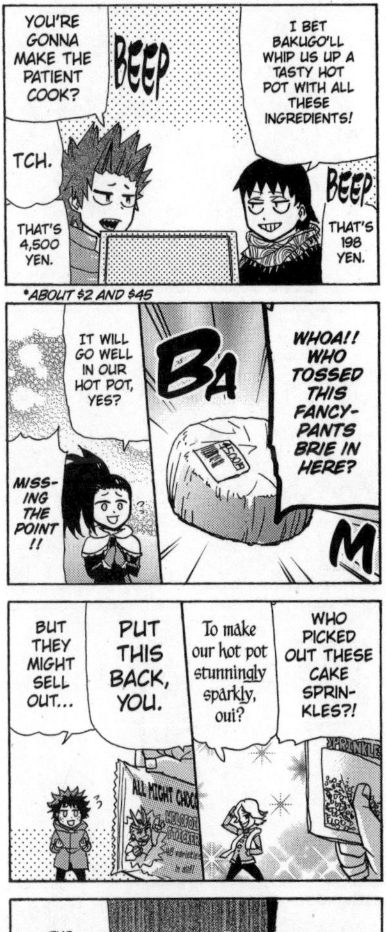
I BET BAKUGO'LL WHIP US UP A TASTY HOT POT WITH ALL THESE INGREDIENTS!
BEEP
YOU'RE GONNA MAKE THE PATIENT COOK?
BEEP
THAT'S 198 YEN.
TCH.
THAT'S 4,500 YEN.
WHOA!! WHO TOSSED THIS FANCY-PANTS BRIE IN HERE?
BA
IT WILL GO WELL IN OUR HOT POT, YES?
M
MISS-ING THE POINT!!
WHO PICKED OUT THESE CAKE SPRIN-KLES?!
SPRINKLES
To make our hot pot stunningly sparkly, oui?
PUT THIS BACK, YOU.
BUT THEY MIGHT SELL OUT...
ALL MIGHT CHOC
DAMMIT!! WHO SNUCK A PLAIN OL' TOOTH-BRUSH IN HERE?!
TOOTHBRUSH
THE BRISTLES ON MINE ARE ALL WORN OUT...
SO BUY A NEW ONE YOUR-SELF!!

*ABOUT $2 AND $45

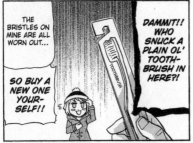

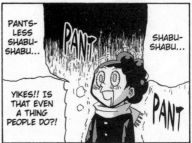

THE FIRST RULE OF HOT POT IS...

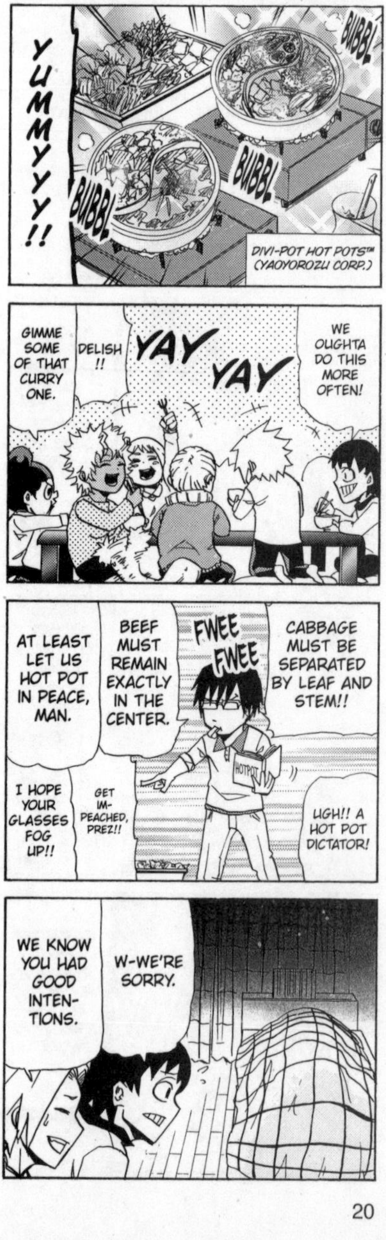
BUBBL
BUBBL
BUBBL
YUMMYYYY!!
DIVI-POT HOT POTS™ (YAOYOROZU CORP.)
WE OUGHTA DO THIS MORE OFTEN!
YAY YAY
DELISH!!
GIMME SOME OF THAT CURRY ONE.
CABBAGE MUST BE SEPARATED BY LEAF AND STEM!!
FWEE FWEE
BEEF MUST REMAIN EXACTLY IN THE CENTER.
AT LEAST LET US HOT POT IN PEACE, MAN.
HOTPOT
UGH!! A HOT POT DICTATOR!
GET IM-PEACHED, PREZ!!
I HOPE YOUR GLASSES FOG UP!!
W-WE'RE SORRY.
WE KNOW YOU HAD GOOD INTEN-TIONS.

MORE GOOD INTENTIONS

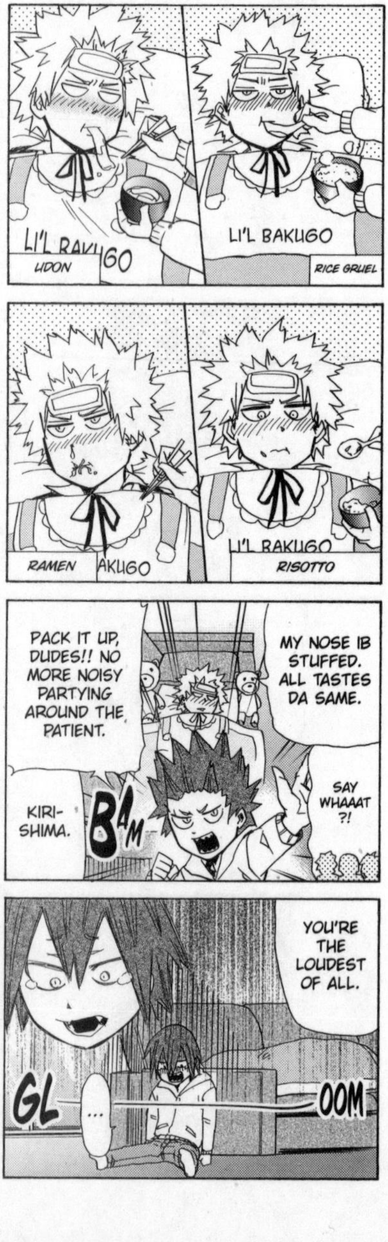
LI'L BAKUGO
RICE GRUEL
LI'L BAKUGO
UDON
LI'L BAKUGO
RISOTTO
AKUGO
RAMEN
MY NOSE IB STUFFED. ALL TASTES DA SAME.
PACK IT UP, DUDES!! NO MORE NOISY PARTYING AROUND THE PATIENT.
SAY WHAAAT?!
BAM
KIRI-SHIMA.
YOU'RE THE LOUDEST OF ALL.
GL OOM
...

Mama Sato

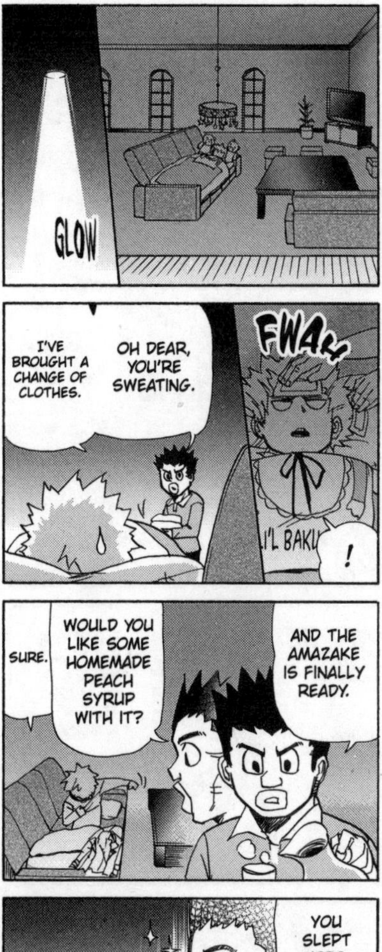
GLOW
FWAH
OH DEAR, YOU'RE SWEATING.
I'VE BROUGHT A CHANGE OF CLOTHES.
I'L BAKU
!
AND THE AMAZAKE IS FINALLY READY.
WOULD YOU LIKE SOME HOMEMADE PEACH SYRUP WITH IT?
SURE.
YOU SLEPT HERE, KIRI-SHIMA?
SHINE
THROUGH BLEARY EYES AT 2 A.M., SATO LOOKED LIKE A MOMMY SENT BY HEAVEN.

Actually, Best Served Cold

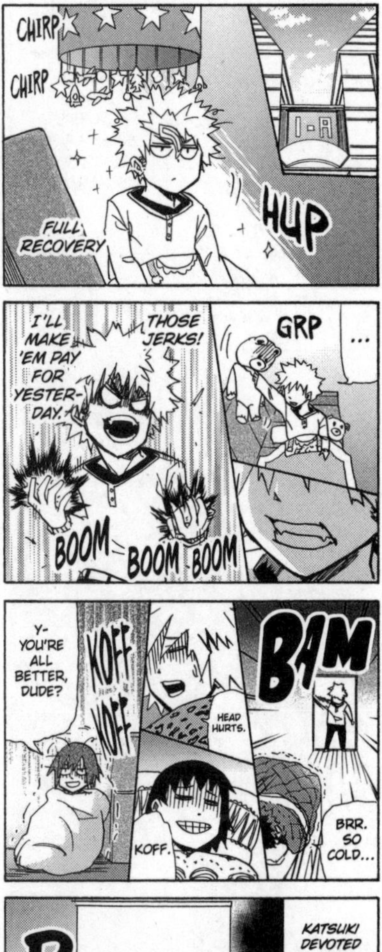
CHIRP
CHIRP
HUP
FULL RECOVERY
GRP
...
THOSE JERKS!
I'LL MAKE 'EM PAY FOR YESTER-DAY.
BOOM
BOOM
BOOM
BAM
HEAD HURTS.
KOFF
KOFF
Y-YOU'RE ALL BETTER, DUDE?
BRR. SO COLD...
KOFF.
KATSUKI DEVOTED HIMSELF TO NURSING THEM BACK TO HEALTH...
DOOOM
...SO HE COULD BEAT THE SNOT OUT OF THEM.

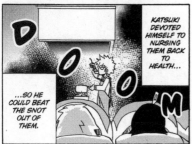

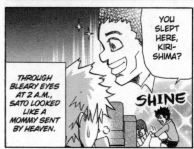

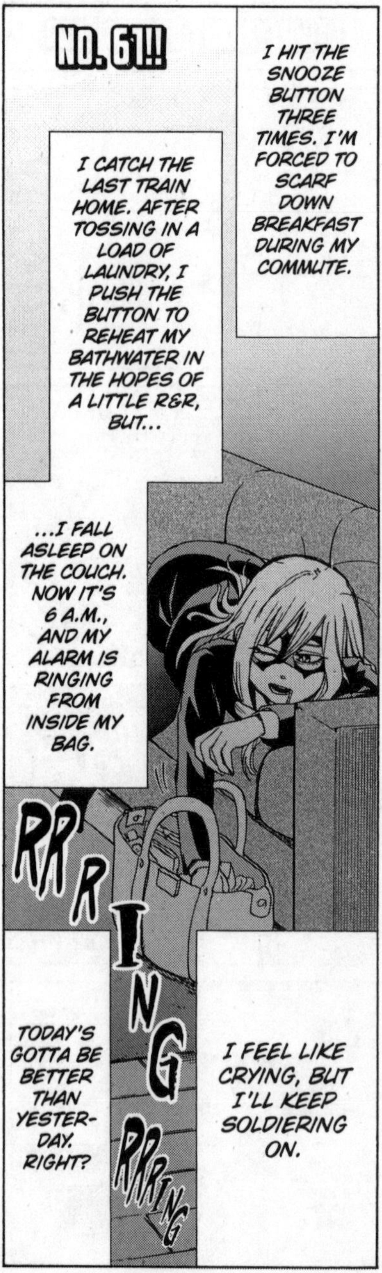
NO. 61!!
I HIT THE SNOOZE BUTTON THREE TIMES. I'M FORCED TO SCARF DOWN BREAKFAST DURING MY COMMUTE.
I CATCH THE LAST TRAIN HOME. AFTER TOSSING IN A LOAD OF LAUNDRY, I PUSH THE BUTTON TO REHEAT MY BATHWATER IN THE HOPES OF A LITTLE R&R, BUT...
...I FALL ASLEEP ON THE COUCH. NOW IT'S 6 A.M., AND MY ALARM IS RINGING FROM INSIDE MY BAG.
RRR
RING
RRRING
I FEEL LIKE CRYING, BUT I'LL KEEP SOLDIERING ON.
TODAY'S GOTTA BE BETTER THAN YESTER-DAY. RIGHT?

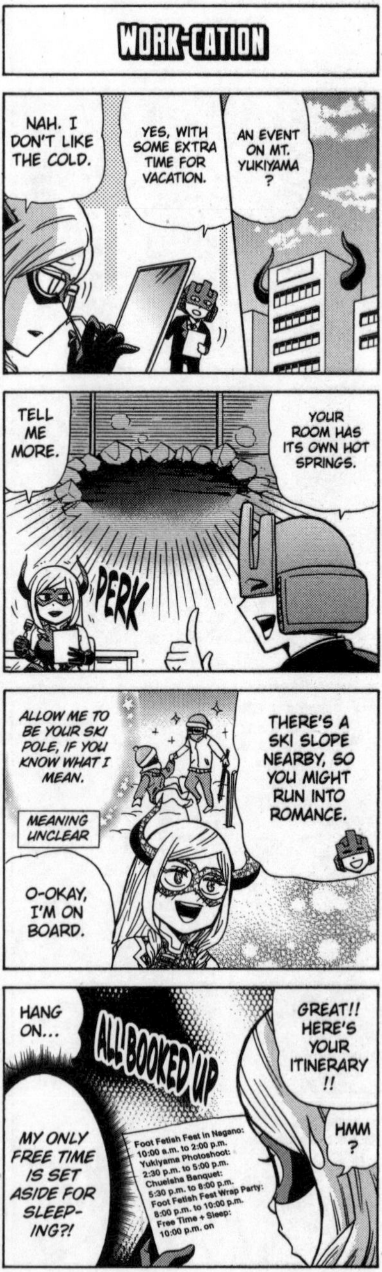
WORK-CATION
AN EVENT ON MT. YUKIYAMA?
YES, WITH SOME EXTRA TIME FOR VACATION.
NAH. I DON'T LIKE THE COLD.
YOUR ROOM HAS ITS OWN HOT SPRINGS.
TELL ME MORE.
PERK
THERE'S A SKI SLOPE NEARBY, SO YOU MIGHT RUN INTO ROMANCE.
ALLOW ME TO BE YOUR SKI POLE, IF YOU KNOW WHAT I MEAN.
MEANING UNCLEAR
O-OKAY, I'M ON BOARD.
GREAT!! HERE'S YOUR ITINERARY!!
HMM?
Foot Fetish Fest in Nagano: 10:00 a.m. to 2:00 p.m.
Yukiyama Photoshoot: 2:30 p.m. to 5:00 p.m.
Chueisha Banquet: 5:30 p.m. to 8:00 p.m.
Foot Fetish Fest Wrap Party: 8:00 p.m. to 10:00 p.m.
Free Time + Sleep: 10:00 p.m. on
HANG ON...
ALL-BOOKED UP
MY ONLY FREE TIME IS SET ASIDE FOR SLEEP-ING?!

ONE MAN'S TORTURE...

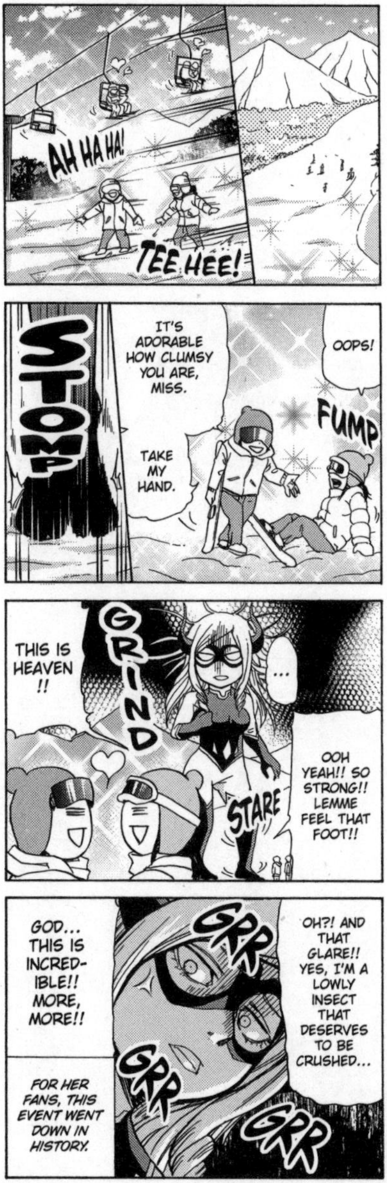
AH HA HA!
TEE HEE!
OOPS!
FUMP
IT'S ADORABLE HOW CLUMSY YOU ARE, MISS.
TAKE MY HAND.
STOMP
...
GRIND
THIS IS HEAVEN!!
OOH YEAH!! SO STRONG!! LEMME FEEL THAT FOOT!!
STARE
OH?! AND THAT GLARE!! YES, I'M A LOWLY INSECT THAT DESERVES TO BE CRUSHED...
GRR
GRR
GRR
GOD... THIS IS INCRED-IBLE!! MORE, MORE!!
FOR HER FANS, THIS EVENT WENT DOWN IN HISTORY.

MT. LADY'S NO GOOD VERY BAD DAY

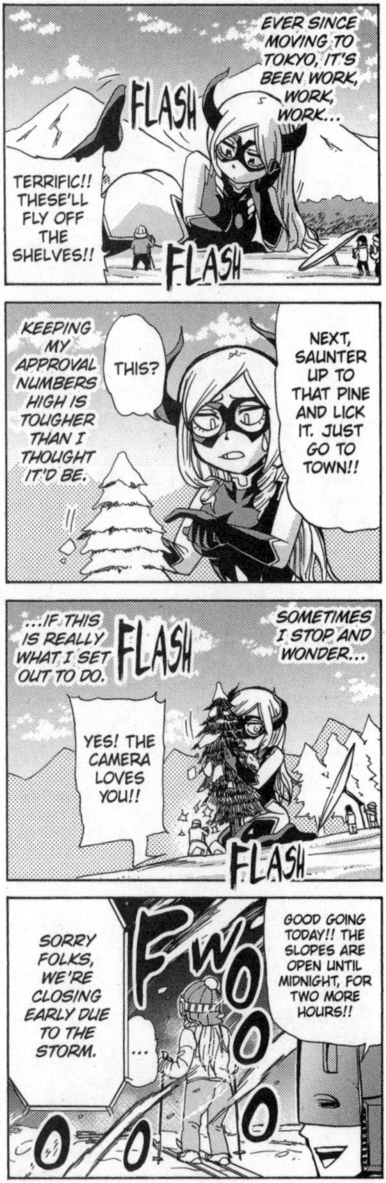
EVER SINCE MOVING TO TOKYO, IT'S BEEN WORK, WORK, WORK...
FLASH
TERRIFIC!! THESE'LL FLY OFF THE SHELVES!!
FLASH
NEXT, SAUNTER UP TO THAT PINE AND LICK IT. JUST GO TO TOWN!!
THIS?
KEEPING MY APPROVAL NUMBERS HIGH IS TOUGHER THAN I THOUGHT IT'D BE.
SOMETIMES I STOP AND WONDER...
FLASH
...IF THIS IS REALLY WHAT I SET OUT TO DO.
YES! THE CAMERA LOVES YOU!!
FLASH
GOOD GOING TODAY!! THE SLOPES ARE OPEN UNTIL MIDNIGHT, FOR TWO MORE HOURS!!
FWOOOOO
SORRY FOLKS, WE'RE CLOSING EARLY DUE TO THE STORM.
...

GRIZZLED

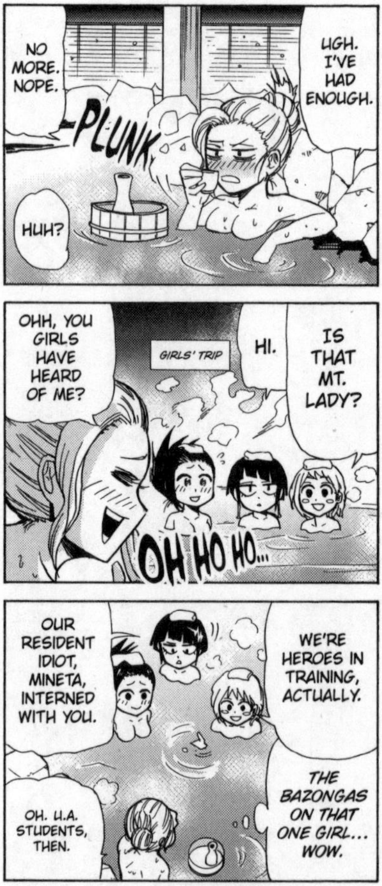
UGH. I'VE HAD ENOUGH.
NO MORE. NOPE.
PLUNK
HUH?
IS THAT MT. LADY?
HI.
GIRLS' TRIP
OHH, YOU GIRLS HAVE HEARD OF ME?
OH HO HO...
WE'RE HEROES IN TRAINING, ACTUALLY.
OUR RESIDENT IDIOT, MINETA, INTERNED WITH YOU.
THE BAZONGAS ON THAT ONE GIRL... WOW.
OH. U.A. STUDENTS, THEN.
WELL? WHAT DOES A PERKY TRIO WITH BRIGHT FUTURES...
...WANT FROM A THIRD-RATE WASHED-UP SPINSTER LIKE ME?
H-HUH? SHE'D RATHER WE WERE JUST FANS?!
PTOOIE

QUARTER-LIFE CRISIS

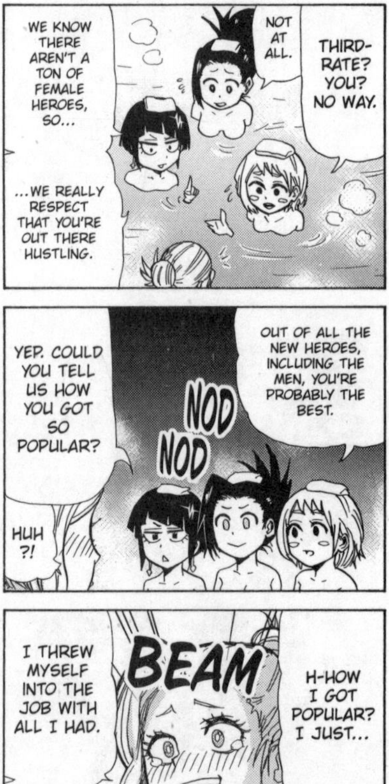
THIRD-RATE? YOU? NO WAY.
NOT AT ALL.
WE KNOW THERE AREN'T A TON OF FEMALE HEROES, SO...
...WE REALLY RESPECT THAT YOU'RE OUT THERE HUSTLING.
OUT OF ALL THE NEW HEROES, INCLUDING THE MEN, YOU'RE PROBABLY THE BEST.
NOD NOD
YEP. COULD YOU TELL US HOW YOU GOT SO POPULAR?
HUH?!
H-HOW I GOT POPULAR? I JUST...
BEAM
I THREW MYSELF INTO THE JOB WITH ALL I HAD.
IT'S THE ONLY WAY TO STAY AFLOAT.
SOMETIMES IT FEELS... LIKE THE JOB'S ALL I HAVE.
SOB
IT'S HARD OUT THERE FOR A PRO...
PLIP PLIP
I'M SORRY... UGH, I'M A MESS...
LOOK AWAY...

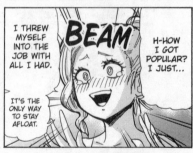

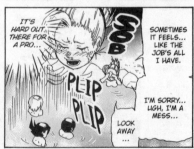

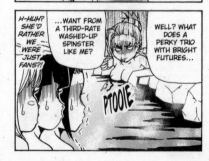

UNPAID OVERTIME

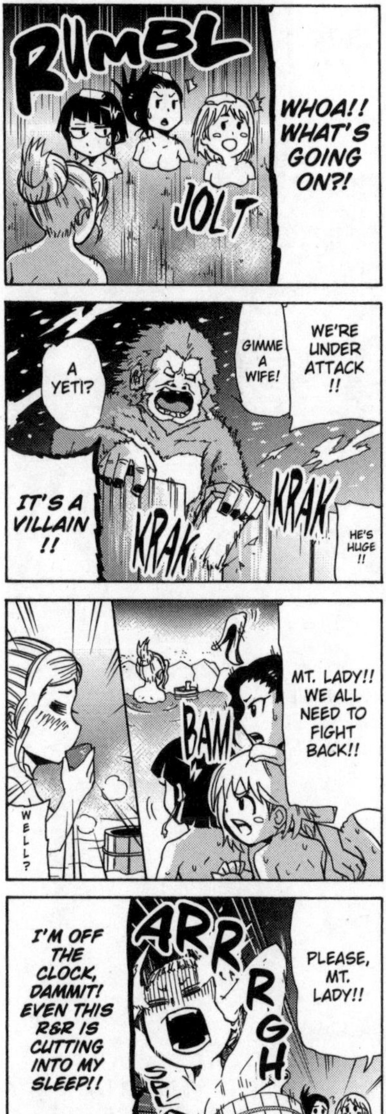
WHOA!! WHAT'S GOING ON?!
RUMBL
JOLT
WE'RE UNDER ATTACK!!
GIMME A WIFE!
A YETI?
HE'S HUGE!!
KRAK
KRAK
IT'S A VILLAIN!!
MT. LADY!! WE ALL NEED TO FIGHT BACK!!
BAM
WELL...?
PLEASE, MT. LADY!!
ARRRGH
I'M OFF THE CLOCK, DAMMIT! EVEN THIS R&R IS CUTTING INTO MY SLEEP!!
SPLASH
HUH?!

CALL TO ACTION

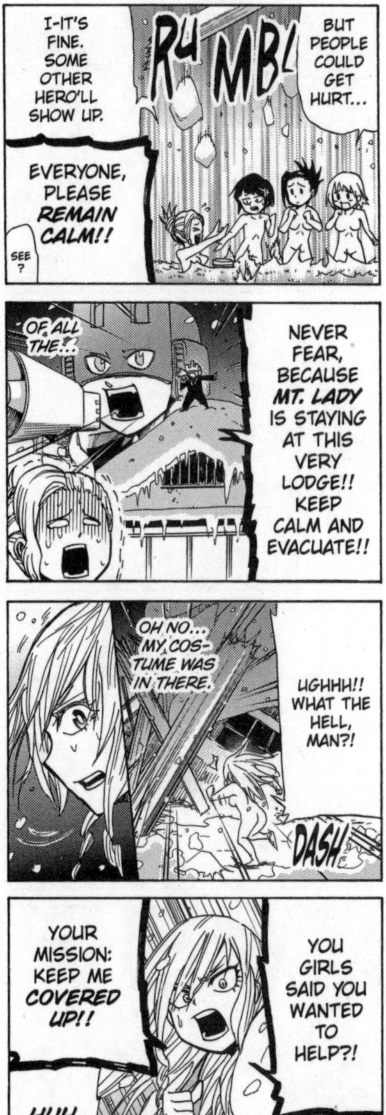
BUT PEOPLE COULD GET HURT...
RUMBL
I-IT'S FINE. SOME OTHER HERO'LL SHOW UP.
EVERYONE, PLEASE REMAIN CALM!!
SEE?
NEVER FEAR, BECAUSE MT. LADY IS STAYING AT THIS VERY LODGE!! KEEP CALM AND EVACUATE!!
OF ALL THE...
UGHHH!! WHAT THE HELL, MAN?!
OH NO... MY COSTUME WAS IN THERE.
DASH
YOU GIRLS SAID YOU WANTED TO HELP?!
YOUR MISSION: KEEP ME COVERED UP!!
HUH?!

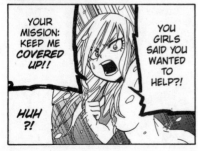

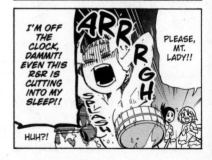

LADY-ON-YETI ACTION SCENE

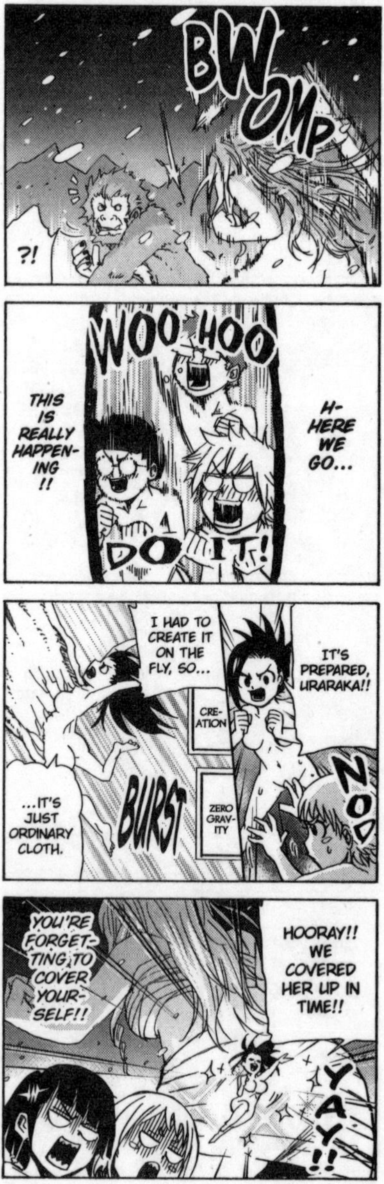
BWOMP
?!
H-HERE WE GO...
WOO HOO
THIS IS REALLY HAPPENING!!
DO IT!
IT'S PREPARED, URARAKA!!
I HAD TO CREATE IT ON THE FLY, SO...
CREATION
NOD
ZERO GRAVITY
BURST
...IT'S JUST ORDINARY CLOTH.
HOORAY!! WE COVERED HER UP IN TIME!!
YOU'RE FORGETTING TO COVER YOURSELF!!
YAY!!

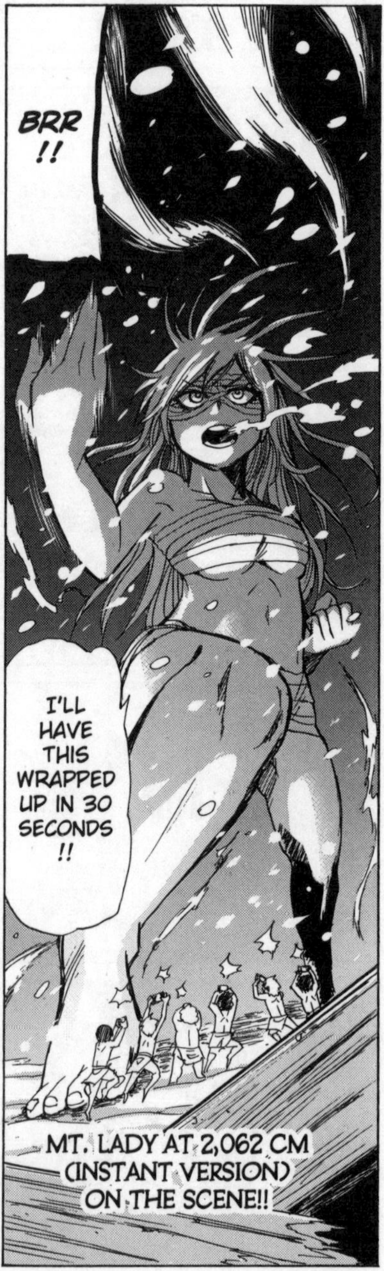
BRR!!
I'LL HAVE THIS WRAPPED UP IN 30 SECONDS!!
MT. LADY AT 2,062 CM (INSTANT VERSION) ON THE SCENE!!

Censorship-no-Jutsu

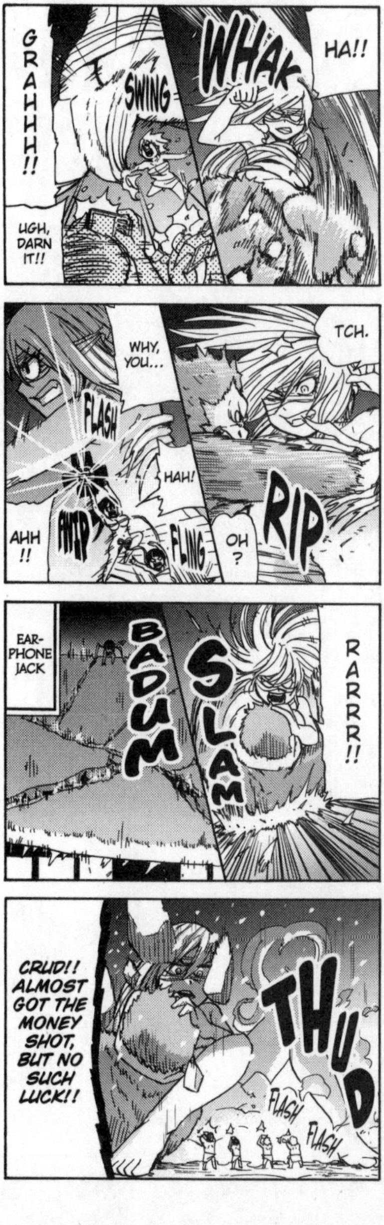
HA!!
WHAK
SWING
GRAHHHH!!
UGH, DARN IT!!
TCH.
WHY, YOU...
FLASH
RIP
OH?
FLING
HAH!
WHIP
AHH!!
RARRR!!
SLAM
BADUM
EARPHONE JACK
THUD
FLASH
FLASH
CRUD!! ALMOST GOT THE MONEY SHOT, BUT NO SUCH LUCK!!

The Endless Cycle of Sacrifice

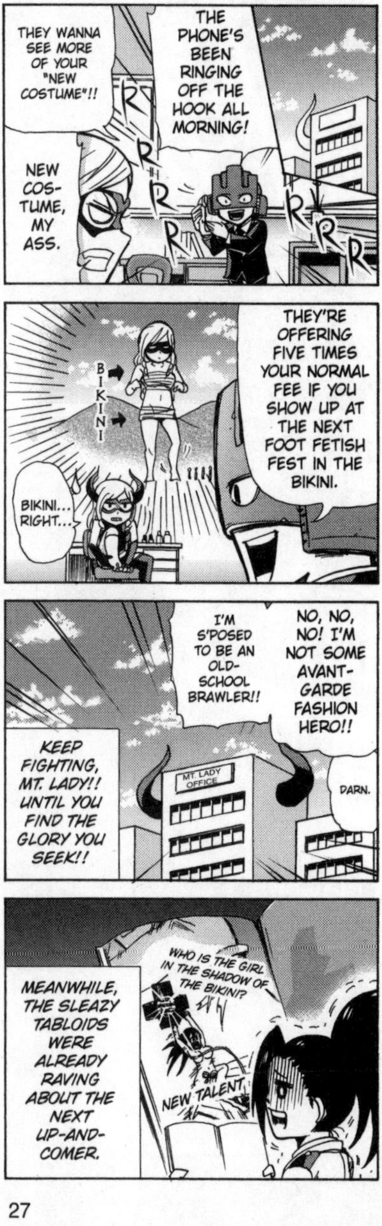
THE PHONE'S BEEN RINGING OFF THE HOOK ALL MORNING!
THEY WANNA SEE MORE OF YOUR "NEW COSTUME"!!
NEW COSTUME, MY ASS.
THEY'RE OFFERING FIVE TIMES YOUR NORMAL FEE IF YOU SHOW UP AT THE NEXT FOOT FETISH FEST IN THE BIKINI.
BIKINI
BIKINI... RIGHT...
NO, NO, NO! I'M NOT SOME AVANT-GARDE FASHION HERO!!
I'M S'POSED TO BE AN OLD-SCHOOL BRAWLER!!
DARN.
MT. LADY OFFICE
KEEP FIGHTING, MT. LADY!! UNTIL YOU FIND THE GLORY YOU SEEK!!
WHO IS THE GIRL IN THE SHADOW OF THE BIKINI!?
NEW TALENT
MEANWHILE, THE SLEAZY TABLOIDS WERE ALREADY RAVING ABOUT THE NEXT UP-AND-COMER.

MY HERO ACADEMIA: SMASH!!

CHARACTER PROFILES!!

THE PROFILES OF THE CHARACTERS IN *SMASH!!* CONTINUE!!
THESE GOOFY FOLKS ARE LIVING
THEIR LIVES AS THEY PLEASE!!
YES, IT'S THAT GOOD OLD
PLUS ULTRA SPIRIT!!

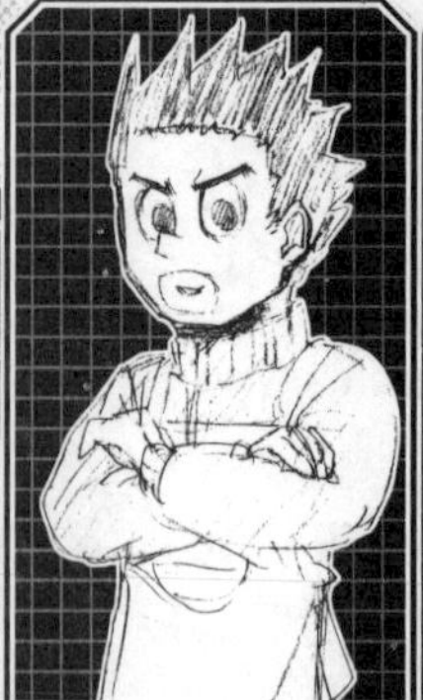

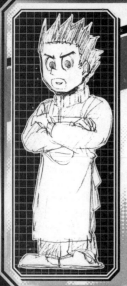

RIKIDO SATO

THIS SACCHARINE MUSCLEMAN WHIPS UP SCRUMPTIOUS SWEETS!! YOU'VE NEVER MET A RIPPED GUY SO KIND, RELIABLE AND DOMESTIC!!

HE RARELY MAKES HIMSELF THE CENTER OF ATTENTION, BUT HE'S ALWAYS READY WITH A PRIMO REACTION TO THE OTHERS' GAGS!! EVERY CLASS NEEDS A GUY LIKE HIM!!

A CHICKEN IN EVERY POT, A CAR IN EVERY GARAGE AND A SATO IN EVERY KITCHEN!!

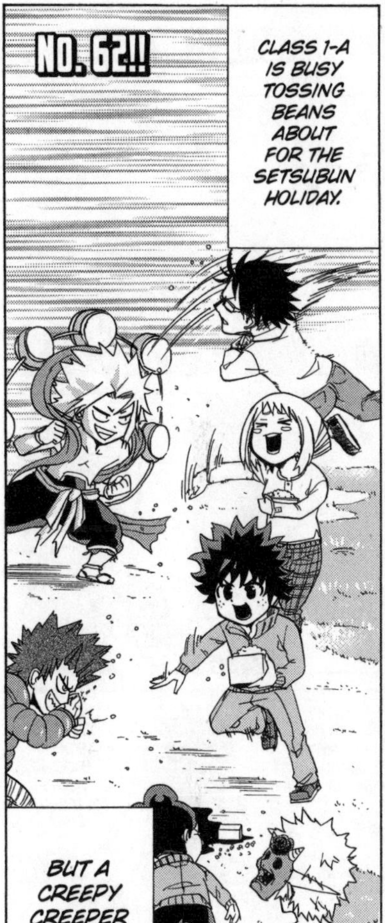
NO. 62!!
CLASS 1-A IS BUSY TOSSING BEANS ABOUT FOR THE SETSUBUN HOLIDAY.
BUT A CREEPY CREEPER WATCHES THEM SILENTLY FROM THE SHADOWS.

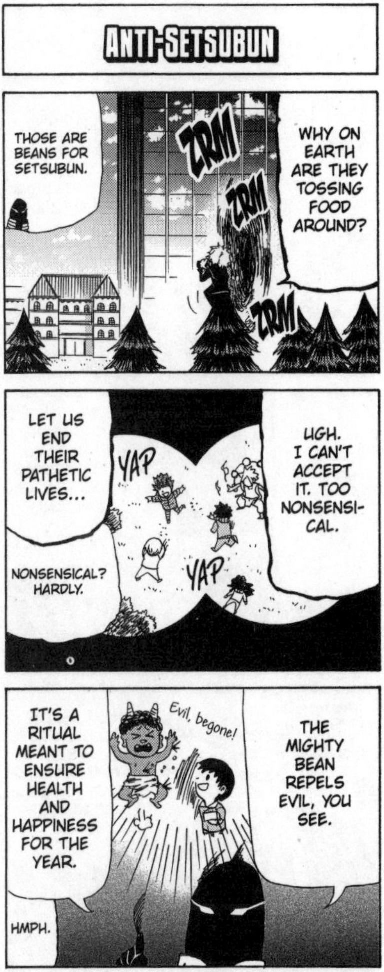
ANTI-SETSUBUN
WHY ON EARTH ARE THEY TOSSING FOOD AROUND?
ZRM
ZRM
ZRM
THOSE ARE BEANS FOR SETSUBUN.
UGH. I CAN'T ACCEPT IT. TOO NONSENSICAL.
LET US END THEIR PATHETIC LIVES...
YAP
YAP
NONSENSICAL? HARDLY.
THE MIGHTY BEAN REPELS EVIL, YOU SEE.
Evil, begone!
IT'S A RITUAL MEANT TO ENSURE HEALTH AND HAPPINESS FOR THE YEAR.
HMPH.
THEN WE NEED A RITUAL TO BRING MORE EVIL INTO THE WORLD.
EVIL
VMM
GOOD
OTHERWISE THE BALANCE IS ALL THROWN OFF.
MAKES SENSE.

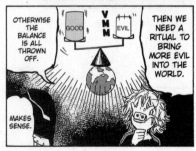

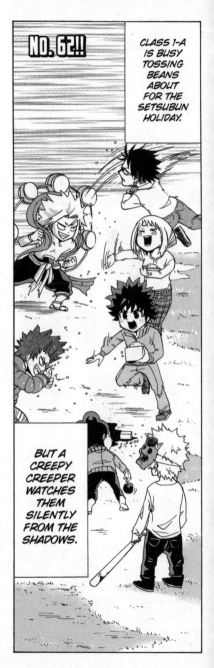

DOUBLE NEGATIVE

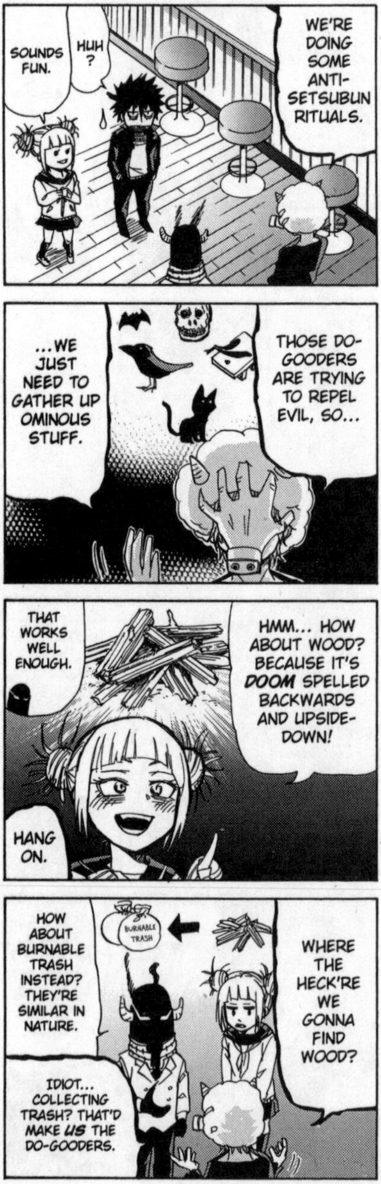
WE'RE DOING SOME ANTI-SETSUBUN RITUALS.
HUH?
SOUNDS FUN.
THOSE DO-GOODERS ARE TRYING TO REPEL EVIL, SO...
...WE JUST NEED TO GATHER UP OMINOUS STUFF.
HMM... HOW ABOUT WOOD? BECAUSE IT'S **DOOM** SPELLED BACKWARDS AND UPSIDE-DOWN!
THAT WORKS WELL ENOUGH.
HANG ON.
WHERE THE HECK'RE WE GONNA FIND WOOD?
BURNABLE TRASH
HOW ABOUT BURNABLE TRASH INSTEAD? THEY'RE SIMILAR IN NATURE.
IDIOT... COLLECTING TRASH? THAT'D MAKE **US** THE DO-GOODERS.

CHARACTERIZATION

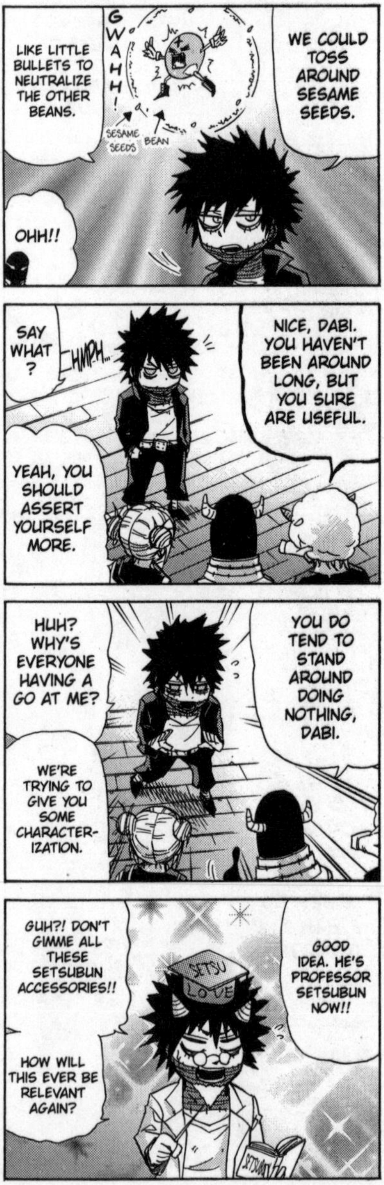
WE COULD TOSS AROUND SESAME SEEDS.
GWAHH!
SESAME SEEDS
BEAN
LIKE LITTLE BULLETS TO NEUTRALIZE THE OTHER BEANS.
OHH!!
NICE, DABI. YOU HAVEN'T BEEN AROUND LONG, BUT YOU SURE ARE USEFUL.
HMPH...
SAY WHAT?
YEAH, YOU SHOULD ASSERT YOURSELF MORE.
YOU DO TEND TO STAND AROUND DOING NOTHING, DABI.
HUH? WHY'S EVERYONE HAVING A GO AT ME?
WE'RE TRYING TO GIVE YOU SOME CHARACTERIZATION.
GOOD IDEA. HE'S PROFESSOR SETSUBUN NOW!!
SETSU LOVE
GUH?! DON'T GIMME ALL THESE SETSUBUN ACCESSORIES!!
HOW WILL THIS EVER BE RELEVANT AGAIN?

Ratings Board

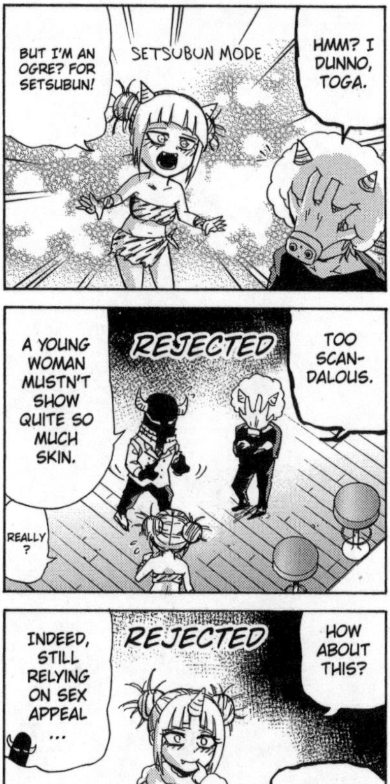
HMM? I DUNNO, TOGA.
SETSUBUN MODE
BUT I'M AN OGRE? FOR SETSUBUN!
TOO SCANDALOUS.
REJECTED
A YOUNG WOMAN MUSTN'T SHOW QUITE SO MUCH SKIN.
REALLY?
HOW ABOUT THIS?
REJECTED
INDEED, STILL RELYING ON SEX APPEAL...
STILL TOO SCANDALOUS. YOU TRYING TO GET US IN TROUBLE...?
FINE... AND THIS?
ACCEPTED
THE LOOK SUITS YOU.
THAT... WORKS.
SO COLLARBONE IS ALL THEY'LL TOLERATE.
SKCH SKCH

Vacurogiri

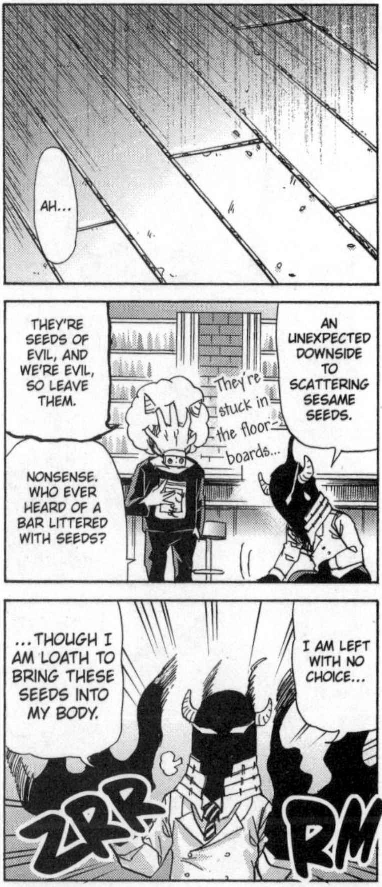
AH...
AN UNEXPECTED DOWNSIDE TO SCATTERING SESAME SEEDS.
They're stuck in the floorboards...
THEY'RE SEEDS OF EVIL, AND WE'RE EVIL, SO LEAVE THEM.
NONSENSE. WHO EVER HEARD OF A BAR LITTERED WITH SEEDS?
I AM LEFT WITH NO CHOICE...
...THOUGH I AM LOATH TO BRING THESE SEEDS INTO MY BODY.
RM
ZRR
WARP GATE
WOW, HOW CONVENIENT!! A MUST-HAVE FOR EVERY HOME!!
ZRRRRM
TNK
TNK

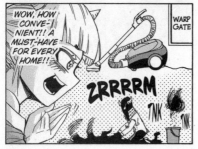

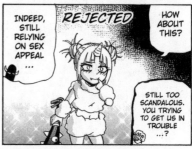

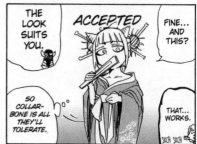

Embracing the Role

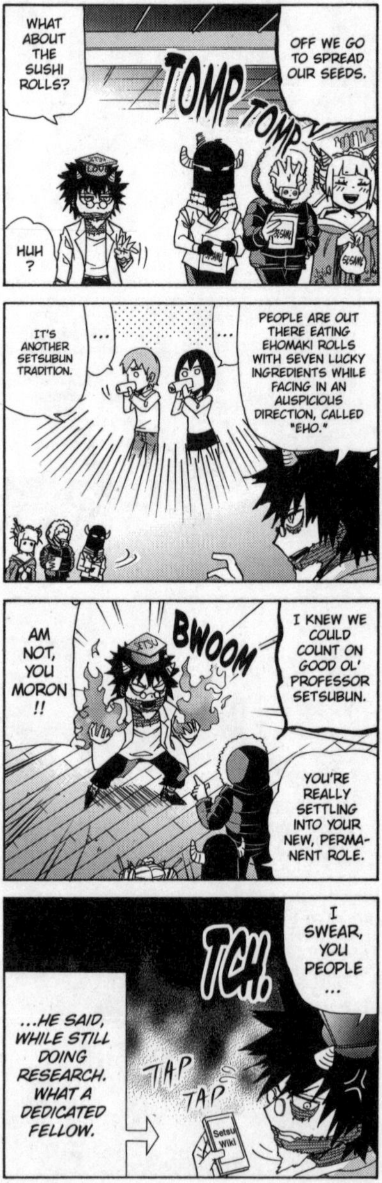
OFF WE GO TO SPREAD OUR SEEDS.
TOMP
TOMP
WHAT ABOUT THE SUSHI ROLLS?
HUH?
PEOPLE ARE OUT THERE EATING EHOMAKI ROLLS WITH SEVEN LUCKY INGREDIENTS WHILE FACING IN AN AUSPICIOUS DIRECTION, CALLED "EHO."
...
...
IT'S ANOTHER SETSUBUN TRADITION.
I KNEW WE COULD COUNT ON GOOD OL' PROFESSOR SETSUBUN.
BWOOM
AM NOT, YOU MORON!!
YOU'RE REALLY SETTLING INTO YOUR NEW, PERMANENT ROLE.
I SWEAR, YOU PEOPLE...
TCH.
...HE SAID, WHILE STILL DOING RESEARCH. WHAT A DEDICATED FELLOW.
TAP
TAP
Setsu Wiki

Winging It

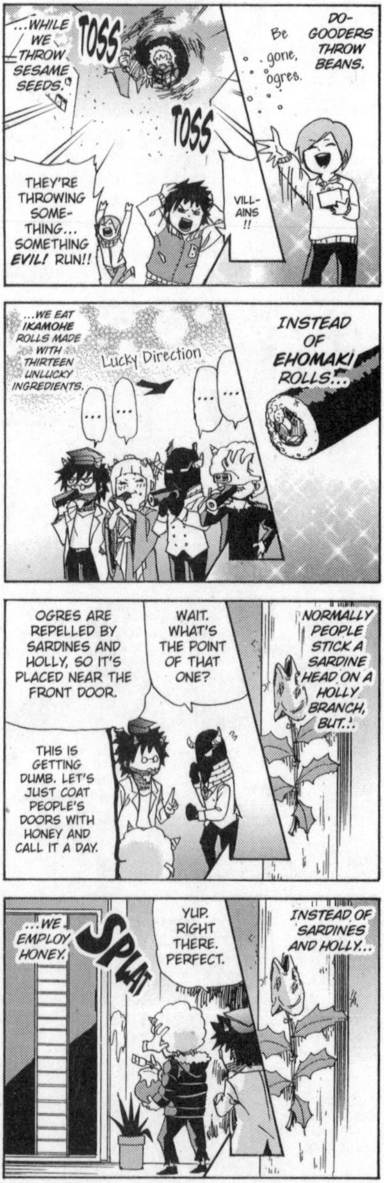
DO-GOODERS THROW BEANS.
Be gone, ogres.
...WHILE WE THROW SESAME SEEDS.
TOSS
TOSS
VILLAINS!!
THEY'RE THROWING SOMETHING... SOMETHING EVIL! RUN!!
INSTEAD OF EHOMAKI ROLLS...
...
...
...
...
Lucky Direction
...WE EAT IKAMOHE ROLLS MADE WITH THIRTEEN UNLUCKY INGREDIENTS.
NORMALLY PEOPLE STICK A SARDINE HEAD ON A HOLLY BRANCH, BUT...
WAIT. WHAT'S THE POINT OF THAT ONE?
OGRES ARE REPELLED BY SARDINES AND HOLLY, SO IT'S PLACED NEAR THE FRONT DOOR.
THIS IS GETTING DUMB. LET'S JUST COAT PEOPLE'S DOORS WITH HONEY AND CALL IT A DAY.
INSTEAD OF SARDINES AND HOLLY...
YUP. RIGHT THERE. PERFECT.
SPLAT
...WE EMPLOY HONEY.

Stumping the Authorities

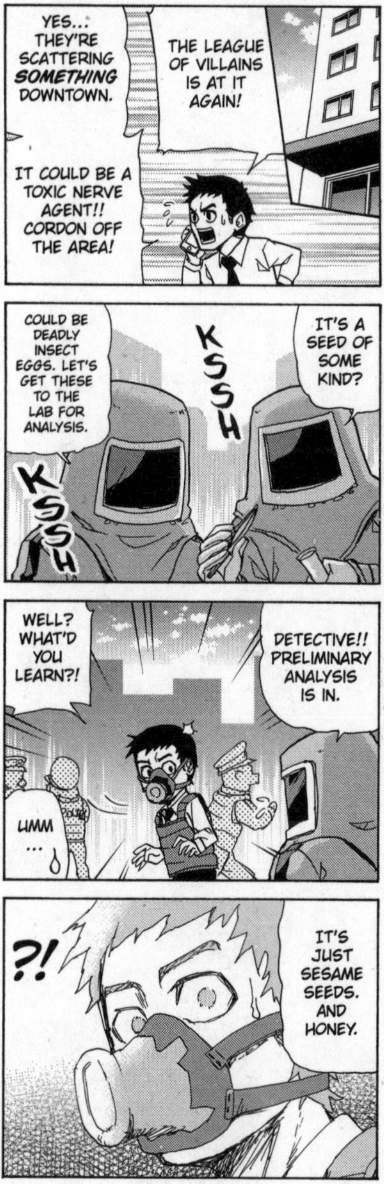
THE LEAGUE OF VILLAINS IS AT IT AGAIN!
YES... THEY'RE SCATTERING *SOMETHING* DOWNTOWN.
IT COULD BE A TOXIC NERVE AGENT!! CORDON OFF THE AREA!
IT'S A SEED OF SOME KIND?
KSSH
COULD BE DEADLY INSECT EGGS. LET'S GET THESE TO THE LAB FOR ANALYSIS.
KSSH
DETECTIVE!! PRELIMINARY ANALYSIS IS IN.
WELL? WHAT'D YOU LEARN?!
UMM ...
IT'S JUST SESAME SEEDS. AND HONEY.
?!

Armchair Investigators

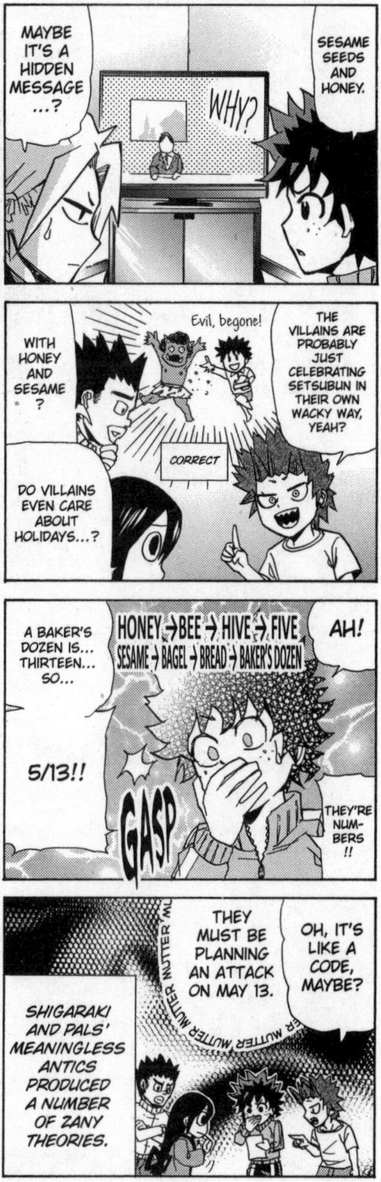
SESAME SEEDS AND HONEY.
WHY?
MAYBE IT'S A HIDDEN MESSAGE ...?
THE VILLAINS ARE PROBABLY JUST CELEBRATING SETSUBUN IN THEIR OWN WACKY WAY, YEAH?
Evil, begone!
WITH HONEY AND SESAME ?
CORRECT
DO VILLAINS EVEN CARE ABOUT HOLIDAYS...?
AH!
HONEY → BEE → HIVE → FIVE
SESAME → BAGEL → BREAD → BAKER'S DOZEN
A BAKER'S DOZEN IS... THIRTEEN... SO...
THEY'RE NUMBERS !!
5/13!!
GASP
OH, IT'S LIKE A CODE, MAYBE?
THEY MUST BE PLANNING AN ATTACK ON MAY 13.
MUTTER MUTTER MUTTER
SHIGARAKI AND PALS' MEANINGLESS ANTICS PRODUCED A NUMBER OF ZANY THEORIES.

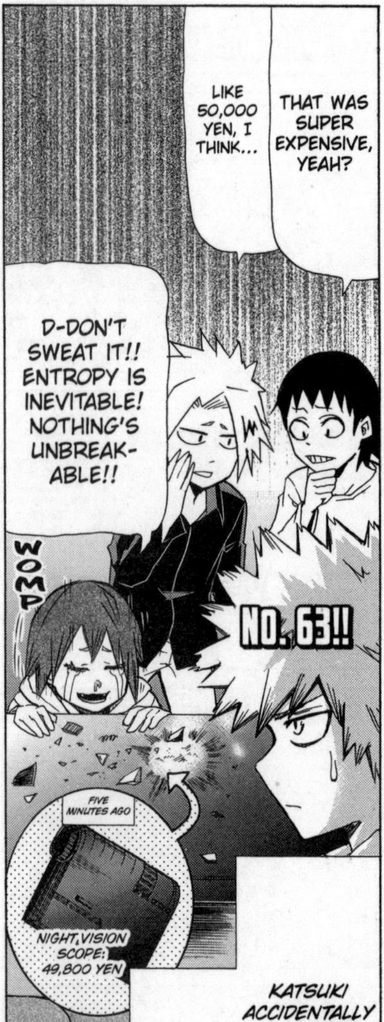
THAT WAS SUPER EXPENSIVE, YEAH?
LIKE 50,000 YEN, I THINK...
D-DON'T SWEAT IT!! ENTROPY IS INEVITABLE! NOTHING'S UNBREAK-ABLE!!
WOMP
NO. 63!!
FIVE MINUTES AGO
NIGHT VISION SCOPE: 49,800 YEN
KATSUKI ACCIDENTALLY SMASHED KIRISHIMA'S NIGHT VISION GEAR.
SECRETLY, HE FEELS GUILTY ABOUT IT.

*ABOUT $498

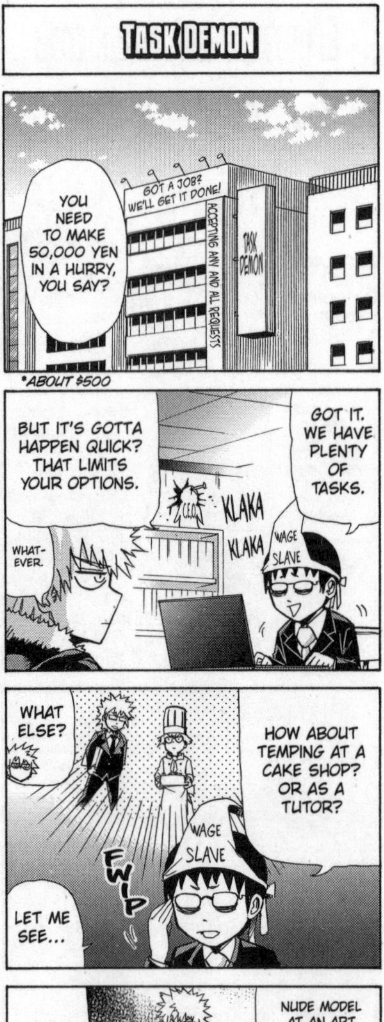
TASK DEMON
GOT A JOB? WE'LL GET IT DONE!
ACCEPTING ANY AND ALL REQUESTS
TASK DEMON
YOU NEED TO MAKE 50,000 YEN IN A HURRY, YOU SAY?
GOT IT. WE HAVE PLENTY OF TASKS.
BUT IT'S GOTTA HAPPEN QUICK? THAT LIMITS YOUR OPTIONS.
C.E.O.
KLAKA
KLAKA
WAGE SLAVE
WHAT-EVER.
HOW ABOUT TEMPING AT A CAKE SHOP? OR AS A TUTOR?
WHAT ELSE?
WAGE SLAVE
FWIP
LET ME SEE...
NUDE MODEL AT AN ART COLLEGE? THAT PAYS 4,000 YEN PER HOUR.
CAKES, PLEASE.
WAGE SLAVE
DOOM

*ABOUT $500

*ABOUT $40

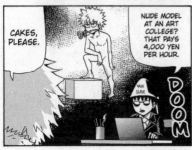

BITTERSWEET

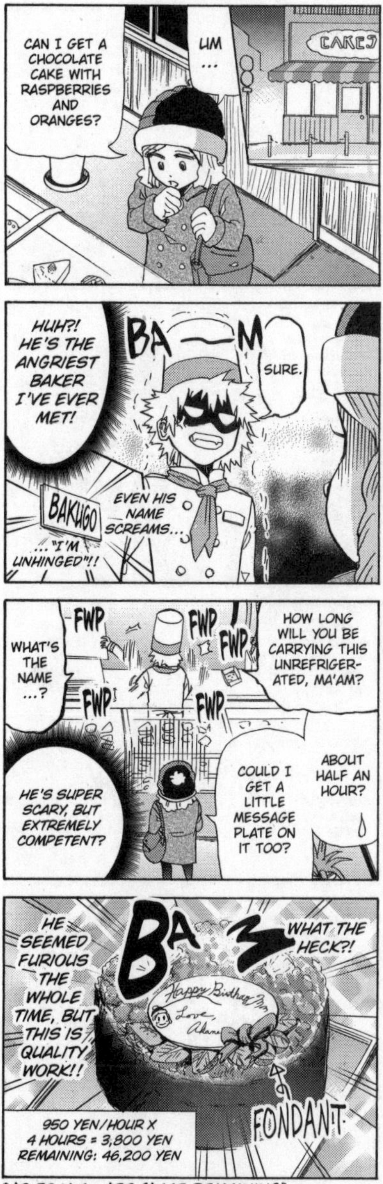
CAKES
UM ...
CAN I GET A CHOCOLATE CAKE WITH RASPBERRIES AND ORANGES?
SURE.
BA—M
HUH?! HE'S THE ANGRIEST BAKER I'VE EVER MET!
EVEN HIS NAME SCREAMS...
BAKUGO
..."I'M UNHINGED"!!
HOW LONG WILL YOU BE CARRYING THIS UNREFRIGERATED, MA'AM?
FWP FWP FWP
WHAT'S THE NAME ...?
FWP FWP FWP
ABOUT HALF AN HOUR?
COULD I GET A LITTLE MESSAGE PLATE ON IT TOO?
HE'S SUPER SCARY, BUT EXTREMELY COMPETENT?
WHAT THE HECK?!
BAM
HE SEEMED FURIOUS THE WHOLE TIME, BUT THIS IS QUALITY WORK!!
Love, Akane
FONDANT
950 YEN/HOUR X 4 HOURS = 3,800 YEN REMAINING: 46,200 YEN

*$9.50 X 4 = $38 ($462 REMAINING)

POSITIVE/NEGATIVE REINFORCEMENT

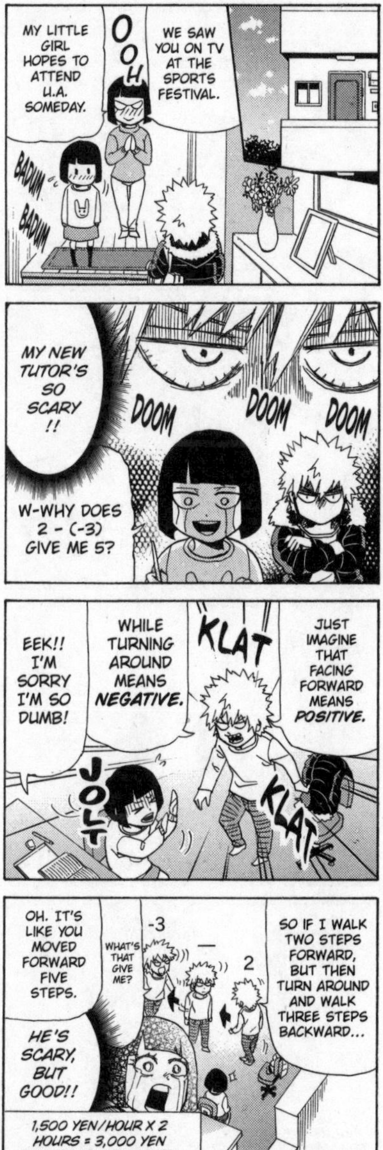
WE SAW YOU ON TV AT THE SPORTS FESTIVAL.
OOH
MY LITTLE GIRL HOPES TO ATTEND U.A. SOMEDAY.
BADUM BADUM
DOOM DOOM DOOM
MY NEW TUTOR'S SO SCARY !!
W-WHY DOES 2 - (-3) GIVE ME 5?
JUST IMAGINE THAT FACING FORWARD MEANS POSITIVE.
KLAT
WHILE TURNING AROUND MEANS NEGATIVE.
EEK!! I'M SORRY I'M SO DUMB!
KLAT
JOLT
SO IF I WALK TWO STEPS FORWARD, BUT THEN TURN AROUND AND WALK THREE STEPS BACKWARD...
2
—
-3
WHAT'S THAT GIVE ME?
OH. IT'S LIKE YOU MOVED FORWARD FIVE STEPS.
HE'S SCARY, BUT GOOD!!
1,500 YEN/HOUR X 2 HOURS = 3,000 YEN REMAINING: 43,200 YEN

*$15 X 2 = $30 ($432 REMAINING)

Rat Race

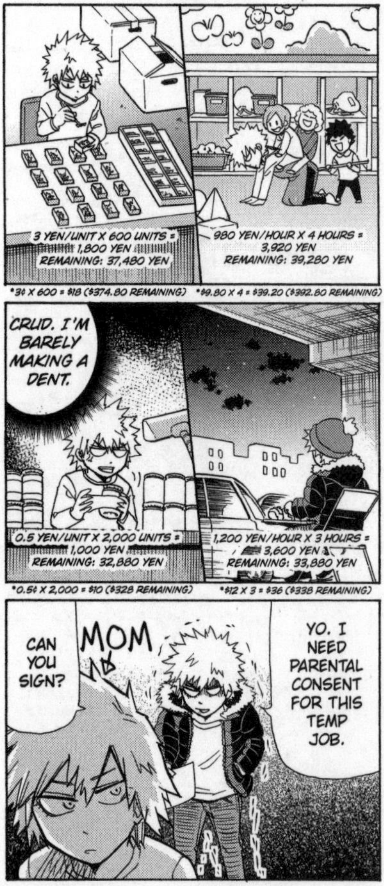
980 YEN/HOUR X 4 HOURS = 3,920 YEN REMAINING: 39,280 YEN
3 YEN/UNIT X 600 UNITS = 1,800 YEN REMAINING: 37,480 YEN
*$9.80 X 4 = $39.20 ($392.80 REMAINING)
*3¢ X 600 = $18 ($374.80 REMAINING)
1,200 YEN/HOUR X 3 HOURS = 3,600 YEN REMAINING: 33,880 YEN
CRUD. I'M BARELY MAKING A DENT.
0.5 YEN/UNIT X 2,000 UNITS = 1,000 YEN REMAINING: 32,880 YEN
*$12 X 3 = $36 ($338 REMAINING)
*0.5¢ X 2,000 = $10 ($328 REMAINING)
YO. I NEED PARENTAL CONSENT FOR THIS TEMP JOB.
MOM
CAN YOU SIGN?
SPARKLE
SPARKLE
4,000 YEN/HOUR X 3 HOURS = 12,000 YEN REMAINING: 20,880 YEN
*$40 X 3 = $120 ($208 REMAINING)

In High Demand

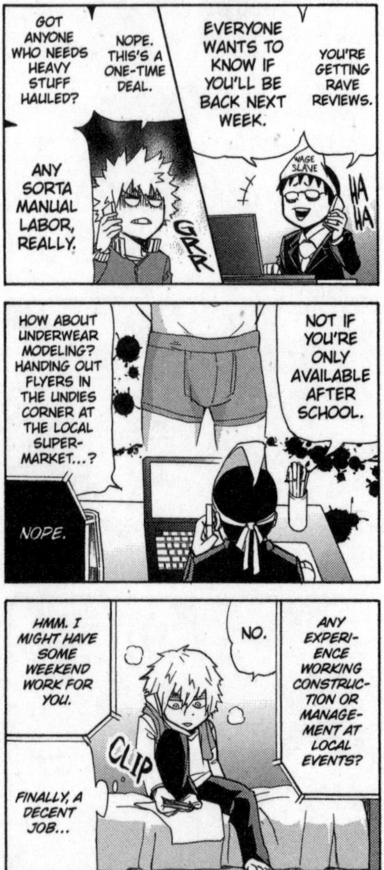
YOU'RE GETTING RAVE REVIEWS.
EVERYONE WANTS TO KNOW IF YOU'LL BE BACK NEXT WEEK.
WAGE SLAVE
HA HA
NOPE. THIS'S A ONE-TIME DEAL.
GOT ANYONE WHO NEEDS HEAVY STUFF HAULED?
ANY SORTA MANUAL LABOR, REALLY.
GRR
NOT IF YOU'RE ONLY AVAILABLE AFTER SCHOOL.
HOW ABOUT UNDERWEAR MODELING? HANDING OUT FLYERS IN THE UNDIES CORNER AT THE LOCAL SUPER-MARKET...?
NOPE.
ANY EXPERI-ENCE WORKING CONSTRUC-TION OR MANAGE-MENT AT LOCAL EVENTS?
NO.
HMM. I MIGHT HAVE SOME WEEKEND WORK FOR YOU.
CLIP
FINALLY, A DECENT JOB...
WEAR THAT AND HELP KIDS INTO THE BOUNCY HOUSE.
SILENT
BEE FEST
...

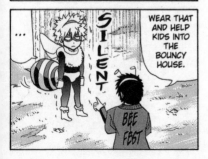

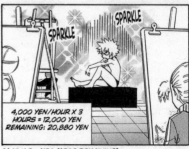

LET SLEEPING BEES LIE

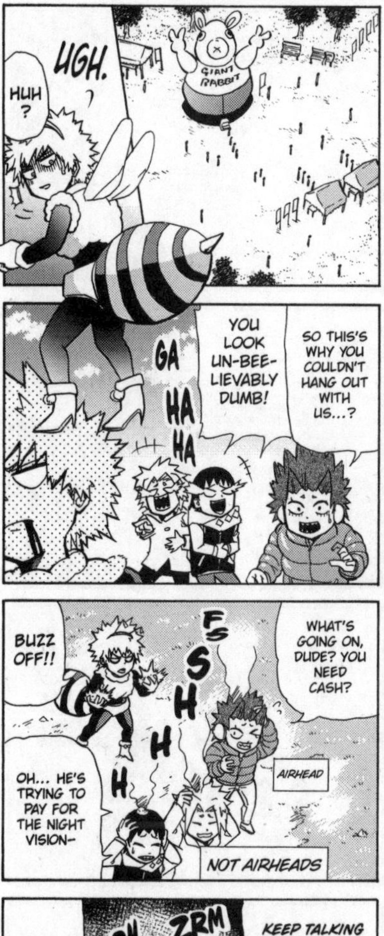
GIANT RABBIT
UGH.
HUH?
SO THIS'S WHY YOU COULDN'T HANG OUT WITH US...?
YOU LOOK UN-BEE-LIEVABLY DUMB!
GA HA HA HA
WHAT'S GOING ON, DUDE? YOU NEED CASH?
FSSHHH
BUZZ OFF!!
AIRHEAD
OH... HE'S TRYING TO PAY FOR THE NIGHT VISION-
NOT AIRHEADS
KEEP TALKING IF YOU WANNA SEE WHAT GRAY MATTER LOOKS LIKE.
ZRM ZRM
UM, UM... "YAYY"? "YAYYY"!!
YAYYY.
SUDDEN AIRHEADS

DARK DEKU

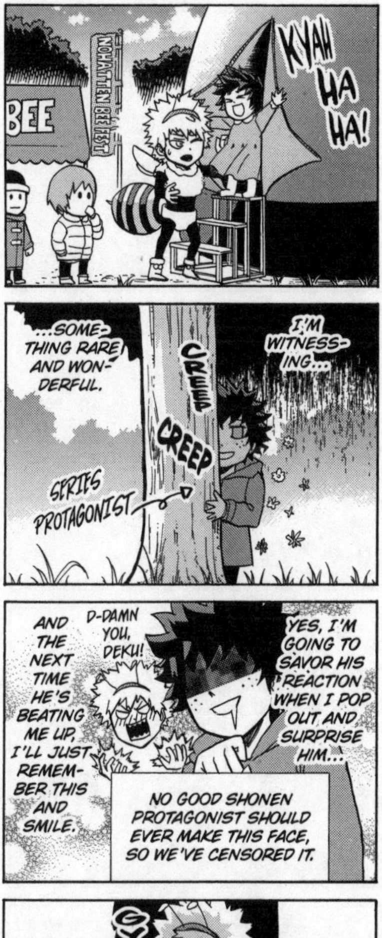
KYAH HA HA!
NOHATTEN BEE FEST
BEE
I'M WITNESSING...
...SOMETHING RARE AND WONDERFUL.
CREEP CREEP
SERIES PROTAGONIST
YES, I'M GOING TO SAVOR HIS REACTION WHEN I POP OUT AND SURPRISE HIM...
D-DAMN YOU, DEKU!
AND THE NEXT TIME HE'S BEATING ME UP, I'LL JUST REMEMBER THIS AND SMILE.
NO GOOD SHONEN PROTAGONIST SHOULD EVER MAKE THIS FACE, SO WE'VE CENSORED IT.
HAVING FUN? ANY LAST WORDS?
GYAHH!
I-I WANNA BE THE GREATEST HERO EVER?
11,000 YEN/DAY X 2 DAYS = 22,000 YEN
50,000 YEN EARNED!!

*$110 X 2 = $220 ($500 EARNED!)

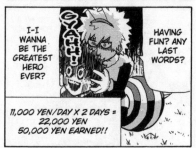

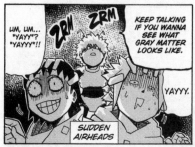

THE PAIN OF DISCRETION

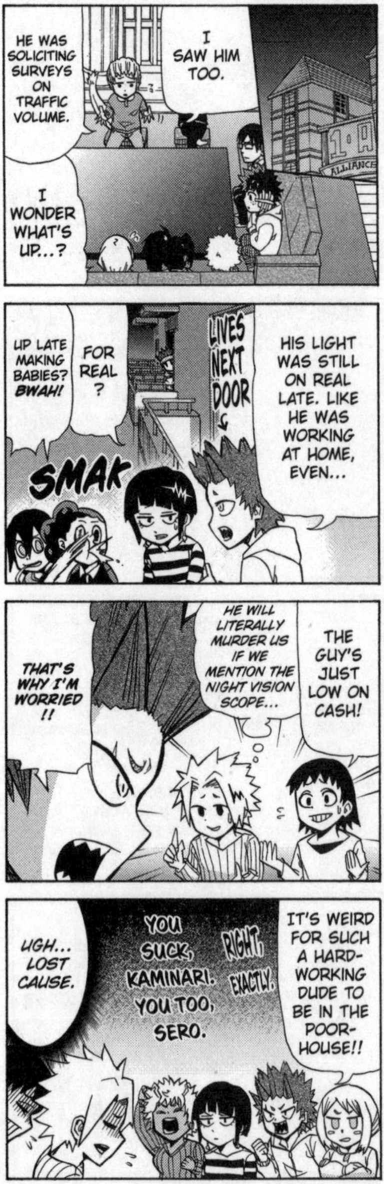
I SAW HIM TOO.
HE WAS SOLICITING SURVEYS ON TRAFFIC VOLUME.
I WONDER WHAT'S UP...?
HIS LIGHT WAS STILL ON REAL LATE. LIKE HE WAS WORKING AT HOME, EVEN...
LIVES NEXT DOOR
FOR REAL?
UP LATE MAKING BABIES? BWAH!
SMAK
THE GUY'S JUST LOW ON CASH!
HE WILL LITERALLY MURDER US IF WE MENTION THE NIGHT VISION SCOPE...
THAT'S WHY I'M WORRIED!!
IT'S WEIRD FOR SUCH A HARD-WORKING DUDE TO BE IN THE POOR-HOUSE!!
RIGHT.
EXACTLY.
YOU SUCK, KAMINARI. YOU TOO, SERO.
UGH... LOST CAUSE.

HUSH MONEY

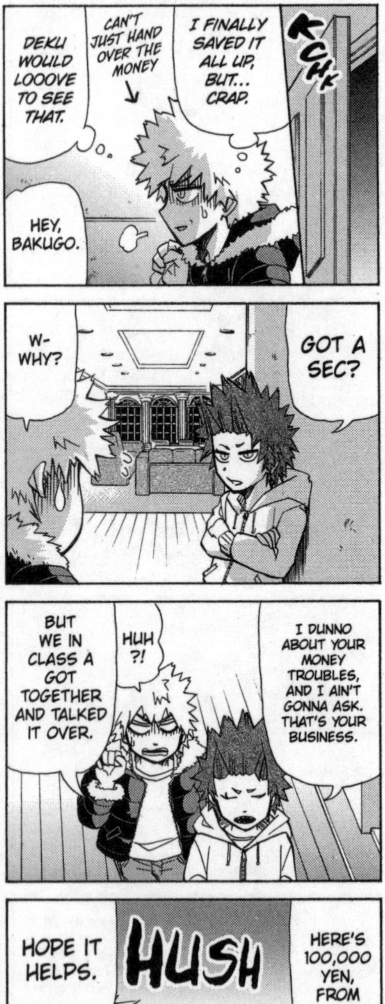
KCHK
I FINALLY SAVED IT ALL UP, BUT... CRAP.
CAN'T JUST HAND OVER THE MONEY
DEKU WOULD LOOOVE TO SEE THAT.
HEY, BAKUGO.
GOT A SEC?
W-WHY?
I DUNNO ABOUT YOUR MONEY TROUBLES, AND I AIN'T GONNA ASK. THAT'S YOUR BUSINESS.
HUH?!
BUT WE IN CLASS A GOT TOGETHER AND TALKED IT OVER.
HERE'S 100,000 YEN, FROM ALL OF US.
HUSH
HOPE IT HELPS.

*ABOUT $1,000

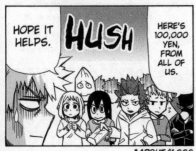

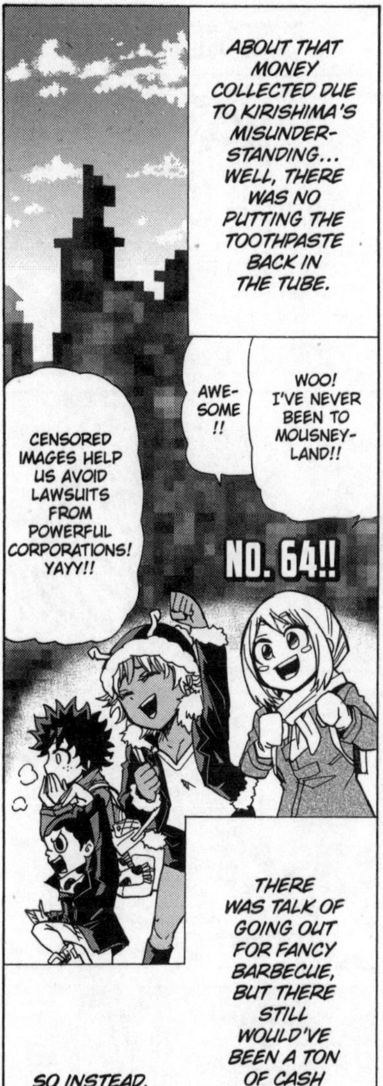
ABOUT THAT MONEY COLLECTED DUE TO KIRISHIMA'S MISUNDERSTANDING... WELL, THERE WAS NO PUTTING THE TOOTHPASTE BACK IN THE TUBE.
WOO! I'VE NEVER BEEN TO MOUSNEYLAND!!
AWESOME!!
CENSORED IMAGES HELP US AVOID LAWSUITS FROM POWERFUL CORPORATIONS! YAYY!!
NO. 64!!
THERE WAS TALK OF GOING OUT FOR FANCY BARBECUE, BUT THERE STILL WOULD'VE BEEN A TON OF CASH LEFT OVER.
SO INSTEAD, WE SETTLED ON A TRIP TO MOUSNEYLAND.

LITIGATION RISK

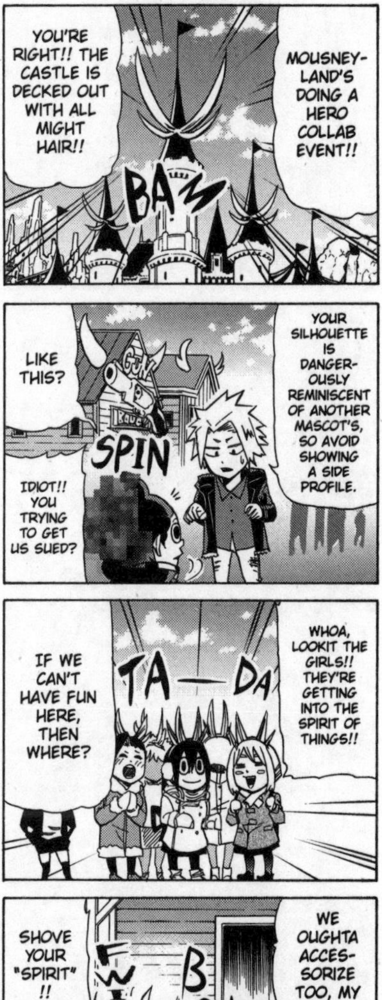
MOUSNEYLAND'S DOING A HERO COLLAB EVENT!!
BAM
YOU'RE RIGHT!! THE CASTLE IS DECKED OUT WITH ALL MIGHT HAIR!!
YOUR SILHOUETTE IS DANGEROUSLY REMINISCENT OF ANOTHER MASCOT'S, SO AVOID SHOWING A SIDE PROFILE.
SPIN
LIKE THIS?
IDIOT!! YOU TRYING TO GET US SUED?
WHOA, LOOKIT THE GIRLS!! THEY'RE GETTING INTO THE SPIRIT OF THINGS!!
TA-DA
IF WE CAN'T HAVE FUN HERE, THEN WHERE?
WE OUGHTA ACCESSORIZE TOO, MY DUDES!!
BOM
FWIP
SHOVE YOUR "SPIRIT"!!

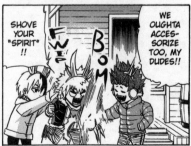

MEMORIES OF BLUE

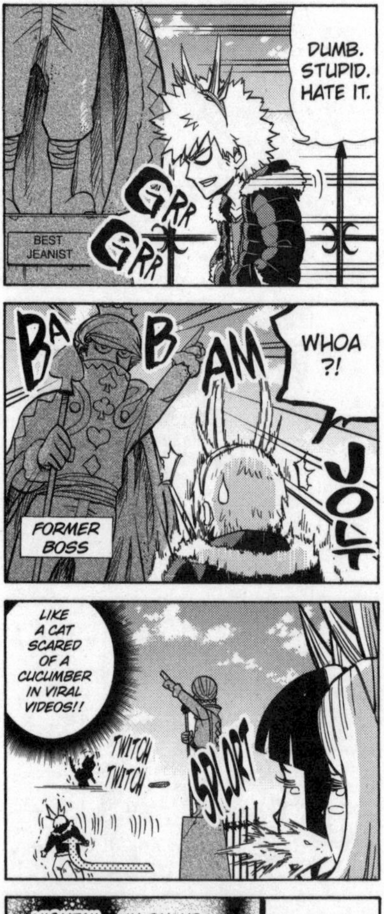
DUMB. STUPID. HATE IT.
GRR
GRR
BEST JEANIST
WHOA ?!
JOLT
BAM
B
BA
FORMER BOSS
SPLORT
TWITCH TWITCH
LIKE A CAT SCARED OF A CUCUMBER IN VIRAL VIDEOS!!
ARE YOU... MOCKING ME...
DOOM
UH-OH, HE HEARD THAT?
HIGHTAIL IT, URARAKA!!
DOOM

SPIRIT PHOTOGRAPHY

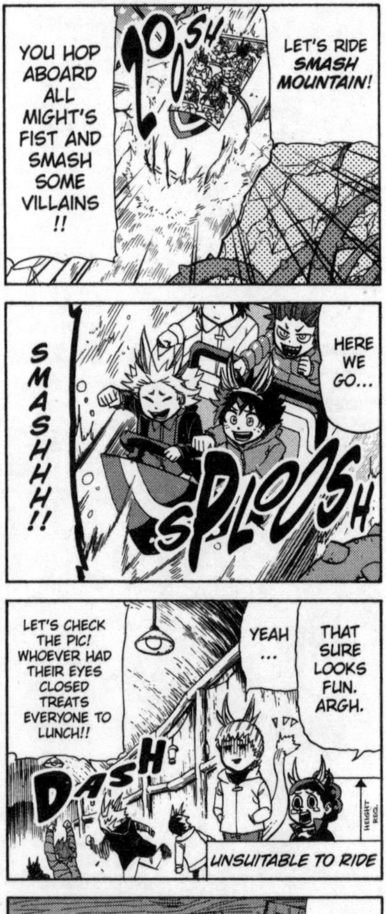
LET'S RIDE SMASH MOUNTAIN!
ZOOSH
YOU HOP ABOARD ALL MIGHT'S FIST AND SMASH SOME VILLAINS !!
HERE WE GO...
SPLOOSH
SMASHHHH!!
THAT SURE LOOKS FUN. ARGH.
YEAH ...
LET'S CHECK THE PIC! WHOEVER HAD THEIR EYES CLOSED TREATS EVERYONE TO LUNCH!!
HEIGHT REQ.
DASH
UNSUITABLE TO RIDE
I APOLO-GIZE.

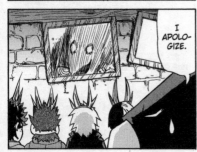

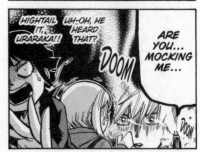

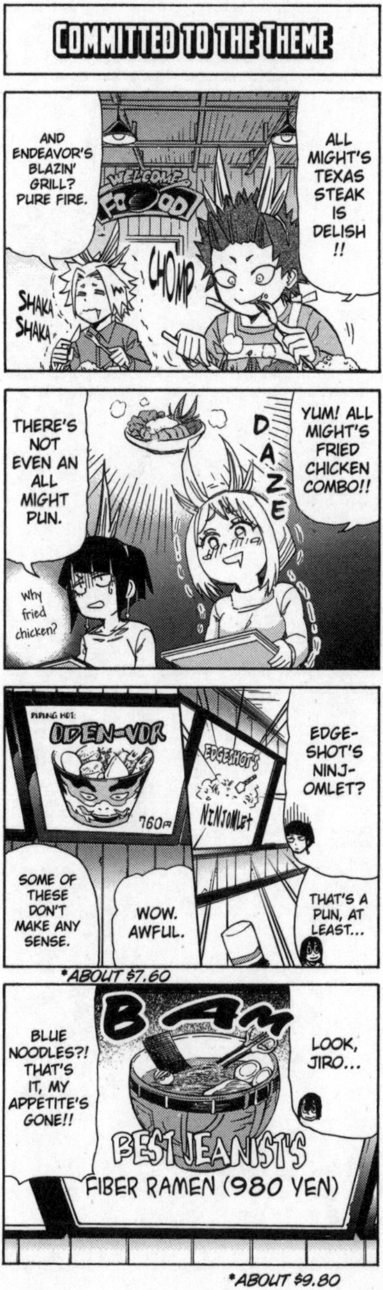
COMMITTED TO THE THEME
ALL MIGHT'S TEXAS STEAK IS DELISH!!
AND ENDEAVOR'S BLAZIN' GRILL? PURE FIRE.
WELCOME FOOD
CHOMP
SHAKA SHAKA
YUM! ALL MIGHT'S FRIED CHICKEN COMBO!!
DAZE
THERE'S NOT EVEN AN ALL MIGHT PUN.
Why fried chicken?
EDGE-SHOT'S NINJ-OMLET?
PIPING HOT:
ODEN-VOR
760円
EDGESHOT'S NINJOMLET
THAT'S A PUN, AT LEAST...
WOW. AWFUL.
SOME OF THESE DON'T MAKE ANY SENSE.
*ABOUT $7.60
LOOK, JIRO...
BAM
BLUE NOODLES?! THAT'S IT, MY APPETITE'S GONE!!
BEST JEANIST'S
FIBER RAMEN (980 YEN)
*ABOUT $9.80

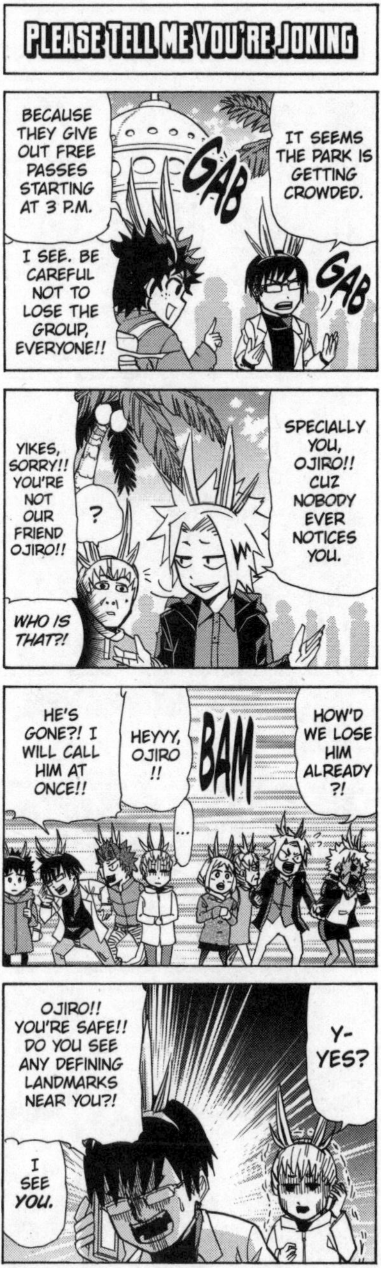
PLEASE TELL ME YOU'RE JOKING
IT SEEMS THE PARK IS GETTING CROWDED.
GAB
BECAUSE THEY GIVE OUT FREE PASSES STARTING AT 3 P.M.
GAB
I SEE. BE CAREFUL NOT TO LOSE THE GROUP, EVERYONE!!
SPECIALLY YOU, OJIRO!! CUZ NOBODY EVER NOTICES YOU.
YIKES, SORRY!! YOU'RE NOT OUR FRIEND OJIRO!!
?
WHO IS THAT?!
HOW'D WE LOSE HIM ALREADY?!
BAM
HEYYY, OJIRO!!
HE'S GONE?! I WILL CALL HIM AT ONCE!!
...
Y-YES?
OJIRO!! YOU'RE SAFE!! DO YOU SEE ANY DEFINING LANDMARKS NEAR YOU?!
I SEE YOU.

The Joyfullest Place on Earth

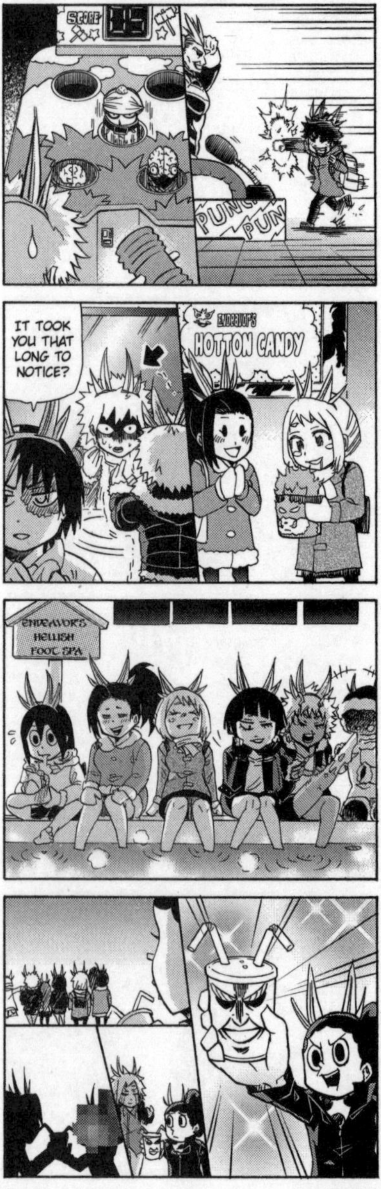

SCORE
IT TOOK YOU THAT LONG TO NOTICE?
ENDEAVOR'S HOTTON CANDY
ENDEAVOR'S HELLISH FOOT SPA

Still Committed to the Theme

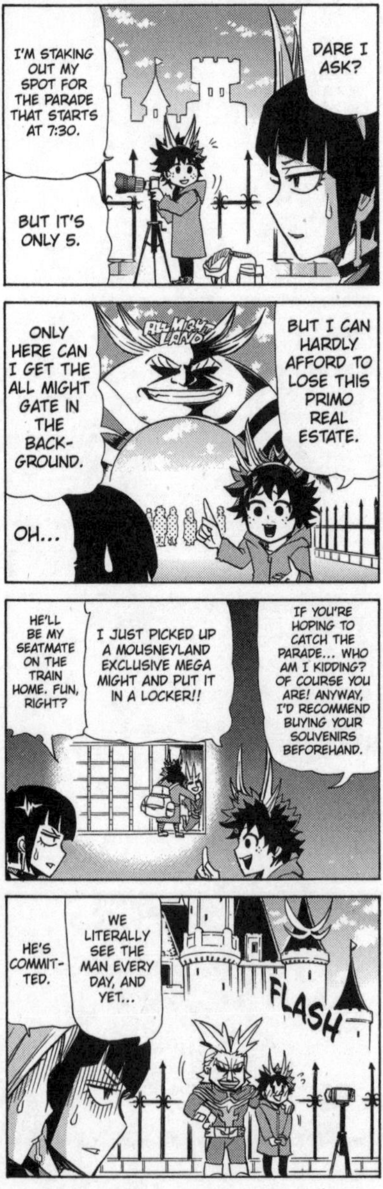

DARE I ASK?
I'M STAKING OUT MY SPOT FOR THE PARADE THAT STARTS AT 7:30.
BUT IT'S ONLY 5.
BUT I CAN HARDLY AFFORD TO LOSE THIS PRIMO REAL ESTATE.
ALL MIGHT LAND
ONLY HERE CAN I GET THE ALL MIGHT GATE IN THE BACK-GROUND.
OH...
IF YOU'RE HOPING TO CATCH THE PARADE... WHO AM I KIDDING? OF COURSE YOU ARE! ANYWAY, I'D RECOMMEND BUYING YOUR SOUVENIRS BEFOREHAND.
I JUST PICKED UP A MOUSNEYLAND EXCLUSIVE MEGA MIGHT AND PUT IT IN A LOCKER!!
HE'LL BE MY SEATMATE ON THE TRAIN HOME. FUN, RIGHT?
FLASH
WE LITERALLY SEE THE MAN EVERY DAY, AND YET...
HE'S COMMIT-TED.

INHERITED SHAME

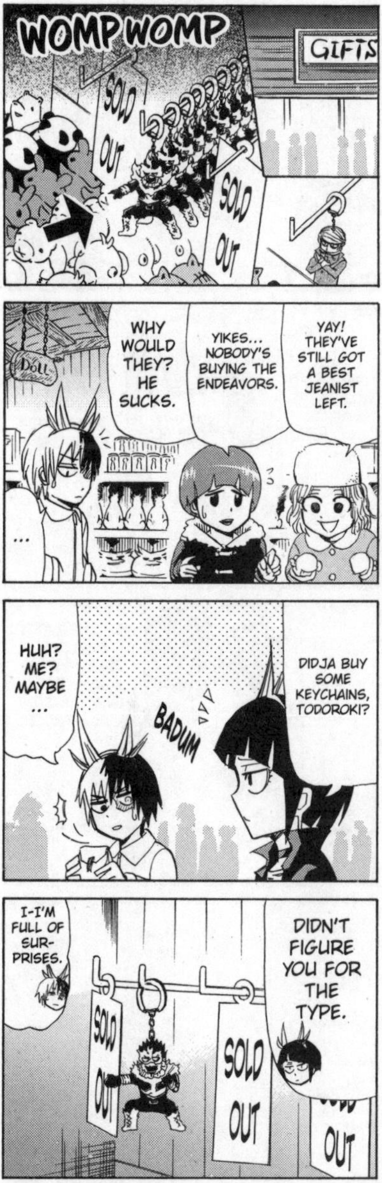
WOMP WOMP
GIFTS
SOLD OUT
SOLD OUT
YAY! THEY'VE STILL GOT A BEST JEANIST LEFT.
YIKES... NOBODY'S BUYING THE ENDEAVORS.
WHY WOULD THEY? HE SUCKS.
DOLL
...
DIDJA BUY SOME KEYCHAINS, TODOROKI?
BADUM
HUH? ME? MAYBE...
DIDN'T FIGURE YOU FOR THE TYPE.
I-I'M FULL OF SUR-PRISES.
SOLD OUT
SOLD OUT
SOLD OUT

MORE LIKE, INSPIREWORKS

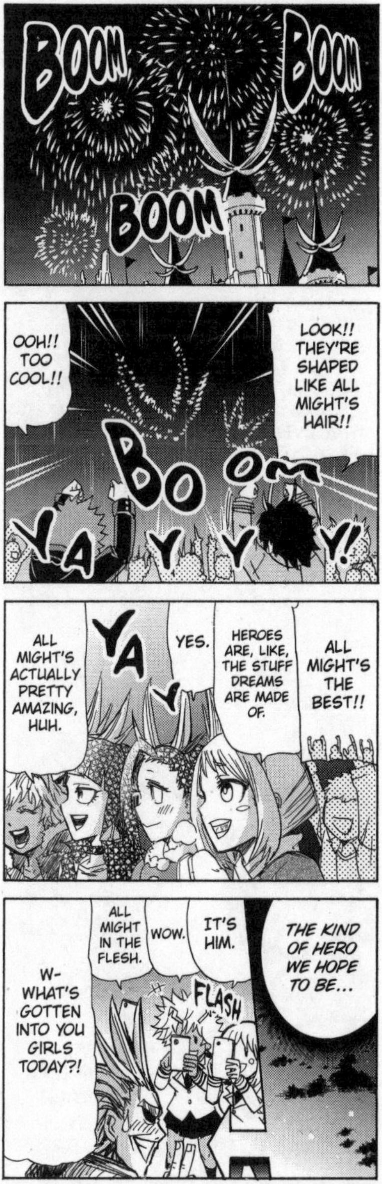
BOOM
BOOM
BOOM
LOOK!! THEY'RE SHAPED LIKE ALL MIGHT'S HAIR!!
OOH!! TOO COOL!!
BOOM
YAYYYY!
ALL MIGHT'S THE BEST!!
HEROES ARE, LIKE, THE STUFF DREAMS ARE MADE OF.
YES.
YAY
ALL MIGHT'S ACTUALLY PRETTY AMAZING, HUH.
THE KIND OF HERO WE HOPE TO BE...
IT'S HIM.
WOW.
ALL MIGHT IN THE FLESH.
FLASH
W-WHAT'S GOTTEN INTO YOU GIRLS TODAY?!

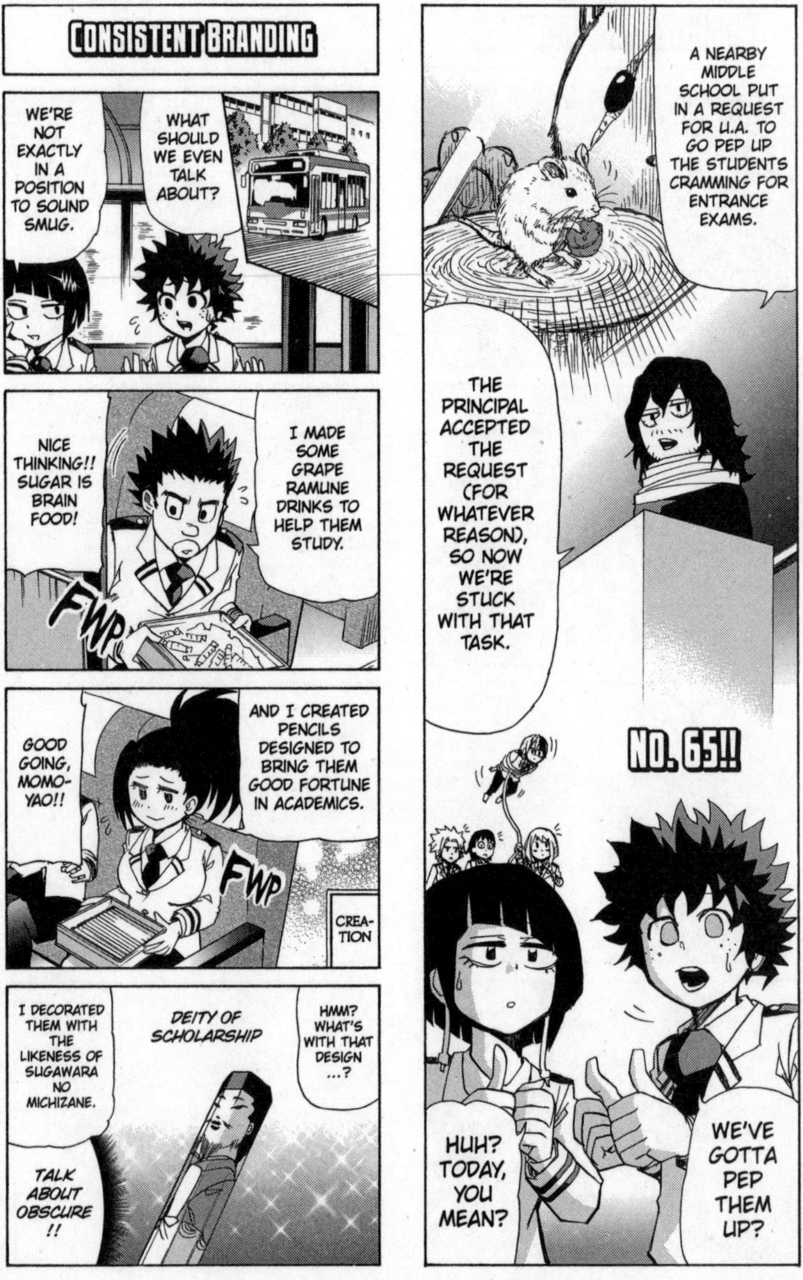
A NEARBY MIDDLE SCHOOL PUT IN A REQUEST FOR U.A. TO GO PEP UP THE STUDENTS CRAMMING FOR ENTRANCE EXAMS.
THE PRINCIPAL ACCEPTED THE REQUEST (FOR WHATEVER REASON), SO NOW WE'RE STUCK WITH THAT TASK.
NO. 65!!
WE'VE GOTTA PEP THEM UP?
HUH? TODAY, YOU MEAN?
CONSISTENT BRANDING
WHAT SHOULD WE EVEN TALK ABOUT?
WE'RE NOT EXACTLY IN A POSITION TO SOUND SMUG.
I MADE SOME GRAPE RAMUNE DRINKS TO HELP THEM STUDY.
NICE THINKING!! SUGAR IS BRAIN FOOD!
FWP
AND I CREATED PENCILS DESIGNED TO BRING THEM GOOD FORTUNE IN ACADEMICS.
GOOD GOING, MOMO-YAO!!
FWP
CREA-TION
HMM? WHAT'S WITH THAT DESIGN ...?
DEITY OF SCHOLARSHIP
I DECORATED THEM WITH THE LIKENESS OF SUGAWARA NO MICHIZANE.
TALK ABOUT OBSCURE !!

Booby Prizes

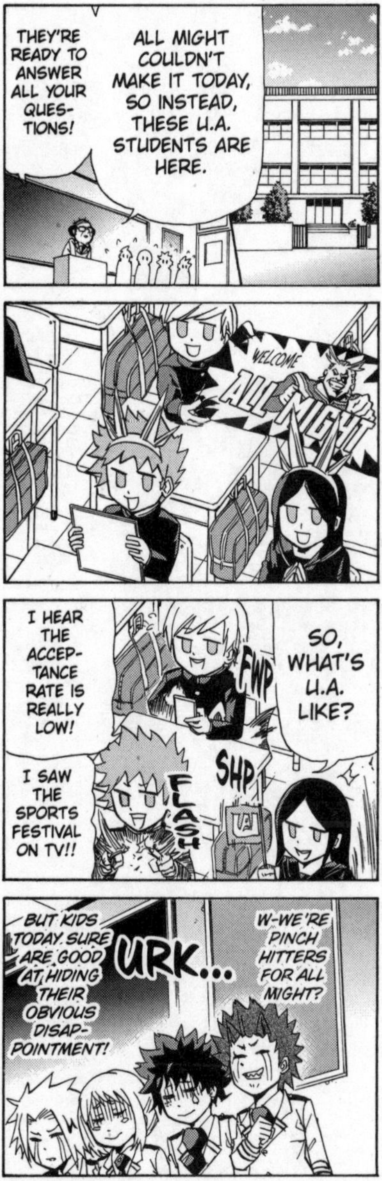
ALL MIGHT COULDN'T MAKE IT TODAY, SO INSTEAD, THESE U.A. STUDENTS ARE HERE.
THEY'RE READY TO ANSWER ALL YOUR QUES-TIONS!
WELCOME ALL MIGHT
SO, WHAT'S U.A. LIKE?
FWP
I HEAR THE ACCEP-TANCE RATE IS REALLY LOW!
SHP
FLASH
I SAW THE SPORTS FESTIVAL ON TV!!
W-WE'RE PINCH HITTERS FOR ALL MIGHT?
URK...
BUT KIDS TODAY SURE ARE GOOD AT HIDING THEIR OBVIOUS DISAP-POINTMENT!

Bootstrappin'

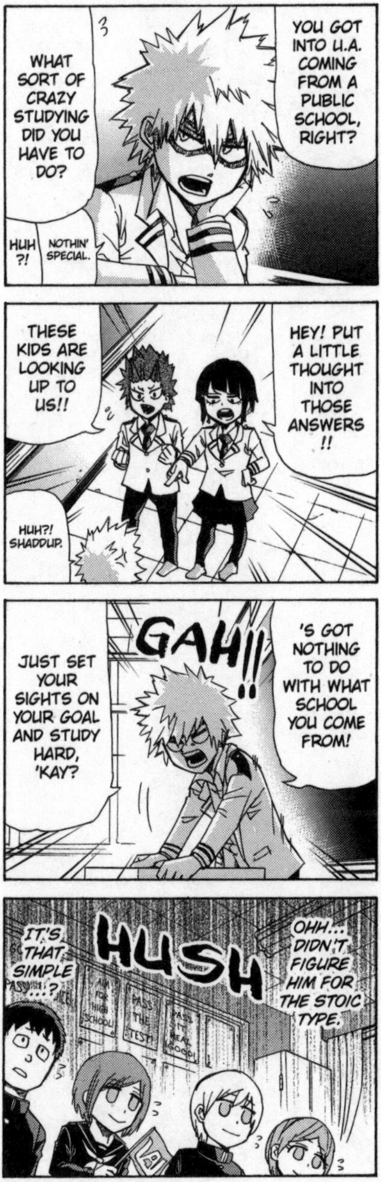
YOU GOT INTO U.A. COMING FROM A PUBLIC SCHOOL, RIGHT?
WHAT SORT OF CRAZY STUDYING DID YOU HAVE TO DO?
NOTHIN' SPECIAL.
HUH ?!
HEY! PUT A LITTLE THOUGHT INTO THOSE ANSWERS !!
THESE KIDS ARE LOOKING UP TO US!!
HUH?! SHADDUP.
'S GOT NOTHING TO DO WITH WHAT SCHOOL YOU COME FROM!
GAH!!
JUST SET YOUR SIGHTS ON YOUR GOAL AND STUDY HARD, 'KAY?
OHH... DIDN'T FIGURE HIM FOR THE STOIC TYPE.
HUSH
IT'S THAT SIMPLE ...?
AIM FOR HIGH SCHOOL
PASS THE TEST!
PASS IT REAL GOOD!

Dim Bulb's Guide to Test Taking

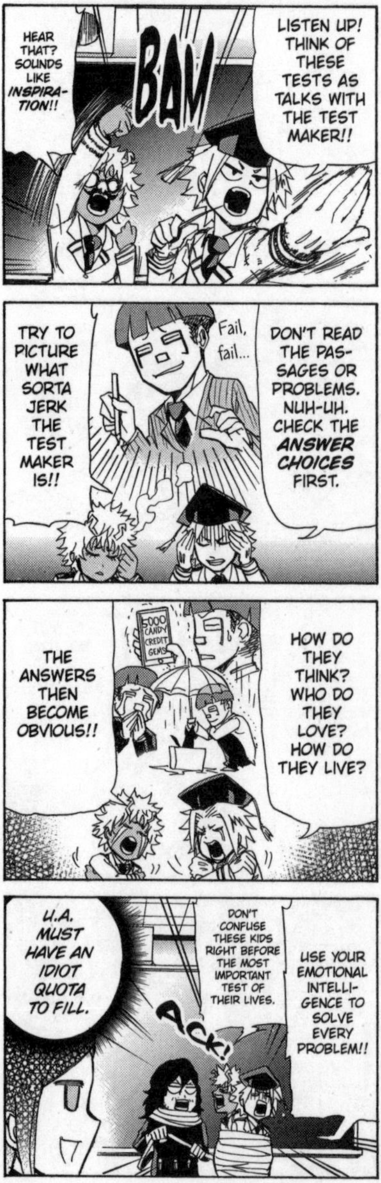
LISTEN UP! THINK OF THESE TESTS AS TALKS WITH THE TEST MAKER!!
BAM
HEAR THAT? SOUNDS LIKE INSPIRATION!!
DON'T READ THE PAS-SAGES OR PROBLEMS. NUH-UH. CHECK THE ANSWER CHOICES FIRST.
Fail, fail...
TRY TO PICTURE WHAT SORTA JERK THE TEST MAKER IS!!
HOW DO THEY THINK? WHO DO THEY LOVE? HOW DO THEY LIVE?
5000 CANDY CREDIT GEMS
THE ANSWERS THEN BECOME OBVIOUS!!
USE YOUR EMOTIONAL INTELLI-GENCE TO SOLVE EVERY PROBLEM!!
DON'T CONFUSE THESE KIDS RIGHT BEFORE THE MOST IMPORTANT TEST OF THEIR LIVES.
ACK!
U.A. MUST HAVE AN IDIOT QUOTA TO FILL.

Unrelatable

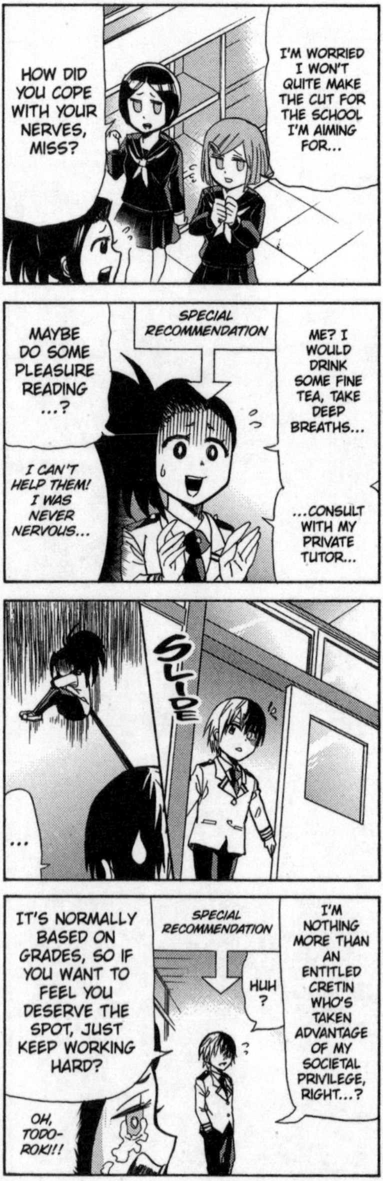
I'M WORRIED I WON'T QUITE MAKE THE CUT FOR THE SCHOOL I'M AIMING FOR...
HOW DID YOU COPE WITH YOUR NERVES, MISS?
ME? I WOULD DRINK SOME FINE TEA, TAKE DEEP BREATHS...
SPECIAL RECOMMENDATION
MAYBE DO SOME PLEASURE READING ...?
...CONSULT WITH MY PRIVATE TUTOR...
I CAN'T HELP THEM! I WAS NEVER NERVOUS...
SLIDE
...
I'M NOTHING MORE THAN AN ENTITLED CRETIN WHO'S TAKEN ADVANTAGE OF MY SOCIETAL PRIVILEGE, RIGHT...?
SPECIAL RECOMMENDATION
HUH ?
IT'S NORMALLY BASED ON GRADES, SO IF YOU WANT TO FEEL YOU DESERVE THE SPOT, JUST KEEP WORKING HARD?
OH, TODO-ROKI!!

His 15 Minutes of Fame

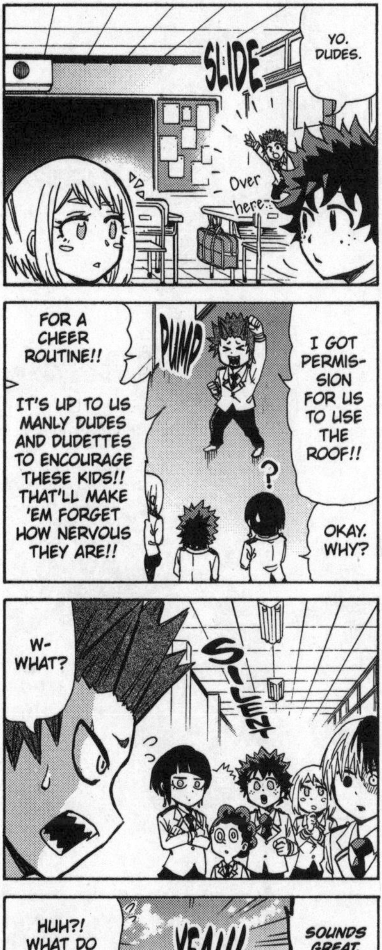
YO. DUDES.
SLIDE
Over here.
I GOT PERMISSION FOR US TO USE THE ROOF!!
OKAY. WHY?
PUMP
FOR A CHEER ROUTINE!!
IT'S UP TO US MANLY DUDES AND DUDETTES TO ENCOURAGE THESE KIDS!! THAT'LL MAKE 'EM FORGET HOW NERVOUS THEY ARE!!
SILENT
W-WHAT?
SOUNDS GREAT, KIRISHIMA!!
YEAH!
HUH?! WHAT DO I DO TOMORROW, THEN?
IT'S LIKE YOUR WHOLE LIFE'S BEEN LEADING UP TO TODAY!!
NEVER MIND THAT. JUST BASK IN THE GLORY OF THIS MOMENT.
YOU'RE BUMMING ME OUT!!

Kiricheera

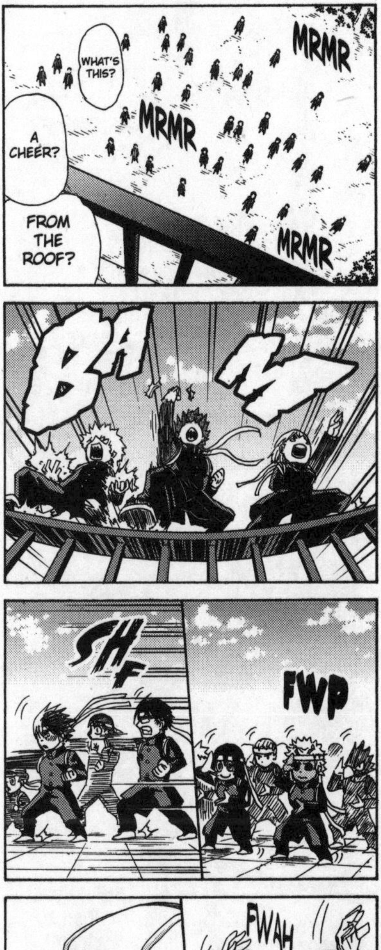
MRMR
WHAT'S THIS?
MRMR
A CHEER?
FROM THE ROOF?
MRMR
BAM
FWP
SHF
FWAH
DOOM

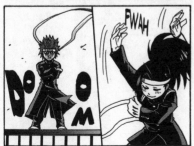

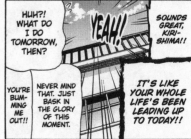

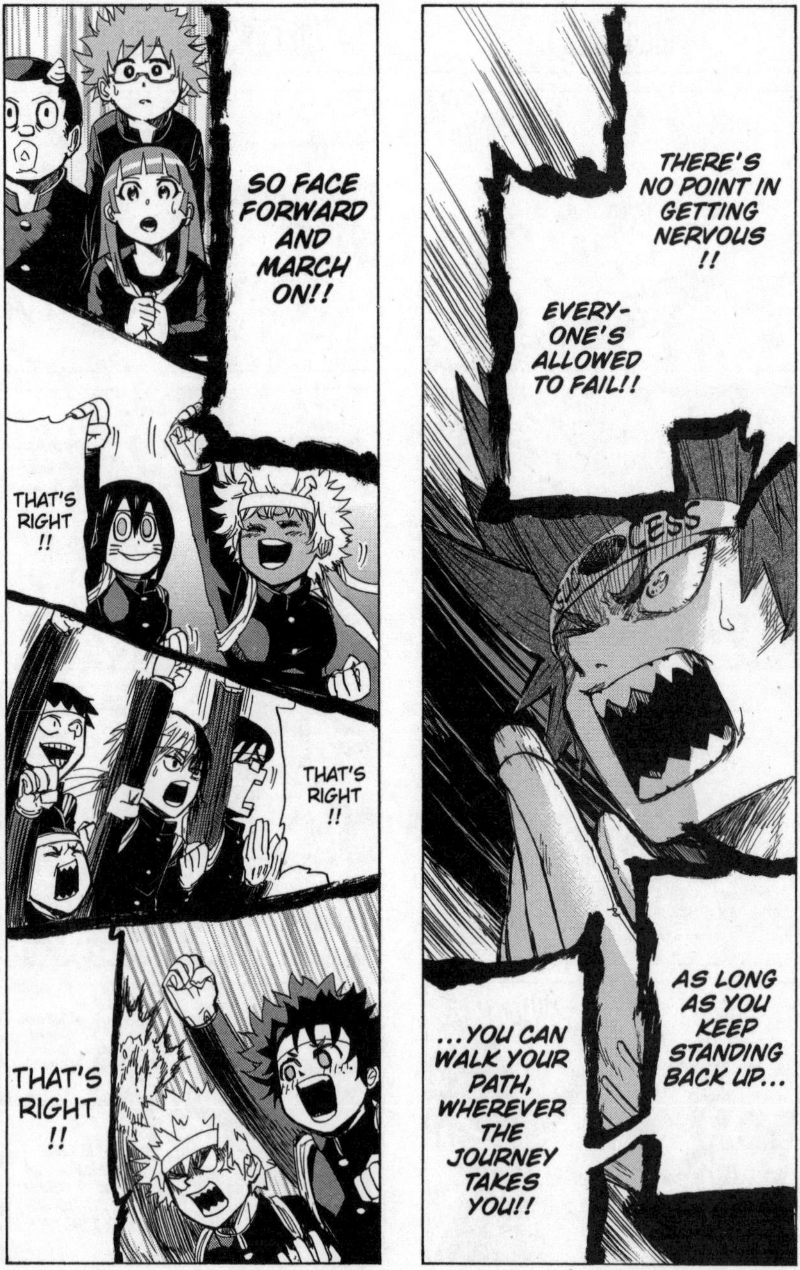

THERE'S NO POINT IN GETTING NERVOUS!!
EVERYONE'S ALLOWED TO FAIL!!
AS LONG AS YOU KEEP STANDING BACK UP...
...YOU CAN WALK YOUR PATH, WHEREVER THE JOURNEY TAKES YOU!!
SO FACE FORWARD AND MARCH ON!!
THAT'S RIGHT!!
THAT'S RIGHT!!
THAT'S RIGHT!!

It's Okay

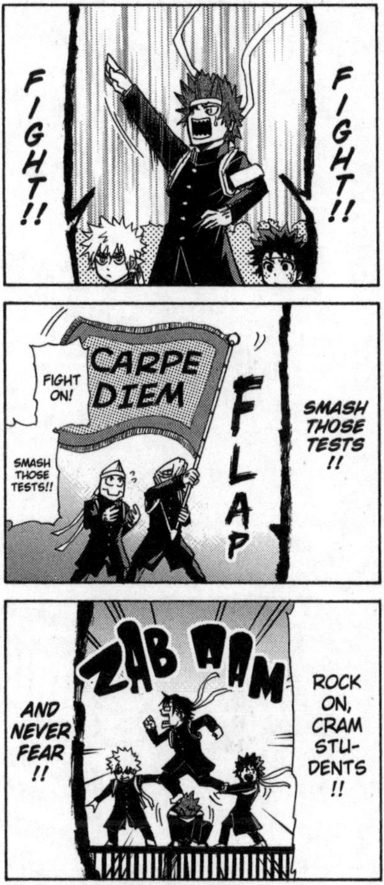
FIGHT!!
FIGHT!!
SMASH THOSE TESTS!!
FLAP
CARPE DIEM
FIGHT ON!
SMASH THOSE TESTS!!
ROCK ON, CRAM STUDENTS!!
ZAB AAM
AND NEVER FEAR!!
HA HA, WUZZAT?
THE EMERGENCY EXIT LOGO?
THEY'RE SAYING IT'S OKAY TO RUN AWAY?
CLAP
CLAP
CLAP
EITHER WAY, I'M FEELING ALL PUMPED UP.

Great Minds, Part 1

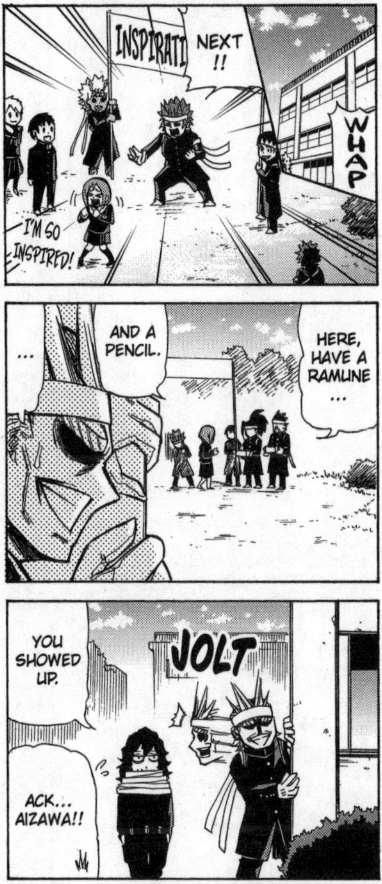
WHAP
NEXT!!
INSPIRATI
I'M SO INSPIRED!
HERE, HAVE A RAMUNE...
AND A PENCIL.
...
JOLT
YOU SHOWED UP.
ACK... AIZAWA!!
YEAH, I FOUND THE TIME AFTER ALL, BUT IT LOOKS LIKE I HAD THE SAME PLAN AS THE KIDS...?
FRET
THEY'RE DOING JUST FINE ON THEIR OWN, SO GO HOME.
FRET
OUCH!!

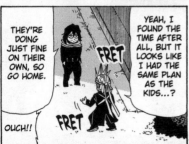

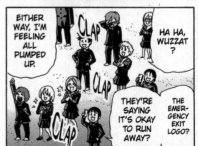

MINA ASHIDO

THE QUINTESSENTIAL HAPPY-GO-LUCKY GIRL!! ANYONE ASHIDO SETS HER SIGHTS ON IS GONNA BE SMILING BEFORE LONG!! SHE DOESN'T SWEAT THE SMALL STUFF. WHOEVER CAME UP WITH SAYING "POLLYANNA" OUGHTA REPLACE IT WITH "POLLYMINA"!!

HER QUIRK'S PRETTY DANGEROUS, BUT SHE'S GOT INNATELY GOOD SENSES AND REFLEXES THAT ALLOW FOR SOLID CONTROL OVER HER ACID, SO NOBODY EVER REALLY HAS TO WORRY...

TORU HAGAKURE

INVISIBLE!! WHICH IS WHY SHE'S ALWAYS TRYING SO AGGRESSIVELY HARD TO BE SEEN!! WHY'RE SO MANY OF THE GIRLS IN THIS SERIES SO RIDICULOUSLY CHEERY...? SHE'D PROBABLY CURL UP INTO A BALL AND DIE IF PEOPLE STOPPED NOTICING HER FOR REAL, BUT THIS GIRL IS LIKABLE ENOUGH TO MAKE YOU DOUBT THE EXPRESSION "APPEARANCES ARE EVERYTHING"!!

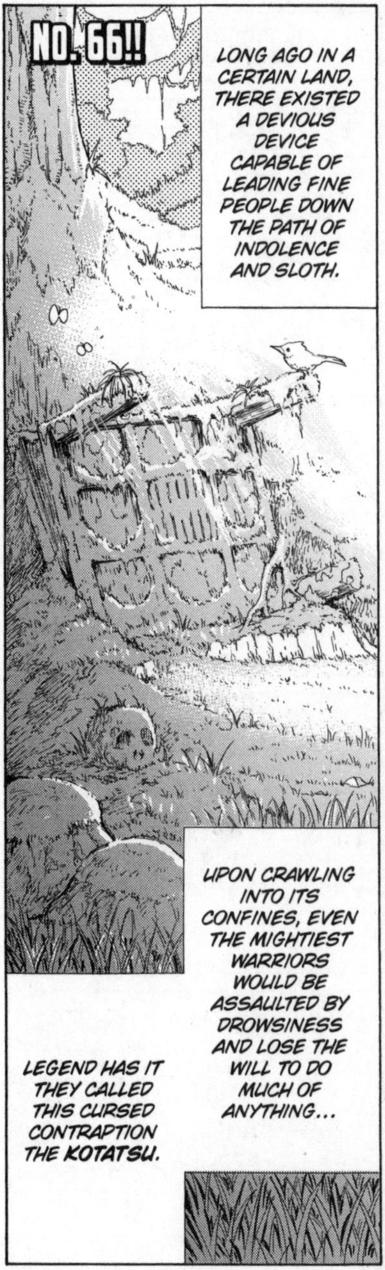
No. 66!!
LONG AGO IN A CERTAIN LAND, THERE EXISTED A DEVIOUS DEVICE CAPABLE OF LEADING FINE PEOPLE DOWN THE PATH OF INDOLENCE AND SLOTH.
UPON CRAWLING INTO ITS CONFINES, EVEN THE MIGHTIEST WARRIORS WOULD BE ASSAULTED BY DROWSINESS AND LOSE THE WILL TO DO MUCH OF ANYTHING...
LEGEND HAS IT THEY CALLED THIS CURSED CONTRAPTION THE KOTATSU.

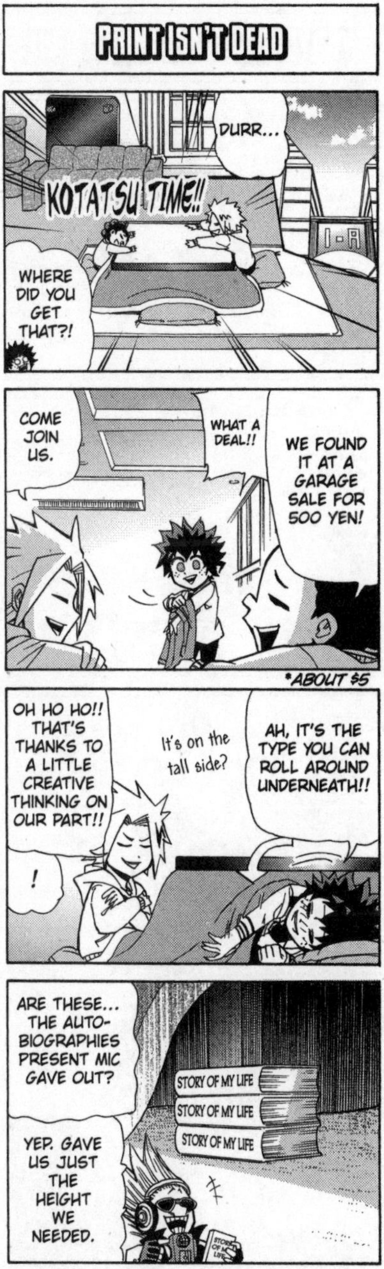
PRINT ISN'T DEAD
DURR...
KOTATSU TIME!!
WHERE DID YOU GET THAT?!
WE FOUND IT AT A GARAGE SALE FOR 500 YEN!
WHAT A DEAL!!
COME JOIN US.
*ABOUT $5
AH, IT'S THE TYPE YOU CAN ROLL AROUND UNDERNEATH!!
It's on the tall side?
OH HO HO!! THAT'S THANKS TO A LITTLE CREATIVE THINKING ON OUR PART!!
!
ARE THESE... THE AUTO-BIOGRAPHIES PRESENT MIC GAVE OUT?
STORY OF MY LIFE
STORY OF MY LIFE
STORY OF MY LIFE
YEP. GAVE US JUST THE HEIGHT WE NEEDED.

YAOYOROZU'S LEARNING CURVE

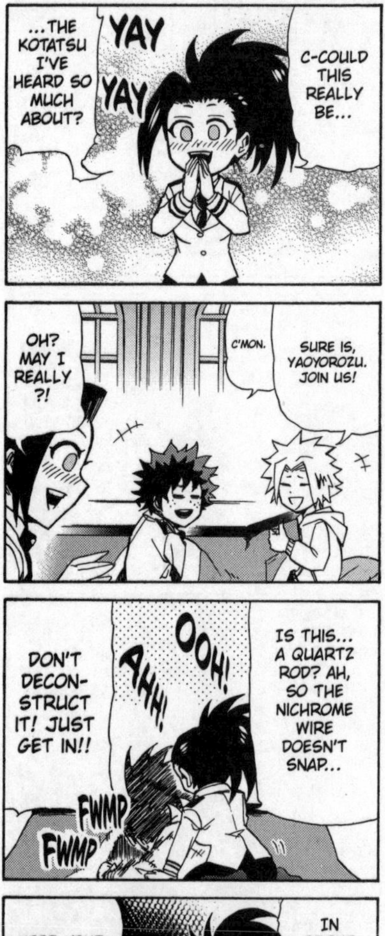
C-COULD THIS REALLY BE...
YAY
YAY
...THE KOTATSU I'VE HEARD SO MUCH ABOUT?
SURE IS, YAOYOROZU. JOIN US!
C'MON.
OH? MAY I REALLY ?!
IS THIS... A QUARTZ ROD? AH, SO THE NICHROME WIRE DOESN'T SNAP...
OOH!
AHH!
DON'T DECON-STRUCT IT! JUST GET IN!!
FWMP
FWMP
IN FRONT OF YOU BOYS?
KEEP YOUR SKIRT ON!! MAYBE YOU SHOULD FIGURE OUT HOW KOTATSU WORK!
SHP

COUP D'IDA, PART 2

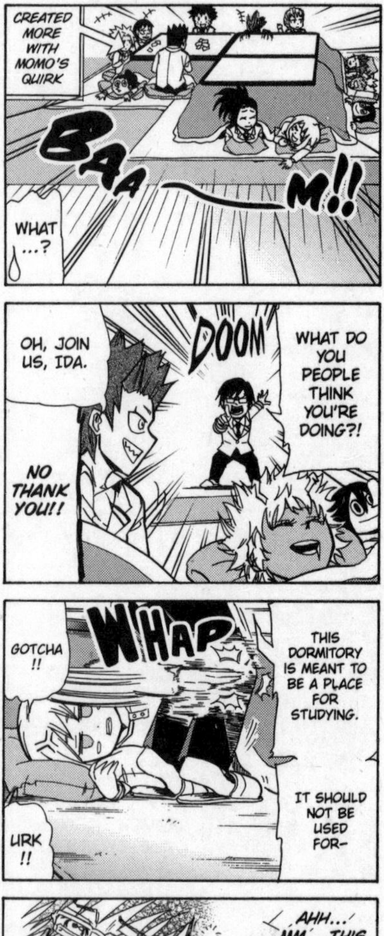
CREATED MORE WITH MOMO'S QUIRK
BAA—M!!
WHAT ...?
WHAT DO YOU PEOPLE THINK YOU'RE DOING?!
DOOM
OH, JOIN US, IDA.
NO THANK YOU!!
THIS DORMITORY IS MEANT TO BE A PLACE FOR STUDYING.
WHAP
GOTCHA !!
IT SHOULD NOT BE USED FOR-
URK !!
AHH... MM... THIS DELICIOUS WARMTH... CANNOT... RESIST...
MELT
IDA HAS FALLEN.

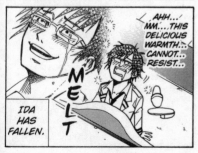

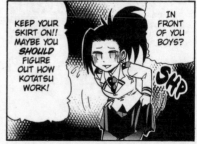

Obvious Punch Line

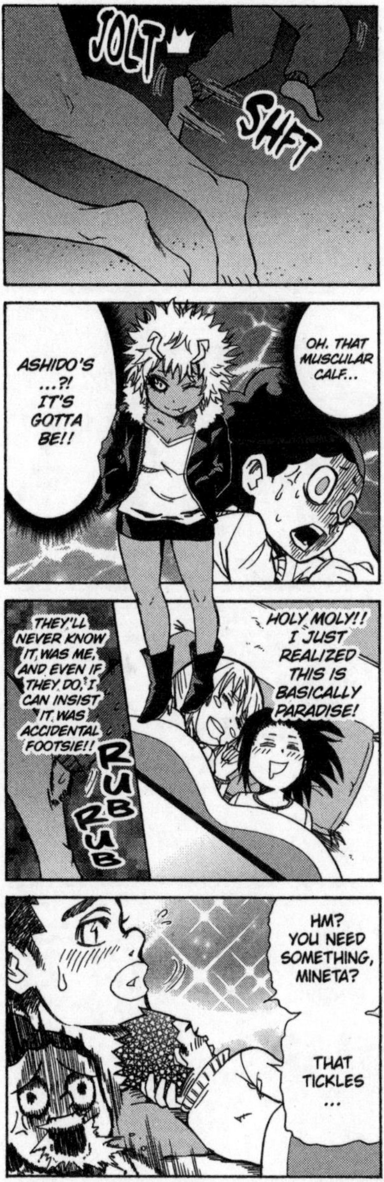
JOLT
SHFT
OH. THAT MUSCULAR CALF...
ASHIDO'S ...?! IT'S GOTTA BE!!
HOLY MOLY!! I JUST REALIZED THIS IS BASICALLY PARADISE!
THEY'LL NEVER KNOW IT WAS ME, AND EVEN IF THEY DO, I CAN INSIST IT WAS ACCIDENTAL FOOTSIE!!
RUB RUB
HM? YOU NEED SOMETHING, MINETA?
THAT TICKLES ...

Land of the Languid

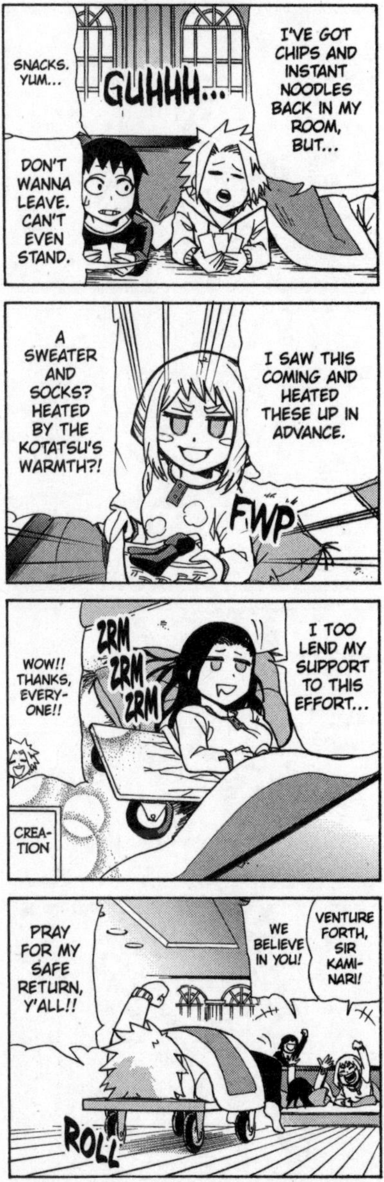
I'VE GOT CHIPS AND INSTANT NOODLES BACK IN MY ROOM, BUT...
SNACKS. YUM...
GUHHH...
DON'T WANNA LEAVE. CAN'T EVEN STAND.
I SAW THIS COMING AND HEATED THESE UP IN ADVANCE.
A SWEATER AND SOCKS? HEATED BY THE KOTATSU'S WARMTH?!
FWP
I TOO LEND MY SUPPORT TO THIS EFFORT...
ZRM ZRM ZRM
WOW!! THANKS, EVERY-ONE!!
CREA-TION
VENTURE FORTH, SIR KAMI-NARI!
WE BELIEVE IN YOU!
PRAY FOR MY SAFE RETURN, Y'ALL!!
ROLL

WINTER IS HERE

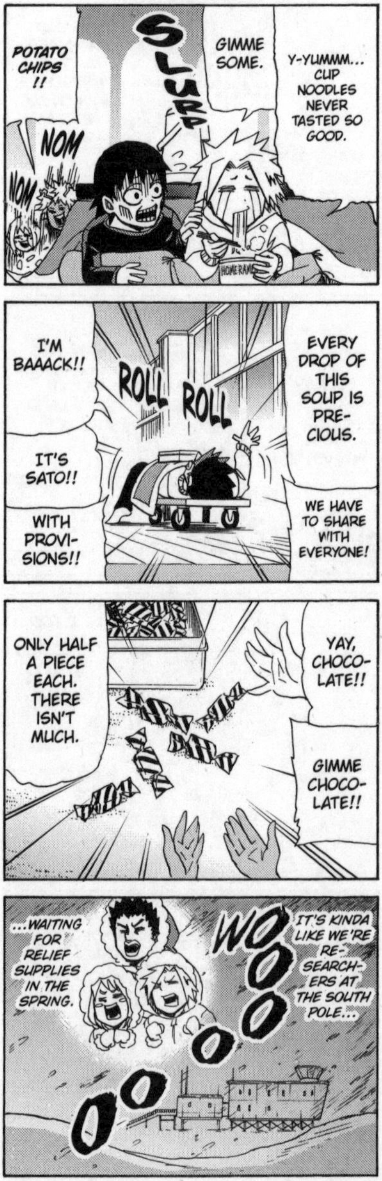
Y-YUMMM... CUP NOODLES NEVER TASTED SO GOOD.
GIMME SOME.
SLURP
POTATO CHIPS !!
NOM
NOM
EVERY DROP OF THIS SOUP IS PRECIOUS.
WE HAVE TO SHARE WITH EVERYONE!
I'M BAAACK!!
ROLL ROLL
IT'S SATO!!
WITH PROVISIONS!!
YAY, CHOCOLATE!!
GIMME CHOCOLATE!!
ONLY HALF A PIECE EACH. THERE ISN'T MUCH.
IT'S KINDA LIKE WE'RE RESEARCHERS AT THE SOUTH POLE...
WOOOOOOO
...WAITING FOR RELIEF SUPPLIES IN THE SPRING.

S.S. *TODOROKI*, ICE-BREAKING SHIP

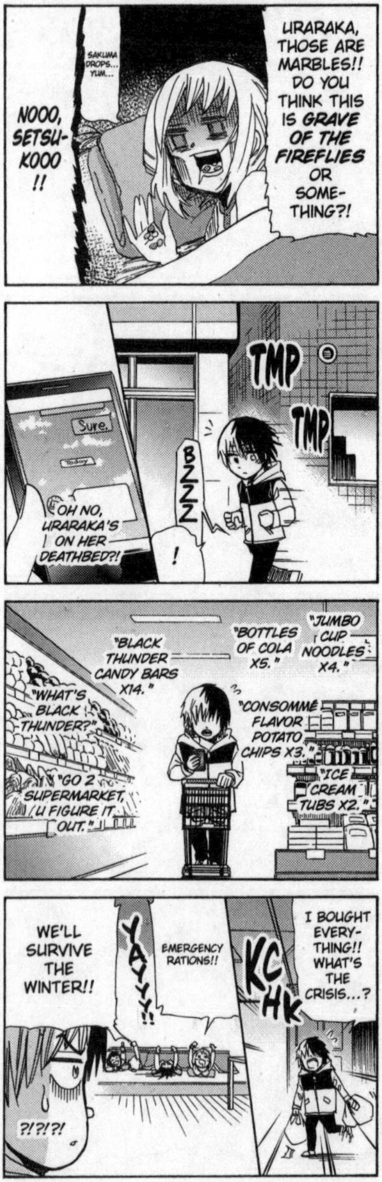
URARAKA, THOSE ARE MARBLES!! DO YOU THINK THIS IS *GRAVE OF THE FIREFLIES* OR SOMETHING?!
SAKUMA DROPS... YUM...
NOOO, SETSUKOOO !!
TMP
TMP
BZZZ
Sure.
Today
!
OH NO, URARAKA'S ON HER DEATHBED?!
"JUMBO CUP NOODLES X4."
"BOTTLES OF COLA X5."
"BLACK THUNDER CANDY BARS X14."
"CONSOMMÉ FLAVOR POTATO CHIPS X3."
"WHAT'S BLACK THUNDER?"
"ICE CREAM TUBS X2."
"GO 2 SUPERMARKET, U FIGURE IT OUT."
I BOUGHT EVERYTHING!! WHAT'S THE CRISIS...?
KCHK
EMERGENCY RATIONS!!
YAYYY!!
WE'LL SURVIVE THE WINTER!!
?!?!?!

KOTATSU KOLONY

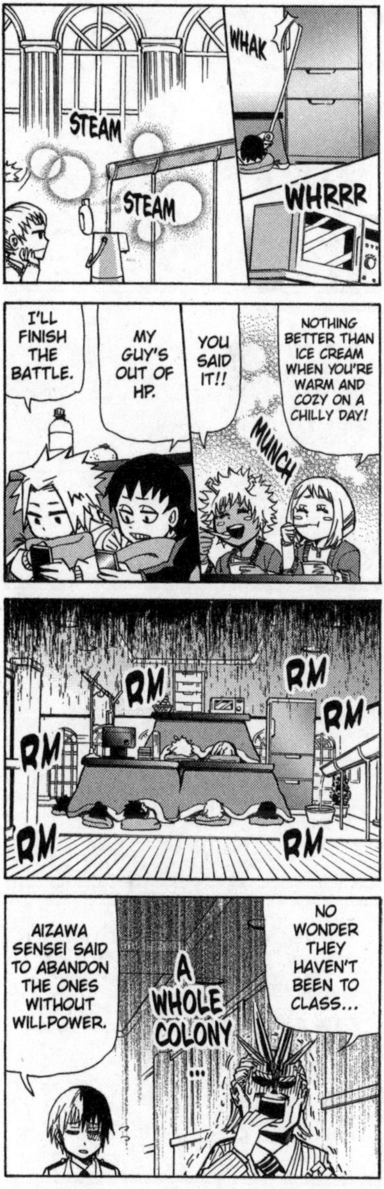
WHAK
WHRRR
STEAM
STEAM
NOTHING BETTER THAN ICE CREAM WHEN YOU'RE WARM AND COZY ON A CHILLY DAY!
MUNCH
YOU SAID IT!!
MY GUY'S OUT OF HP.
I'LL FINISH THE BATTLE.
RM
RM
RM
RM
RM
RM
RM
NO WONDER THEY HAVEN'T BEEN TO CLASS...
A WHOLE COLONY...
AIZAWA SENSEI SAID TO ABANDON THE ONES WITHOUT WILLPOWER.

WHAT DEVILRY

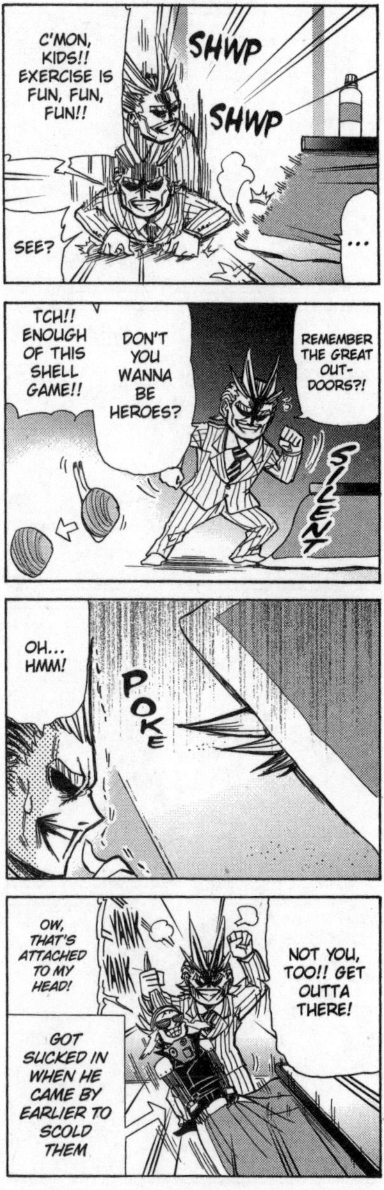
SHWP
SHWP
C'MON, KIDS!! EXERCISE IS FUN, FUN, FUN!!
...
SEE?
REMEMBER THE GREAT OUT-DOORS?!
SILENT
DON'T YOU WANNA BE HEROES?
TCH!! ENOUGH OF THIS SHELL GAME!!
POKE
OH... HMM!
NOT YOU, TOO!! GET OUTTA THERE!
YANK
YANK
OW, THAT'S ATTACHED TO MY HEAD!
GOT SUCKED IN WHEN HE CAME BY EARLIER TO SCOLD THEM

Armored Upgrade Level 2

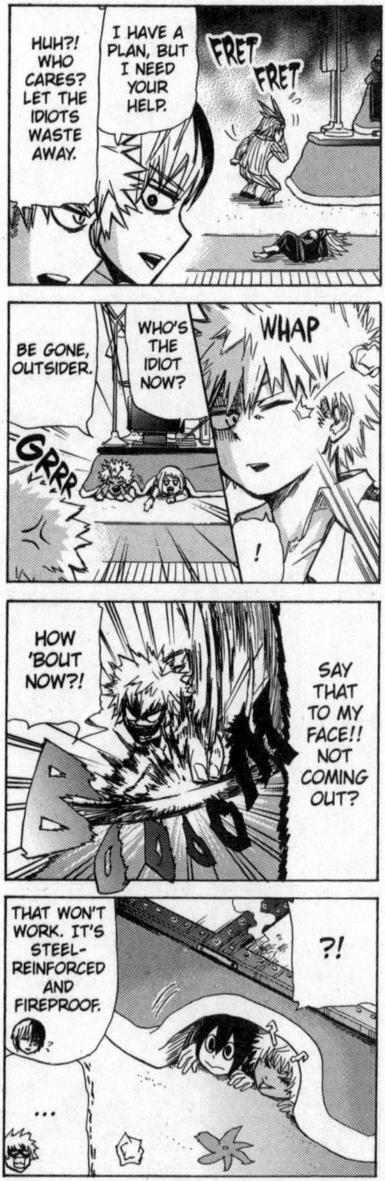
FRET
FRET
I HAVE A PLAN, BUT I NEED YOUR HELP.
HUH?! WHO CARES? LET THE IDIOTS WASTE AWAY.
WHAP
WHO'S THE IDIOT NOW?
BE GONE, OUTSIDER.
GRRR
!
SAY THAT TO MY FACE!! NOT COMING OUT?
HOW 'BOUT NOW?!
?!
THAT WON'T WORK. IT'S STEEL-REINFORCED AND FIREPROOF.
...

Extermination Tactics

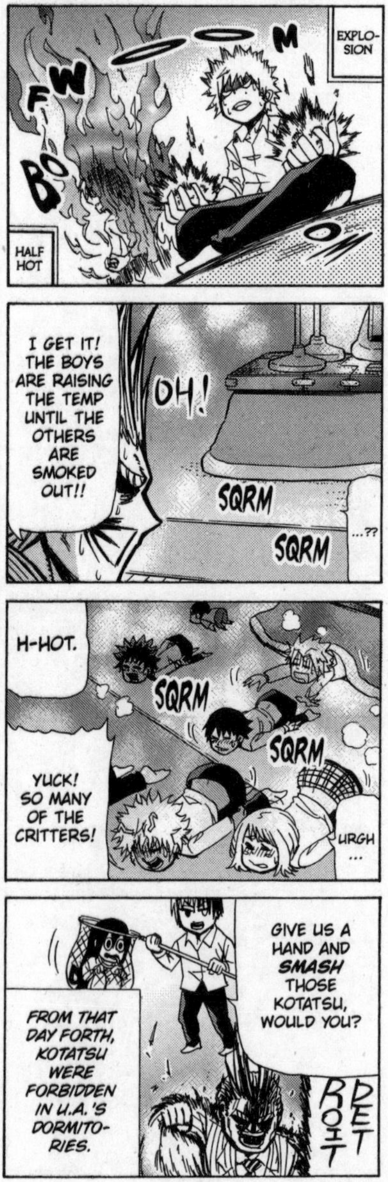
EXPLOSION
FWOOOM
BOOM
HALF HOT
...??
SQRM
SQRM
OH!
I GET IT! THE BOYS ARE RAISING THE TEMP UNTIL THE OTHERS ARE SMOKED OUT!!
H-HOT.
SQRM
SQRM
YUCK! SO MANY OF THE CRITTERS!
URGH...
DETROIT
GIVE US A HAND AND SMASH THOSE KOTATSU, WOULD YOU?
!
!
FROM THAT DAY FORTH, KOTATSU WERE FORBIDDEN IN U.A.'S DORMITORIES.

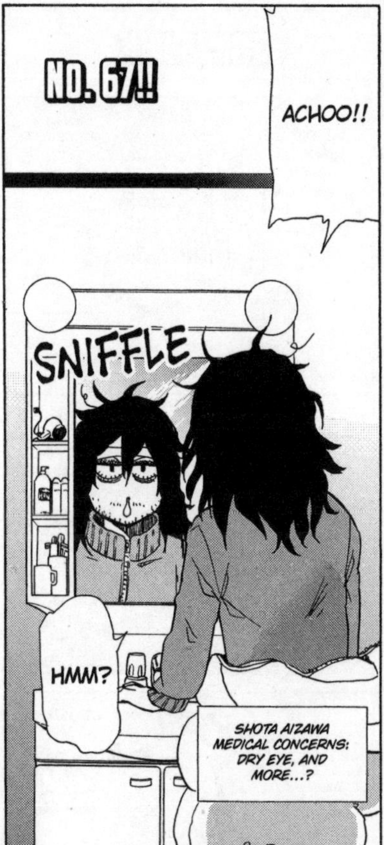

NO. 67!!
ACHOO!!
SNIFFLE
HMM?
SHOTA AIZAWA MEDICAL CONCERNS: DRY EYE, AND MORE...?
WARMER WEATHER BRINGS THE EVER-DREADED ALLERGY-INDUCING POLLEN.

YAYYY FEVER

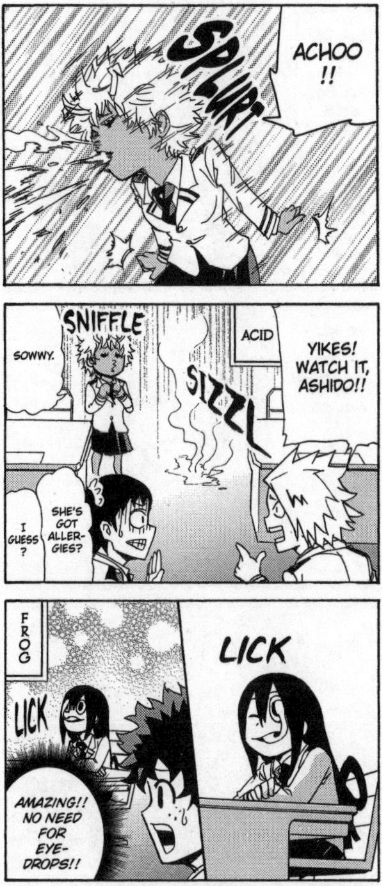

ACHOO !!
SPLURT
YIKES! WATCH IT, ASHIDO!!
ACID
SIZZL
SNIFFLE
SOWWY.
SHE'S GOT ALLER-GIES?
I GUESS?
LICK
FROG
LICK
AMAZING!! NO NEED FOR EYE-DROPS!!
GET OUTTA HERE, POLLEN PUNK!!
WHAP
I'M SUFFERING TOO, Y'KNOW?
YOUR STATIC ELECTRICITY IS ATTRACTING IT!!
WHAP
ELECTRIFI-CATION
POOR GUY.

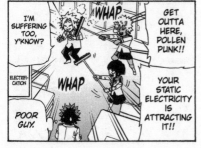

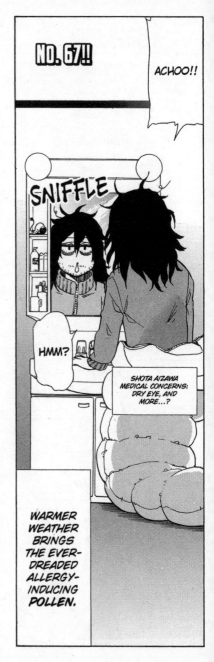

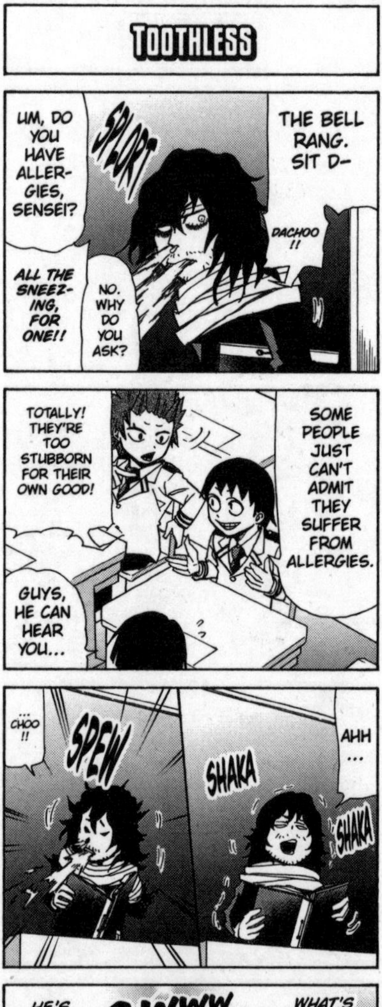
TOOTHLESS
THE BELL RANG. SIT D-
DACHOO!!
SPLORT
UM, DO YOU HAVE ALLER-GIES, SENSEI?
NO. WHY DO YOU ASK?
ALL THE SNEEZ-ING, FOR ONE!!
SOME PEOPLE JUST CAN'T ADMIT THEY SUFFER FROM ALLERGIES.
TOTALLY! THEY'RE TOO STUBBORN FOR THEIR OWN GOOD!
GUYS, HE CAN HEAR YOU...
AHH...
SHAKA
SHAKA
SPEW
...CHOO!!
WHAT'S THIS?
AWWW
HE'S NOT SCARY AT ALL ANY-MORE!!
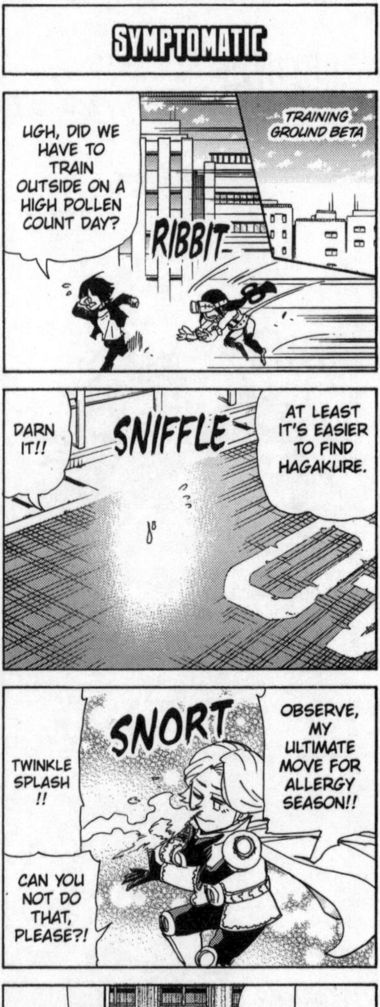
SYMPTOMATIC
TRAINING GROUND BETA
RIBBIT
UGH, DID WE HAVE TO TRAIN OUTSIDE ON A HIGH POLLEN COUNT DAY?
AT LEAST IT'S EASIER TO FIND HAGAKURE.
SNIFFLE
DARN IT!!
OBSERVE, MY ULTIMATE MOVE FOR ALLERGY SEASON!!
SNORT
TWINKLE SPLASH!!
CAN YOU NOT DO THAT, PLEASE?!
ARE YOU DOING OKAY, TOKOYAMI?
I AM, BUT...
DARK SHADOW
EYES... ITCHY...
HE DOESN'T HAVE A BODY THOUGH!

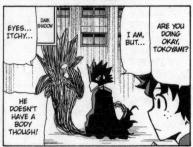

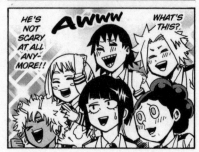

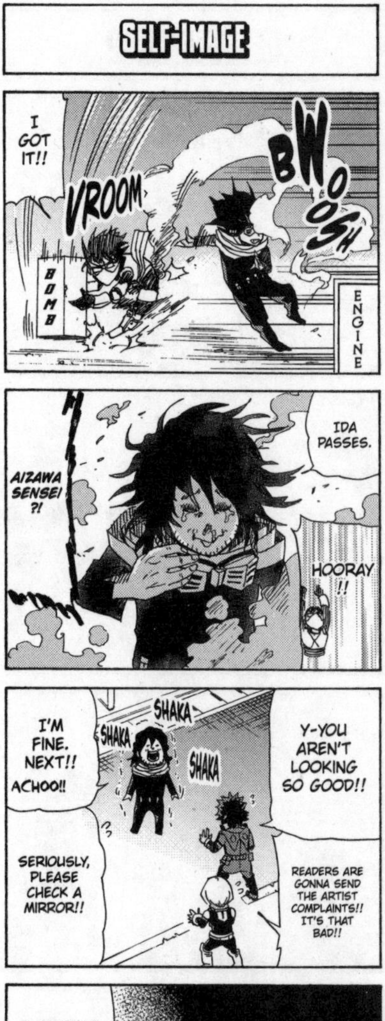
SELF-IMAGE
BWOOSH
I GOT IT!!
VROOM
ENGINE
BOMB
IDA PASSES.
HOORAY!!
AIZAWA SENSEI?!
Y-YOU AREN'T LOOKING SO GOOD!!
SHAKA
SHAKA
I'M FINE. NEXT!!
SHAKA
ACHOO!!
READERS ARE GONNA SEND THE ARTIST COMPLAINTS!! IT'S THAT BAD!!
SERIOUSLY, PLEASE CHECK A MIRROR!!
I ALWAYS LOOK LIKE THIS.
...
DOES HE EVEN OWN A MIRROR?!

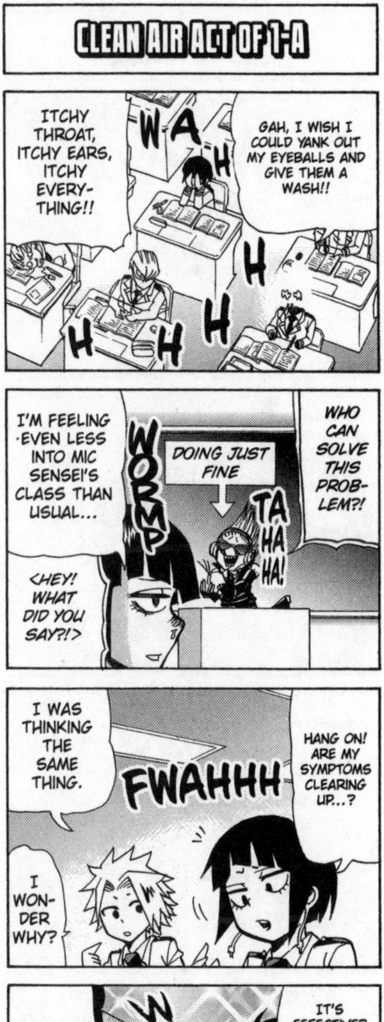
CLEAN AIR ACT OF 1-A
GAH, I WISH I COULD YANK OUT MY EYEBALLS AND GIVE THEM A WASH!!
WAH
ITCHY THROAT, ITCHY EARS, ITCHY EVERY-THING!!
H H H H
WHO CAN SOLVE THIS PROB-LEM?!
TAHAHA!
DOING JUST FINE
WORMP
I'M FEELING EVEN LESS INTO MIC SENSEI'S CLASS THAN USUAL...
<HEY! WHAT DID YOU SAY?!>
HANG ON! ARE MY SYMPTOMS CLEARING UP...?
FWAHHH
I WAS THINKING THE SAME THING.
I WON-DER WHY?
IT'S EFFECTIVE? HOW WONDER-FUL...
WHRRR
I'VE NEVER CREATED THIS DEVICE BEFORE.
CREATION: AIR PURIFIER
YESSS!! THAT'S OUR GUARD-IAN ANGEL, MOMO-YAO!!

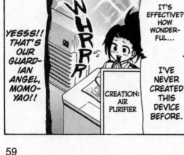

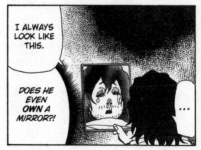

The Road to Hell

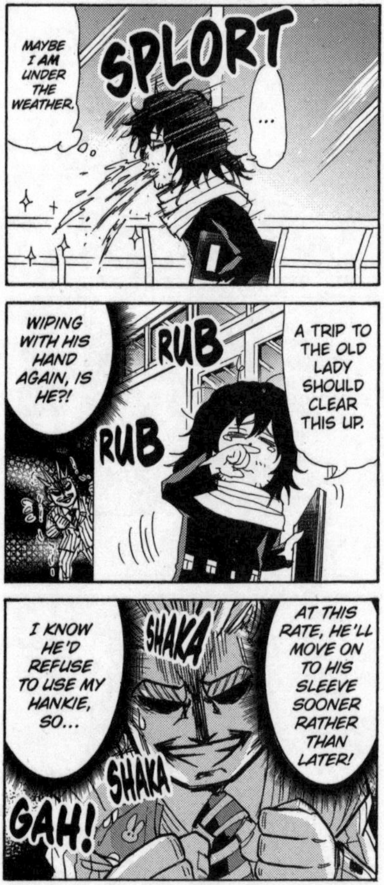
SPLORT
...
MAYBE I AM UNDER THE WEATHER.
A TRIP TO THE OLD LADY SHOULD CLEAR THIS UP.
RUB
RUB
WIPING WITH HIS HAND AGAIN, IS HE?!
AT THIS RATE, HE'LL MOVE ON TO HIS SLEEVE SOONER RATHER THAN LATER!
SHAKA
I KNOW HE'D REFUSE TO USE MY HANKIE, SO...
SHAKA
GAH!
A-AIZAWA!! HERE'S SOME TOILET PAPER! FROM THE BATHROOM!
SHWIP
IT'S NOT A PERSONAL GIFT FROM ME, SO YOU HAVE NO EXCUSE NOT TO USE IT!
?
DON'T REMOVE SCHOOL PROPERTY FROM ITS PROPER LOCATION, PLEASE.
GAH!!

Sadoprankism

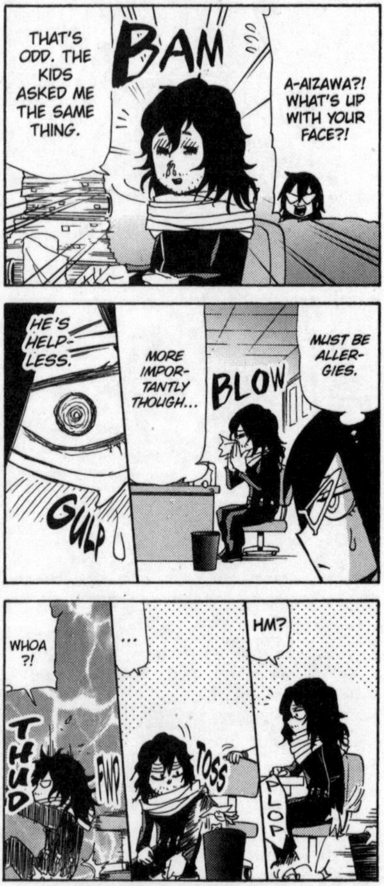
A-AIZAWA?! WHAT'S UP WITH YOUR FACE?!
BAM
THAT'S ODD. THE KIDS ASKED ME THE SAME THING.
MUST BE ALLERGIES.
BLOW
MORE IMPORTANTLY THOUGH...
HE'S HELPLESS.
GULP
HM?
...
TOSS
PLOP
FWP
WHOA ?!
THUD
C-CARE TO EXPLAIN YOURSELF?!
SHIVER
S-SORRY. I HAD TO...
EXCUSE ME?!

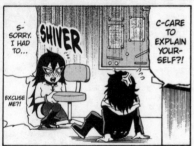

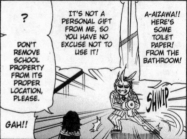

SHORTSIGHTED

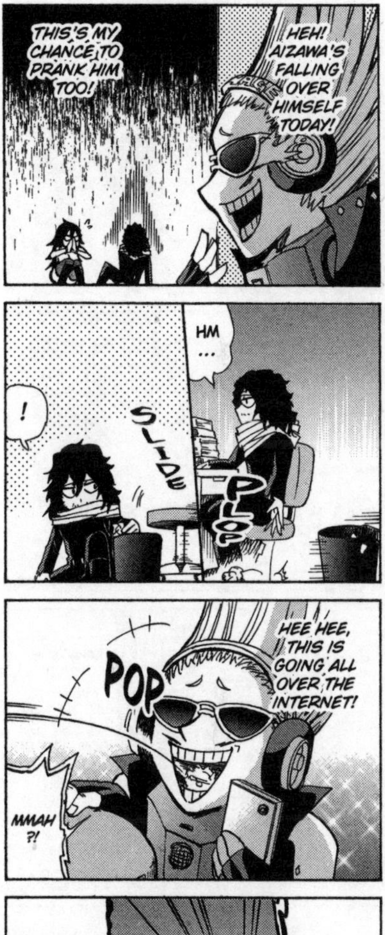
HEH! AIZAWA'S FALLING OVER HIMSELF TODAY!
THIS'S MY CHANCE TO PRANK HIM TOO!
HM ...
SLIDE
PLOP
!
HEE HEE, THIS IS GOING ALL OVER THE INTERNET!
POP
MMAH ?!
HORK!! HORK!!
YOU'RE 30 YEARS OLD. ACT LIKE IT!
HUH?! I THOUGHT WE WERE BESTIES!

A RATIONAL SOLUTION

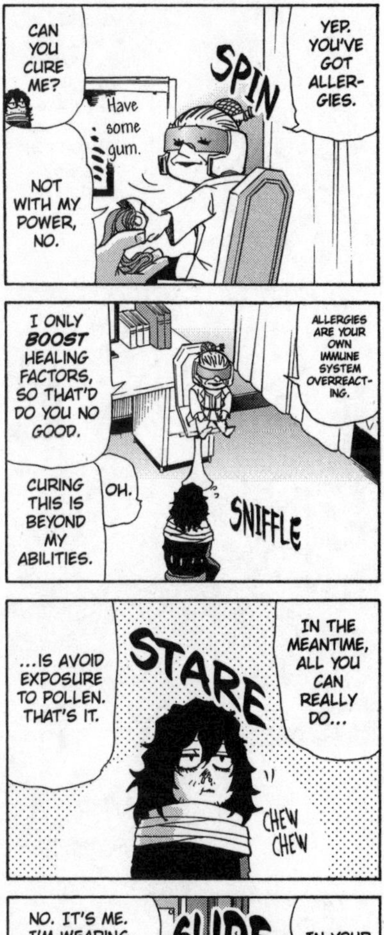
YEP. YOU'VE GOT ALLERGIES.
SPIN
CAN YOU CURE ME?
Have some gum.
NOT WITH MY POWER, NO.
ALLERGIES ARE YOUR OWN IMMUNE SYSTEM OVERREACTING.
I ONLY BOOST HEALING FACTORS, SO THAT'D DO YOU NO GOOD.
OH.
CURING THIS IS BEYOND MY ABILITIES.
SNIFFLE
IN THE MEANTIME, ALL YOU CAN REALLY DO...
STARE
...IS AVOID EXPOSURE TO POLLEN. THAT'S IT.
CHEW CHEW
IN YOUR SEATS. NOW.
SLIDE
NO. IT'S ME. I'M WEARING THIS UNTIL POLLEN SEASON IS OVER.
HUH? THIRTEEN SENSEI?!
ACK... AIZAWA SENSEI!?

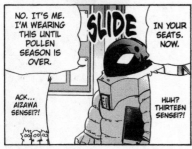

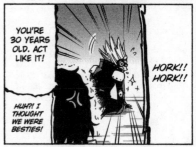

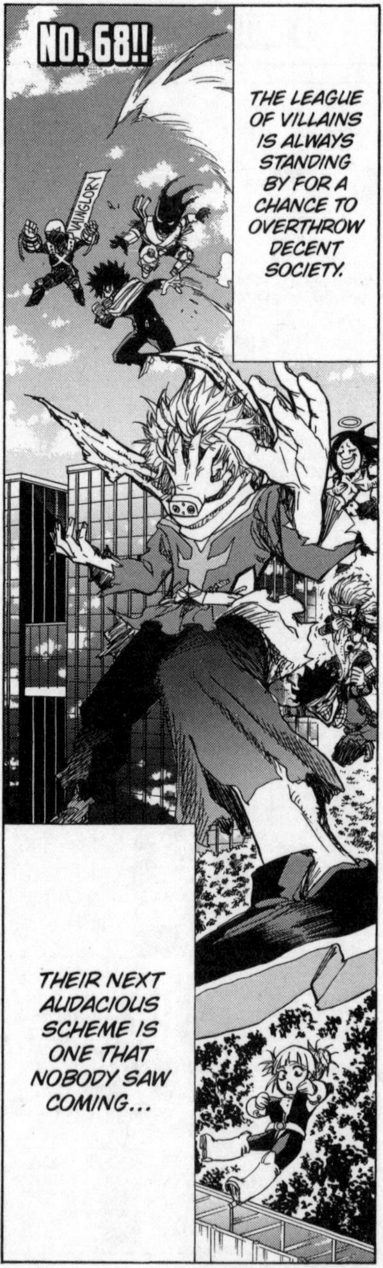
NO. 68!!
THE LEAGUE OF VILLAINS IS ALWAYS STANDING BY FOR A CHANCE TO OVERTHROW DECENT SOCIETY.
VAINGLORY
THEIR NEXT AUDACIOUS SCHEME IS ONE THAT NOBODY SAW COMING...

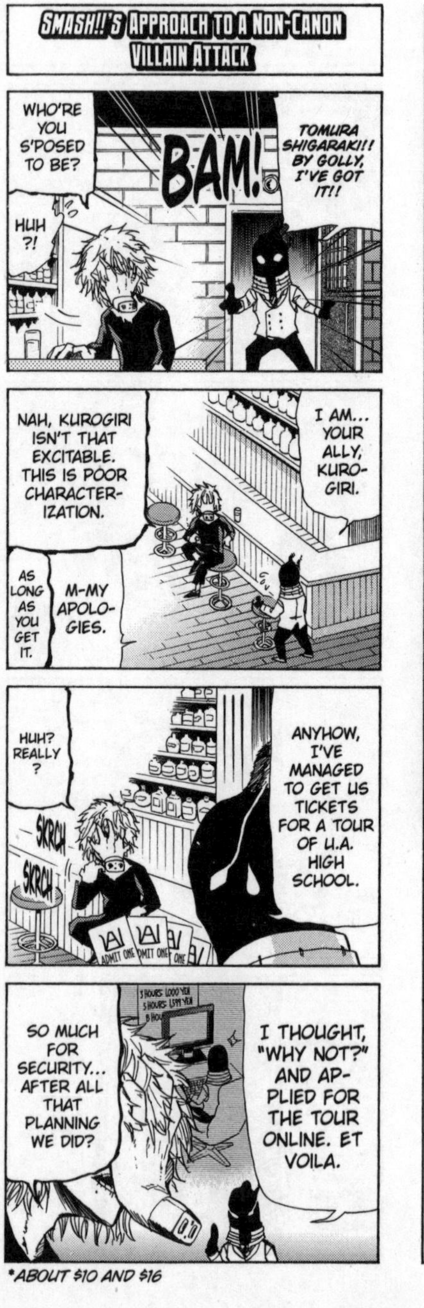
SMASH!!'S APPROACH TO A NON-CANON VILLAIN ATTACK
TOMURA SHIGARAKI!! BY GOLLY, I'VE GOT IT!!
BAM!
WHO'RE YOU S'POSED TO BE?
HUH ?!
I AM... YOUR ALLY, KURO-GIRI.
NAH, KUROGIRI ISN'T THAT EXCITABLE. THIS IS POOR CHARACTER-IZATION.
M-MY APOLO-GIES.
AS LONG AS YOU GET IT.
ANYHOW, I'VE MANAGED TO GET US TICKETS FOR A TOUR OF U.A. HIGH SCHOOL.
HUH? REALLY ?
SKRCH
SKRCH
ADMIT ONE
3 HOURS 1,000 YEN
5 HOURS 1,599 YEN
I THOUGHT, "WHY NOT?" AND AP-PLIED FOR THE TOUR ONLINE. ET VOILA.
SO MUCH FOR SECURITY... AFTER ALL THAT PLANNING WE DID?

*ABOUT $10 AND $16

GUTTER MIND

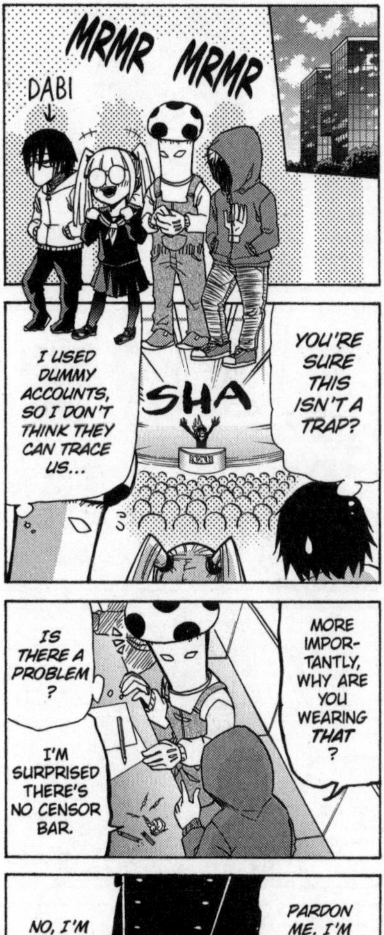
MRMR
MRMR
DABI
YOU'RE SURE THIS ISN'T A TRAP?
SHA
I USED DUMMY ACCOUNTS, SO I DON'T THINK THEY CAN TRACE US...
MORE IMPORTANTLY, WHY ARE YOU WEARING THAT?
IS THERE A PROBLEM?
I'M SURPRISED THERE'S NO CENSOR BAR.
PARDON ME. I'M OFF TO THE BATHROOM.
NO, I'M GOING THERE TO CHANGE!
KLAT KLAT
IF YOU'RE TAKING A DUMP, MAKE IT QUICK.
QUIT IT! YOU'LL JUST DRAW MORE ATTENTION THAT WAY!

RECYCLED CONTENT

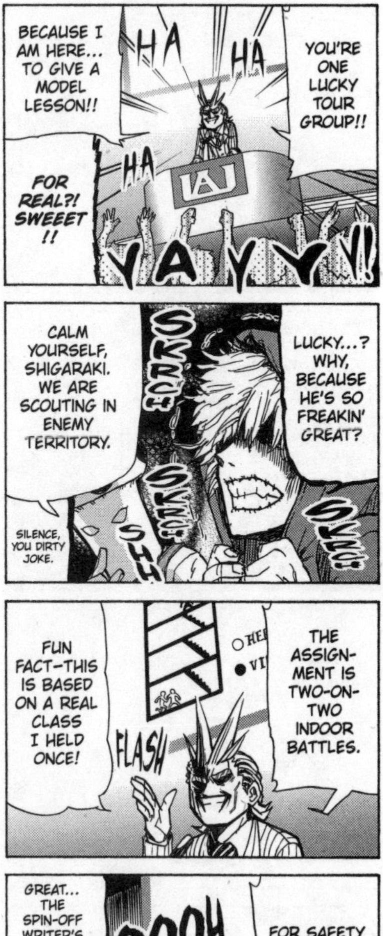
YOU'RE ONE LUCKY TOUR GROUP!!
HA HA
BECAUSE I AM HERE... TO GIVE A MODEL LESSON!!
HA
FOR REAL?! SWEEET!!
YAYYY!
LUCKY...? WHY, BECAUSE HE'S SO FREAKIN' GREAT?
SKRCH
CALM YOURSELF, SHIGARAKI. WE ARE SCOUTING IN ENEMY TERRITORY.
SKRCH SKRCH
SHH
SILENCE, YOU DIRTY JOKE.
THE ASSIGNMENT IS TWO-ON-TWO INDOOR BATTLES.
FUN FACT—THIS IS BASED ON A REAL CLASS I HELD ONCE!
FLASH
FOR SAFETY PURPOSES, THESE CURRENT STUDENTS WILL BE JOINING YOU!
OOOH
GREAT... THE SPIN-OFF WRITER'S FINALLY RUN OUT OF IDEAS.
LET'S JUST TRY TO GET THROUGH THIS, SHIGARAKI.
CLAP CLAP

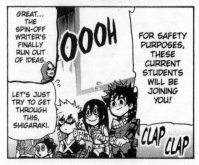

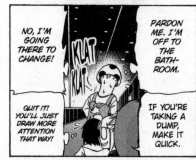

Bakublivious

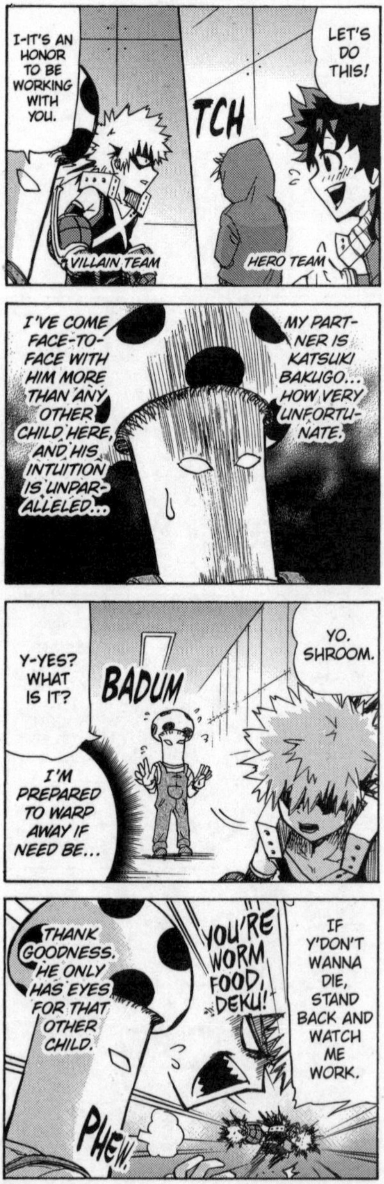
LET'S DO THIS!
TCH
I-IT'S AN HONOR TO BE WORKING WITH YOU.
HERO TEAM
VILLAIN TEAM
MY PARTNER IS KATSUKI BAKUGO... HOW VERY UNFORTUNATE.
I'VE COME FACE-TO-FACE WITH HIM MORE THAN ANY OTHER CHILD HERE, AND HIS INTUITION IS UNPARALLELED...
YO. SHROOM.
BADUM
Y-YES? WHAT IS IT?
I'M PREPARED TO WARP AWAY IF NEED BE...
IF Y'DON'T WANNA DIE, STAND BACK AND WATCH ME WORK.
YOU'RE WORM FOOD, DEKU!
THANK GOODNESS. HE ONLY HAS EYES FOR THAT OTHER CHILD.
PHEW

Let's Kidnap Him Again

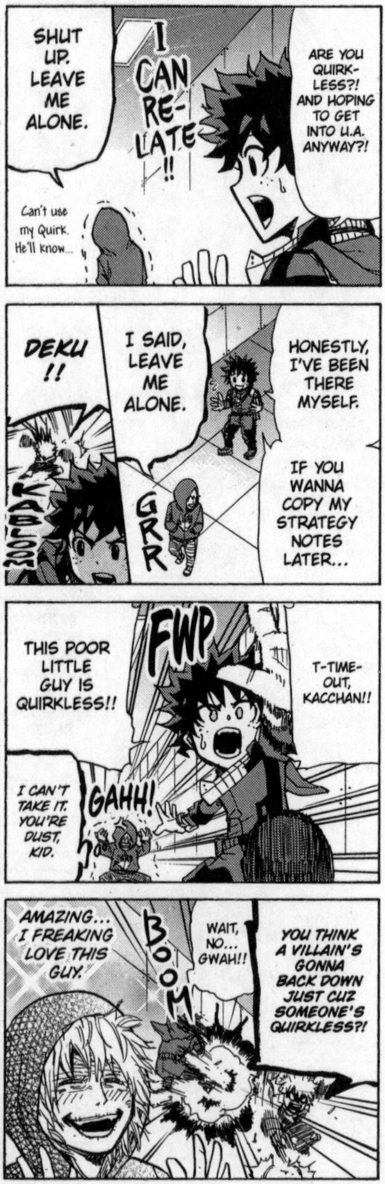
ARE YOU QUIRKLESS?! AND HOPING TO GET INTO U.A. ANYWAY?!
I CAN RELATE!!
SHUT UP. LEAVE ME ALONE.
Can't use my Quirk. He'll know...
HONESTLY, I'VE BEEN THERE MYSELF.
IF YOU WANNA COPY MY STRATEGY NOTES LATER...
I SAID, LEAVE ME ALONE.
GRR
DEKU!!
KABLOOM
T-TIME-OUT, KACCHAN!!
FWP
THIS POOR LITTLE GUY IS QUIRKLESS!!
GAHH!
I CAN'T TAKE IT. YOU'RE DUST, KID.
YOU THINK A VILLAIN'S GONNA BACK DOWN JUST CUZ SOMEONE'S QUIRKLESS?!
WAIT, NO... GWAH!!
BOOM
AMAZING... I FREAKING LOVE THIS GUY.

PRAGMATISM

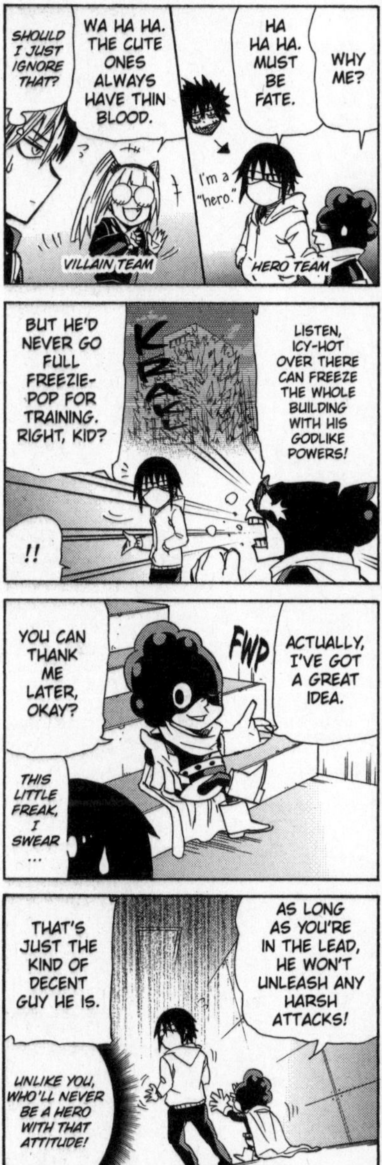
WHY ME?
HA HA HA. MUST BE FATE.
I'm a "hero."
WA HA HA. THE CUTE ONES ALWAYS HAVE THIN BLOOD.
SHOULD I JUST IGNORE THAT?
HERO TEAM
VILLAIN TEAM
LISTEN, ICY-HOT OVER THERE CAN FREEZE THE WHOLE BUILDING WITH HIS GODLIKE POWERS!
BUT HE'D NEVER GO FULL FREEZIE-POP FOR TRAINING. RIGHT, KID?
!!
ACTUALLY, I'VE GOT A GREAT IDEA.
FWP
YOU CAN THANK ME LATER, OKAY?
THIS LITTLE FREAK, I SWEAR...
AS LONG AS YOU'RE IN THE LEAD, HE WON'T UNLEASH ANY HARSH ATTACKS!
THAT'S JUST THE KIND OF DECENT GUY HE IS.
UNLIKE YOU, WHO'LL NEVER BE A HERO WITH THAT ATTITUDE!

YUMMY

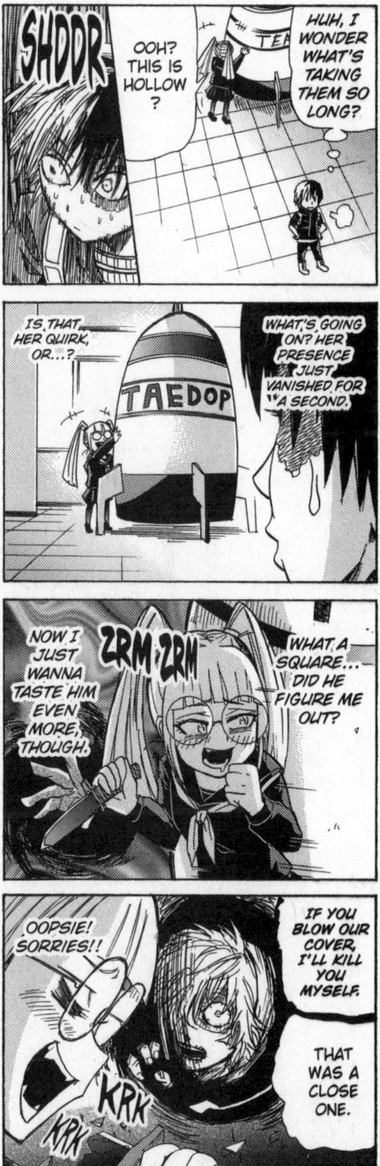
HUH, I WONDER WHAT'S TAKING THEM SO LONG?
OOH? THIS IS HOLLOW?
SHDDR
WHAT'S GOING ON? HER PRESENCE JUST VANISHED FOR A SECOND.
TAEDOP
IS THAT HER QUIRK, OR...?
WHAT A SQUARE... DID HE FIGURE ME OUT?
ZRM ZRM
NOW I JUST WANNA TASTE HIM EVEN MORE, THOUGH.
IF YOU BLOW OUR COVER, I'LL KILL YOU MYSELF.
OOPSIE! SORRIES!!
THAT WAS A CLOSE ONE.
KRK KRK

MODEL STUDENT

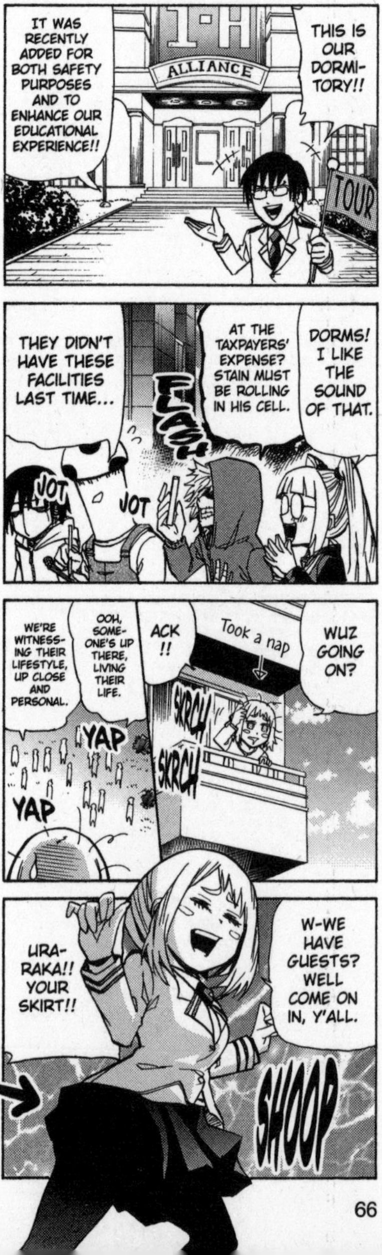
1-H
ALLIANCE
THIS IS OUR DORMITORY!!
IT WAS RECENTLY ADDED FOR BOTH SAFETY PURPOSES AND TO ENHANCE OUR EDUCATIONAL EXPERIENCE!!
TOUR
DORMS! I LIKE THE SOUND OF THAT.
AT THE TAXPAYERS' EXPENSE? STAIN MUST BE ROLLING IN HIS CELL.
FLASH
THEY DIDN'T HAVE THESE FACILITIES LAST TIME...
JOT
JOT
WUZ GOING ON?
Took a nap
ACK !!
OOH, SOME-ONE'S UP THERE, LIVING THEIR LIFE.
WE'RE WITNESSING THEIR LIFESTYLE, UP CLOSE AND PERSONAL.
SKRCH
SKRCH
YAP
YAP
W-WE HAVE GUESTS? WELL COME ON IN, Y'ALL.
URA-RAKA!! YOUR SKIRT!!
SHOOP

MAISON DU LEAGUE

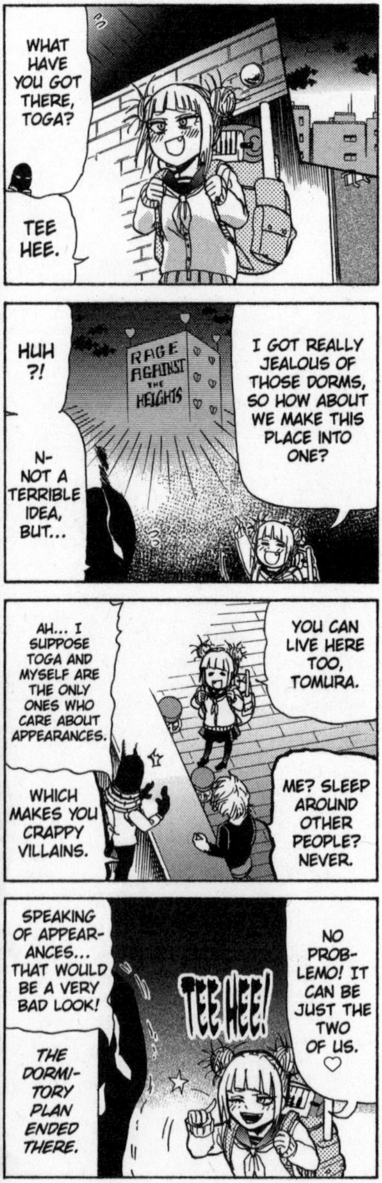
WHAT HAVE YOU GOT THERE, TOGA?
TEE HEE.
I GOT REALLY JEALOUS OF THOSE DORMS, SO HOW ABOUT WE MAKE THIS PLACE INTO ONE?
RAGE AGAINST THE HEIGHTS
HUH ?!
N-NOT A TERRIBLE IDEA, BUT...
YOU CAN LIVE HERE TOO, TOMURA.
AH... I SUPPOSE TOGA AND MYSELF ARE THE ONLY ONES WHO CARE ABOUT APPEARANCES.
ME? SLEEP AROUND OTHER PEOPLE? NEVER.
WHICH MAKES YOU CRAPPY VILLAINS.
SPEAKING OF APPEARANCES... THAT WOULD BE A VERY BAD LOOK!
NO PROBLEMO! IT CAN BE JUST THE TWO OF US. ♡
TEE HEE!
THE DORMITORY PLAN ENDED THERE.

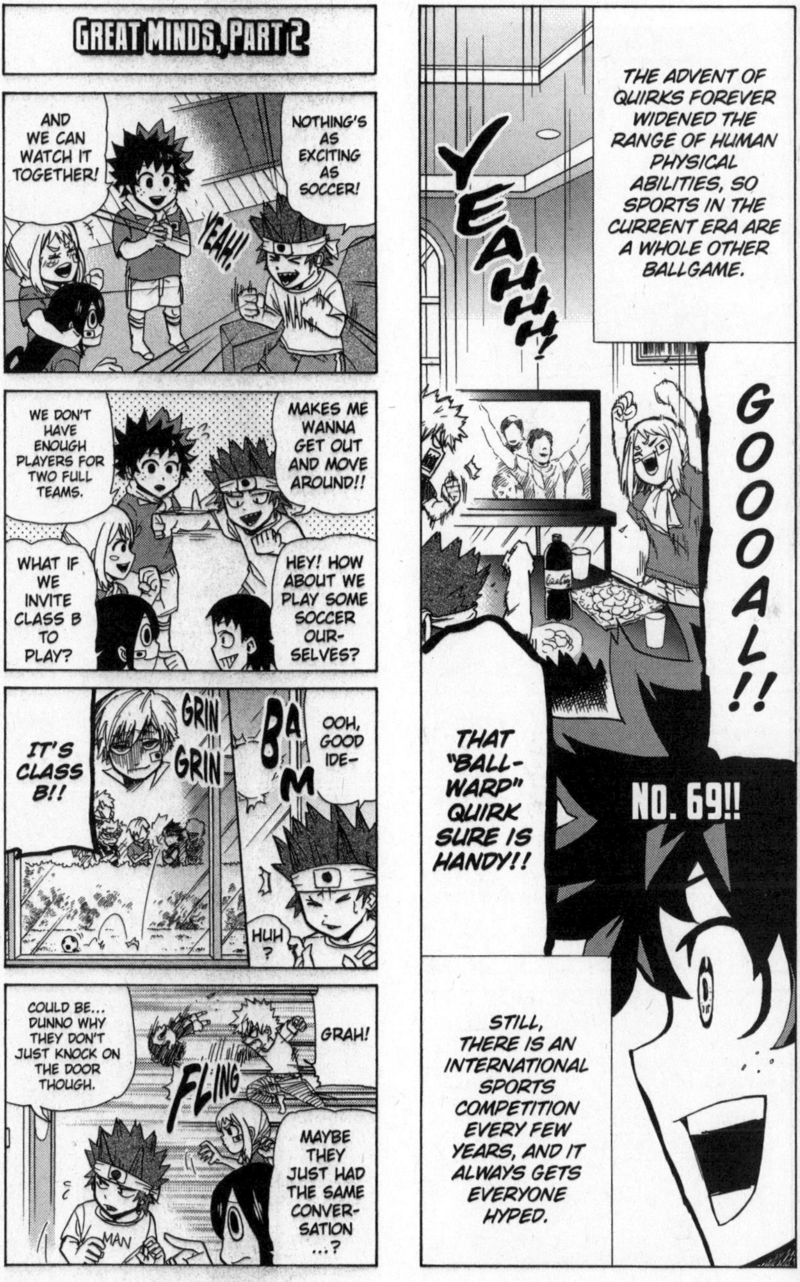
THE ADVENT OF QUIRKS FOREVER WIDENED THE RANGE OF HUMAN PHYSICAL ABILITIES, SO SPORTS IN THE CURRENT ERA ARE A WHOLE OTHER BALLGAME.
YEAHHH!
GOOOAL!!
No. 69!!
THAT "BALL-WARP" QUIRK SURE IS HANDY!!
STILL, THERE IS AN INTERNATIONAL SPORTS COMPETITION EVERY FEW YEARS, AND IT ALWAYS GETS EVERYONE HYPED.
GREAT MINDS, PART 2
NOTHING'S AS EXCITING AS SOCCER!
YEAH!
AND WE CAN WATCH IT TOGETHER!
MAKES ME WANNA GET OUT AND MOVE AROUND!!
HEY! HOW ABOUT WE PLAY SOME SOCCER OUR-SELVES?
WE DON'T HAVE ENOUGH PLAYERS FOR TWO FULL TEAMS.
WHAT IF WE INVITE CLASS B TO PLAY?
OOH, GOOD IDE-
BAM
GRIN GRIN
IT'S CLASS B!!
HUH?
GRAH!
FLING
COULD BE... DUNNO WHY THEY DON'T JUST KNOCK ON THE DOOR THOUGH.
MAYBE THEY JUST HAD THE SAME CONVER-SATION ...?

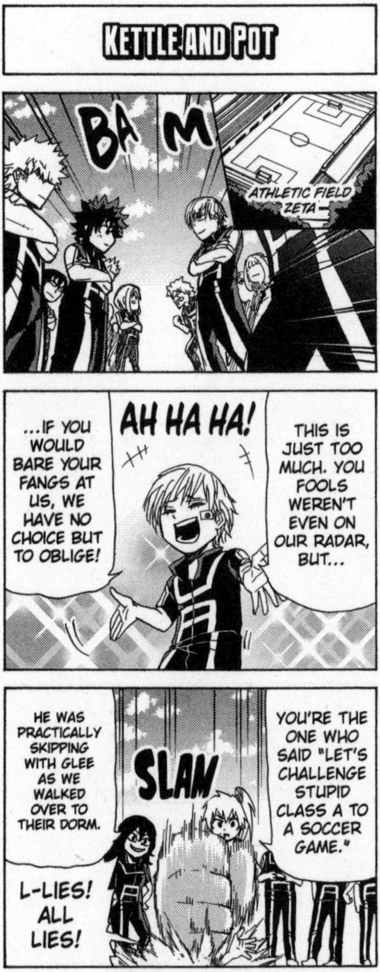
KETTLE AND POT
BAM
ATHLETIC FIELD ZETA
THIS IS JUST TOO MUCH. YOU FOOLS WEREN'T EVEN ON OUR RADAR, BUT...
AH HA HA!
...IF YOU WOULD BARE YOUR FANGS AT US, WE HAVE NO CHOICE BUT TO OBLIGE!
YOU'RE THE ONE WHO SAID "LET'S CHALLENGE STUPID CLASS A TO A SOCCER GAME."
HE WAS PRACTICALLY SKIPPING WITH GLEE AS WE WALKED OVER TO THEIR DORM.
SLAM
L-LIES! ALL LIES!
AND SO WHAT IF I JUMP FOR JOY AT THE THOUGHT OF THEM WEEPING LIKE THE LOSERS THEY ARE...?
THIS GUY'S PERSONALITY SUCKS.
PUT THE STONE DOWN, MR. GLASS HOUSE!!

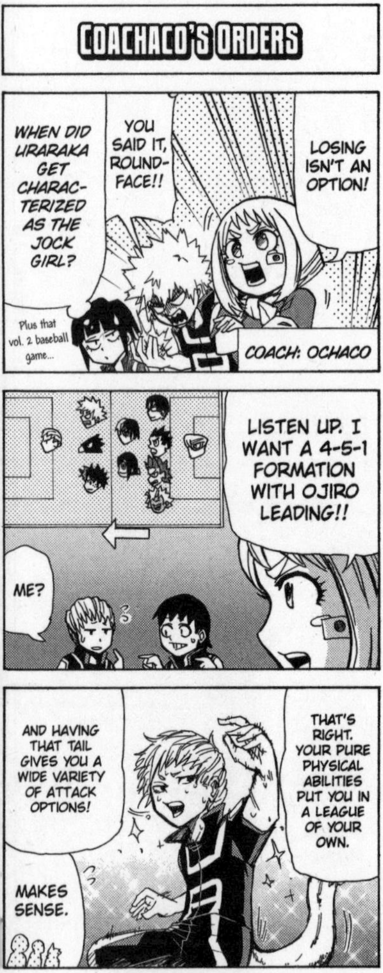
COACHACO'S ORDERS
LOSING ISN'T AN OPTION!
YOU SAID IT, ROUND-FACE!!
WHEN DID URARAKA GET CHARACTERIZED AS THE JOCK GIRL?
COACH: OCHACO
Plus that vol. 2 baseball game...
LISTEN UP. I WANT A 4-5-1 FORMATION WITH OJIRO LEADING!!
ME?
THAT'S RIGHT. YOUR PURE PHYSICAL ABILITIES PUT YOU IN A LEAGUE OF YOUR OWN.
AND HAVING THAT TAIL GIVES YOU A WIDE VARIETY OF ATTACK OPTIONS!
MAKES SENSE.
BUT WE CAN'T HAVE THAT FUR KILLING EVERY HIT.
SO YOU'RE GETTING A MAKEOVER.
POOR OJIRO!!

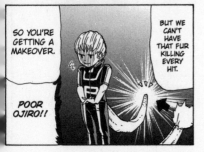

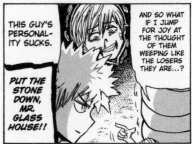

How Offensive, Class A

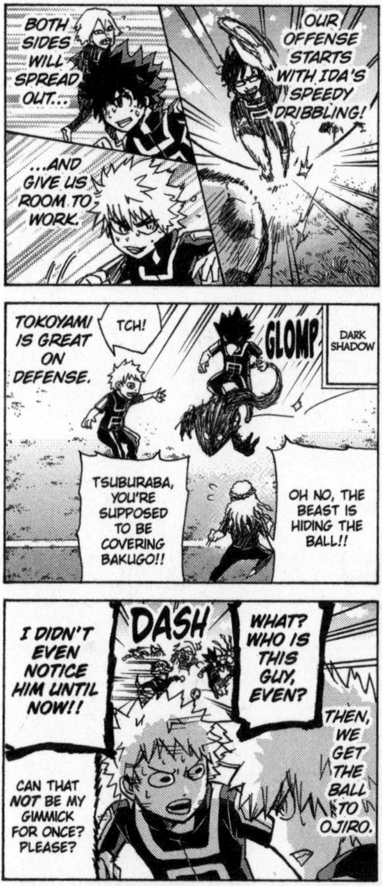
OUR OFFENSE STARTS WITH IDA'S SPEEDY DRIBBLING!
BOTH SIDES WILL SPREAD OUT...
...AND GIVE US ROOM TO WORK.
DARK SHADOW
GLOMP
TCH!
TOKOYAMI IS GREAT ON DEFENSE.
OH NO, THE BEAST IS HIDING THE BALL!!
TSUBURABA, YOU'RE SUPPOSED TO BE COVERING BAKUGO!!
WHAT? WHO IS THIS GUY, EVEN?
DASH
I DIDN'T EVEN NOTICE HIM UNTIL NOW!!
THEN, WE GET THE BALL TO OJIRO.
CAN THAT NOT BE MY GIMMICK FOR ONCE? PLEASE?
GOA-
WHAP
THAT'S JUST NOT FAIR!!
BIG FIST: KENDO'S HANDS GROW REAL, REAL BIG!!

Violations All Around

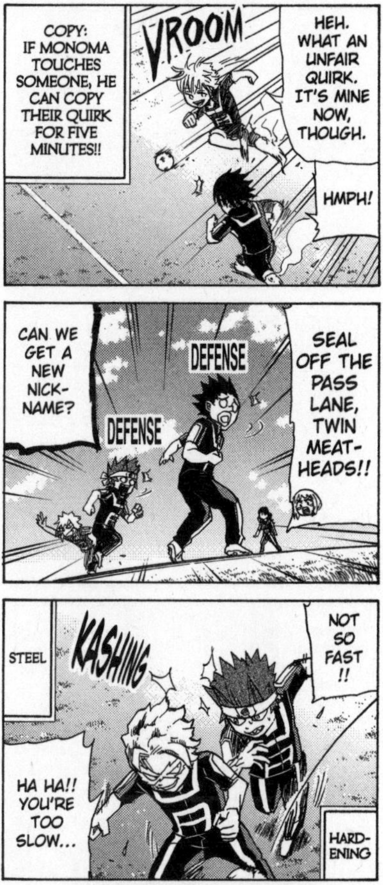
HEH. WHAT AN UNFAIR QUIRK. IT'S MINE NOW, THOUGH.
VROOM
COPY: IF MONOMA TOUCHES SOMEONE, HE CAN COPY THEIR QUIRK FOR FIVE MINUTES!!
HMPH!
SEAL OFF THE PASS LANE, TWIN MEATHEADS!!
DEFENSE
CAN WE GET A NEW NICKNAME?
DEFENSE
NOT SO FAST!!
KASHING
STEEL
HA HA!! YOU'RE TOO SLOW...
HARDENING
HIYAH!!
TALK ABOUT WELL-ARMED!!
BOING
ULTIMATE DEFENSE: THOUSAND-ARMED DEITY

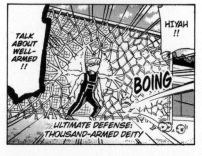

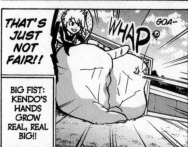

EVERY SPORTS MANGA

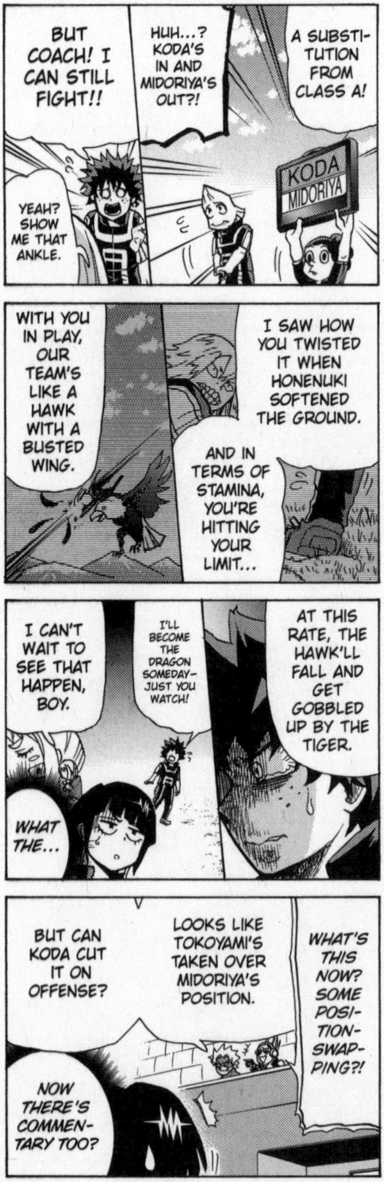
A SUBSTITUTION FROM CLASS A!
HUH...? KODA'S IN AND MIDORIYA'S OUT?!
BUT COACH! I CAN STILL FIGHT!!
KODA
MIDORIYA
YEAH? SHOW ME THAT ANKLE.
I SAW HOW YOU TWISTED IT WHEN HONENUKI SOFTENED THE GROUND.
AND IN TERMS OF STAMINA, YOU'RE HITTING YOUR LIMIT...
WITH YOU IN PLAY, OUR TEAM'S LIKE A HAWK WITH A BUSTED WING.
AT THIS RATE, THE HAWK'LL FALL AND GET GOBBLED UP BY THE TIGER.
I'LL BECOME THE DRAGON SOMEDAY— JUST YOU WATCH!
I CAN'T WAIT TO SEE THAT HAPPEN, BOY.
WHAT THE...
WHAT'S THIS NOW? SOME POSITION-SWAPPING?!
LOOKS LIKE TOKOYAMI'S TAKEN OVER MIDORIYA'S POSITION.
BUT CAN KODA CUT IT ON OFFENSE?
NOW THERE'S COMMENTARY TOO?

B'S BIG SIS

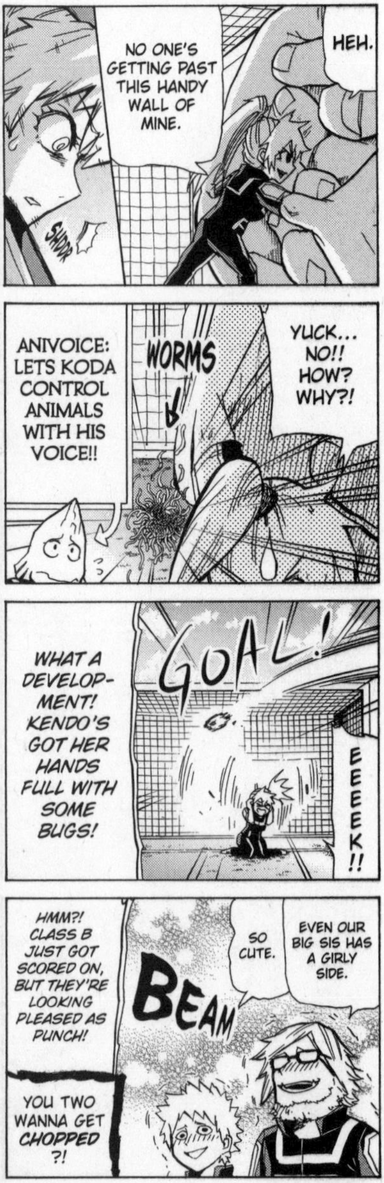
HEH.
NO ONE'S GETTING PAST THIS HANDY WALL OF MINE.
YUCK... NO!! HOW? WHY?!
WORMS
ANIVOICE: LETS KODA CONTROL ANIMALS WITH HIS VOICE!!
GOAL!
EEEEEK!!
WHAT A DEVELOPMENT! KENDO'S GOT HER HANDS FULL WITH SOME BUGS!
EVEN OUR BIG SIS HAS A GIRLY SIDE.
SO CUTE.
BEAM
HMM?! CLASS B JUST GOT SCORED ON, BUT THEY'RE LOOKING PLEASED AS PUNCH!
YOU TWO WANNA GET CHOPPED?!

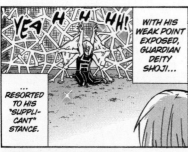

Tossing the Rule Book

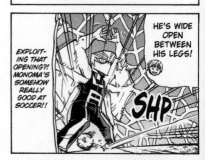

HE'S WIDE OPEN BETWEEN HIS LEGS!
EXPLOITING THAT OPENING?! MONOMA'S SOMEHOW REALLY GOOD AT SOCCER!!
SHP
HMPH.
NO WORMS ARE GONNA SCARE ME OFF AGAIN.
GRITTING HER TEETH? STILL CUTE.
PEEK
TRY SICCING COCKROACHES ON HER.
BADUM
BADUM
OR PIGEONS. THOSE MIGHT WORK.
WHICH TEAM ARE YOU MORONS ON, ANYWAY?!
MIC'S BOOMING COMMENTARY ATTRACTED A STADIUM'S WORTH OF SPECTATORS...
BUZZ
BUZZ
...TURNING THE FRIENDLY SCRIMMAGE BETWEEN CLASSES A AND B INTO A SCHOOLWIDE SPECTACLE.
WITH HIS WEAK POINT EXPOSED, GUARDIAN DEITY SHOJI...
YEAHHHH!
...RESORTED TO HIS "SUPPLICANT" STANCE.
IN THE SECOND HALF OF OVERTIME, CLASS A LAUNCHED ITS NUCLEAR WARHEAD.
SNIFF SNIFF
PANT PANT
LORD PRESERVE ME!!
KA WHIP
RED CARD FOR SHIOZAKI!!
MINETA'S SACRIFICE EARNED HIS TEAM A PENALTY KICK.
TO NO AVAIL, THOUGH.
PONK
RAHH
TCH.
RAHH
MINETA EMBRACED THORNY DOOM FOR NOTHING!!
THIS OVERALL DEADLOCK SENT THE GAME...
RAAHHH
...INTO A PENALTY KICK SHOOT-OUT.

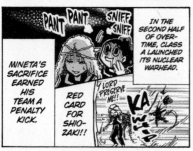

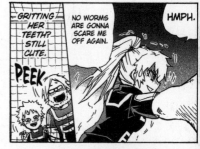

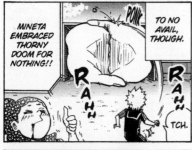

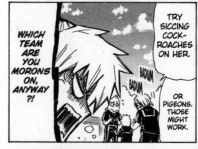

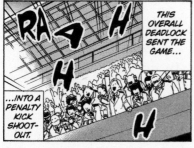

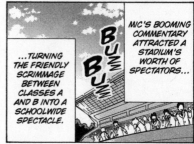

YOU WIN. GET OUT THERE.

IN THAT CASE, YOUR BODY WON'T LAST LONG.

HEH.

I MADE MY PEACE WITH THAT.

PLEASE! I'VE GOT A PLAN.

LET ME KICK TOO, COACH.

NO MEANS NO, KID.

NAH, NOT WITH THAT BUM ANKLE.

ON THIS GREEN PITCH OF DREAMS!!

THANK YOU... IT FEELS LIKE I'M HOME AGAIN.

...AND I AIN'T ABOUT TO LET THAT KINDA TALENT DESTROY ITSELF.

AT LEAST HEAR ME OUT, COACH...

YOU'RE CARRYING THE FUTURE OF JAPAN'S SOCCER DREAMS ON YOUR SHOULDERS...

THIS COACH OCHACO SHTICK AGAIN?

THE REF DECLARES THIS GAME'LL BE DECIDED BY ROCK-PAPER-SCISSORS! THE FIRST ONE TO HAVE THREE VICTORIES WINS!!

THIS JUST IN! THE AUDIENCE AGREES THAT PENALTY KICKS ARE POINTLESS AGAINST GOALIES THIS TOUGH.

I KEEP MY EYE ON THE BALL IN FRONT OF ME AND FIGHT EVERY FIGHT LIKE IT'S MY LAST.

SORRY, COACH, BUT I'M NOT MUCH FOR THINKING AHEAD LIKE THAT.

CLASS B WINS!!

ARGH!!

WE DEMAND A DO-OVER!

FIFTH IN LINE

A	X	X	O	X	–
B	O	O	X	O	–

IF I *LET* MYSELF HESITATE...

...THEN I MIGHT AS WELL QUIT RIGHT NOW!!

THAT'S HOW I'M OUT HERE GETTING STRONGER, COACH. AND IF I HESITATE FOR EVEN A MINUTE...

NEITO MONOMA

HE'S FROM CLASS B!! NOT A, BUT B! GOT IT?

IT'S NOT LIKE THE CLASS B KIDS ARE SLOUCHES, BUT MONOMA IS ALWAYS EAGER TO PROVE HOW SUPERIOR THEY ARE, FOR WHATEVER REASON!! SUCH SOUR GRAPES HAVE GOT TO BE HIDING QUITE THE INFERIORITY COMPLEX...

HE'LL ENGAGE CLASS A IN THE MOST MEANINGLESS CONTESTS, IF THAT'S WHAT IT TAKES. DOESN'T THAT JUST SHOW HOW PETTY HE REALLY IS, THOUGH....? DON'T GIVE UP, MONOMA!! YOU'RE ACTUALLY A PRETTY SKILLED DUDE!!

ITSUKA KENDO

CLASS B'S HONORARY BIG SISTER!!

SHE'S EASYGOING, SPORTSMANLIKE AND HAS KILLER JUDGMENT.

SHE SEEMS LIKE A STRONG ENOUGH PERSON TO MAKE IT OUT THERE ALL ON HER OWN, YET SHE'S THE MOST LOYAL FRIEND YOU'LL EVER FIND. SINCE THIS IS *SMASH!!* , I'M GOING OUT OF MY WAY TO SHOW THE LITTLE CRACKS IN HER ARMOR...

ANYWAY, KENDO IS THE AWESOMEST!!

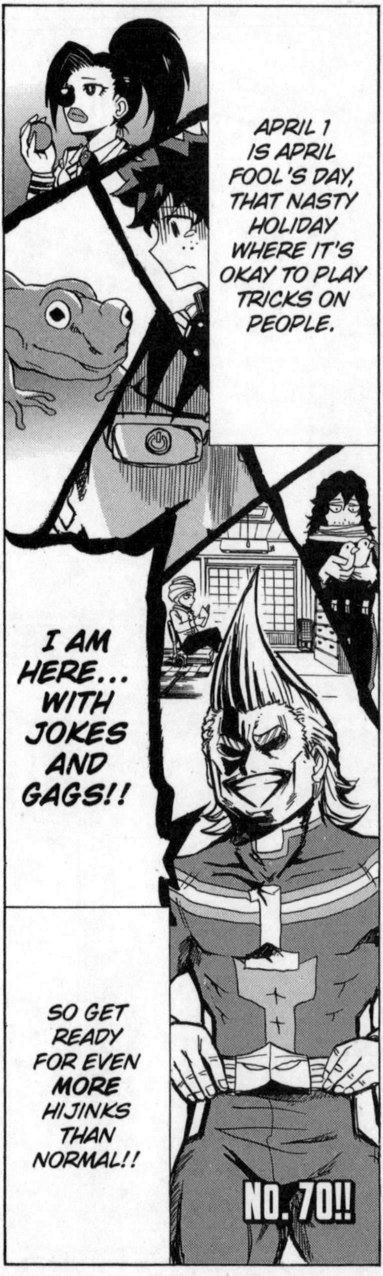
APRIL 1 IS APRIL FOOL'S DAY, THAT NASTY HOLIDAY WHERE IT'S OKAY TO PLAY TRICKS ON PEOPLE.
I AM HERE... WITH JOKES AND GAGS!!
SO GET READY FOR EVEN MORE HIJINKS THAN NORMAL!!
NO. 70!!

THE IMPORTANCE OF PR CONSULTANTS

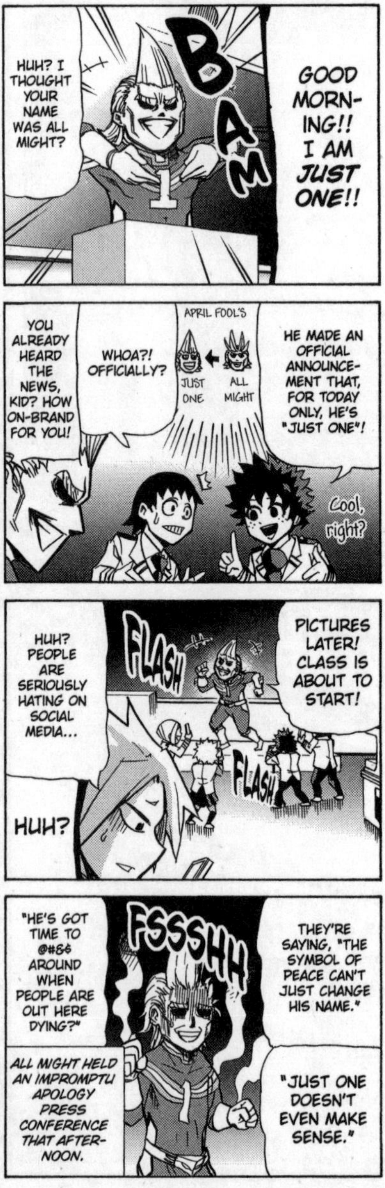
GOOD MORNING!! I AM JUST ONE!!
BAM
HUH? I THOUGHT YOUR NAME WAS ALL MIGHT?
HE MADE AN OFFICIAL ANNOUNCEMENT THAT, FOR TODAY ONLY, HE'S "JUST ONE"!
APRIL FOOL'S
JUST ONE
ALL MIGHT
WHOA?! OFFICIALLY?
YOU ALREADY HEARD THE NEWS, KID? HOW ON-BRAND FOR YOU!
Cool, right?
PICTURES LATER! CLASS IS ABOUT TO START!
FLASH
FLASH
HUH? PEOPLE ARE SERIOUSLY HATING ON SOCIAL MEDIA...
HUH?
THEY'RE SAYING, "THE SYMBOL OF PEACE CAN'T JUST CHANGE HIS NAME."
FSSSHH
"HE'S GOT TIME TO @#&$ AROUND WHEN PEOPLE ARE OUT HERE DYING?"
"JUST ONE DOESN'T EVEN MAKE SENSE."
ALL MIGHT HELD AN IMPROMPTU APOLOGY PRESS CONFERENCE THAT AFTERNOON.

MR. ROBOTO

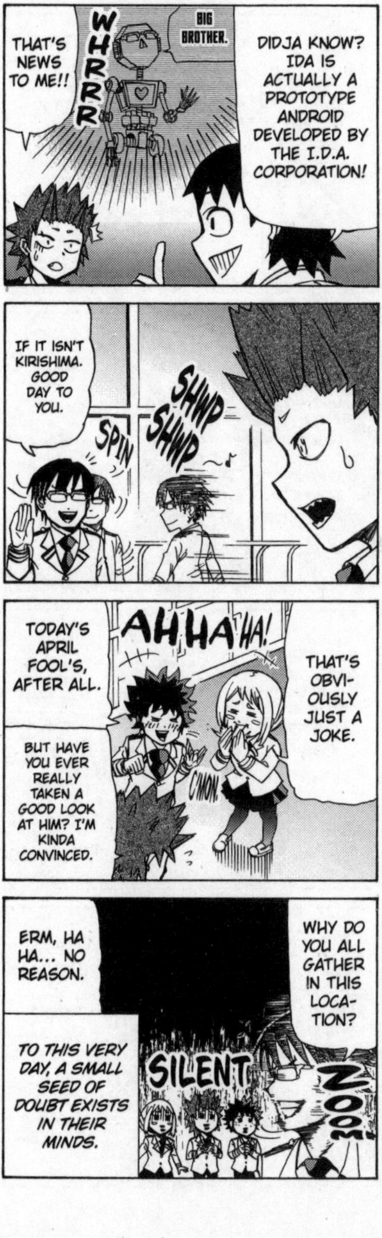
DIDJA KNOW? IDA IS ACTUALLY A PROTOTYPE ANDROID DEVELOPED BY THE I.D.A. CORPORATION!
BIG BROTHER.
WHRRR
THAT'S NEWS TO ME!!
SHWP SHWP
SPIN
IF IT ISN'T KIRISHIMA. GOOD DAY TO YOU.
THAT'S OBVIOUSLY JUST A JOKE.
AH HA HA!
C'MON.
TODAY'S APRIL FOOL'S, AFTER ALL.
BUT HAVE YOU EVER REALLY TAKEN A GOOD LOOK AT HIM? I'M KINDA CONVINCED.
WHY DO YOU ALL GATHER IN THIS LOCATION?
ZOOM
ERM, HA HA... NO REASON.
SILENT
TO THIS VERY DAY, A SMALL SEED OF DOUBT EXISTS IN THEIR MINDS.

FAILURE FROM SUCCESS FROM FAILURE

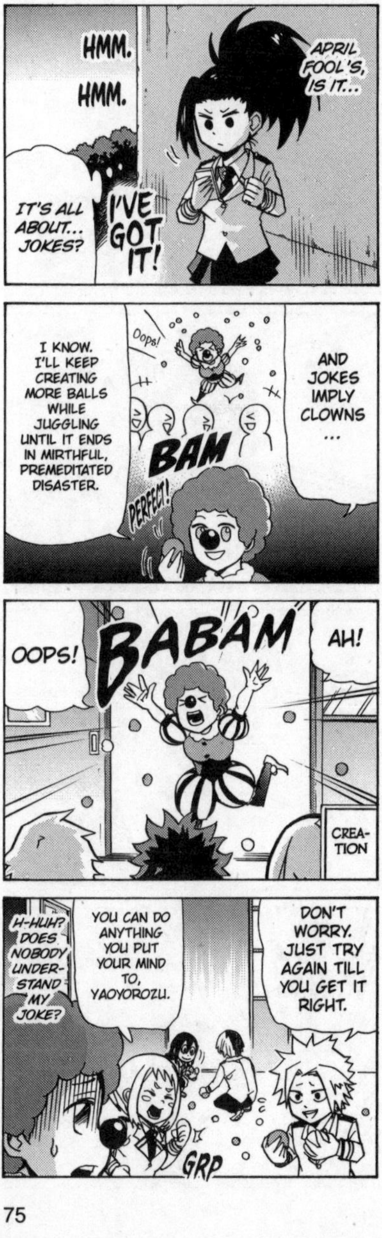
APRIL FOOL'S, IS IT...
HMM.
HMM.
I'VE GOT IT!
IT'S ALL ABOUT... JOKES?
AND JOKES IMPLY CLOWNS ...
Oops!
BAM
PERFECT!
I KNOW. I'LL KEEP CREATING MORE BALLS WHILE JUGGLING UNTIL IT ENDS IN MIRTHFUL, PREMEDITATED DISASTER.
AH!
BABAM
OOPS!
CREATION
DON'T WORRY. JUST TRY AGAIN TILL YOU GET IT RIGHT.
YOU CAN DO ANYTHING YOU PUT YOUR MIND TO, YAOYOROZU.
H-HUH? DOES NOBODY UNDERSTAND MY JOKE?
GRP

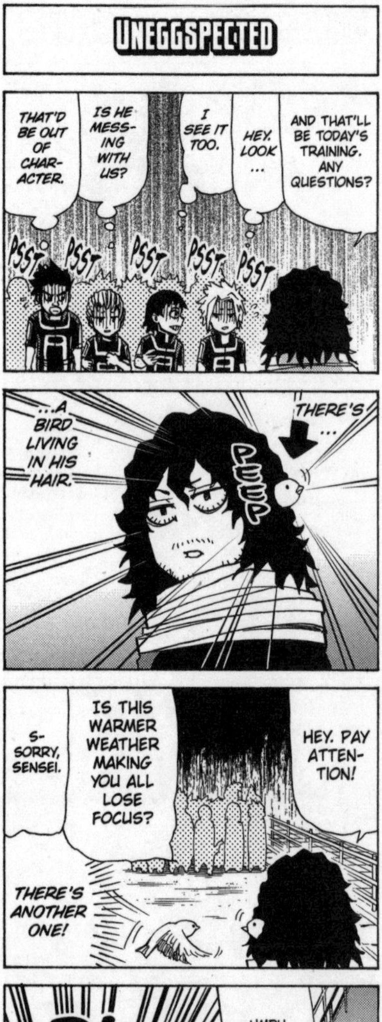
UNEGGSPECTED
AND THAT'LL BE TODAY'S TRAINING. ANY QUESTIONS?
HEY. LOOK...
I SEE IT TOO.
IS HE MESSING WITH US?
THAT'D BE OUT OF CHARACTER.
PSST
PSST
PSST
PSST
PSST
THERE'S...
PEEP
...A BIRD LIVING IN HIS HAIR.
HEY. PAY ATTENTION!
IS THIS WARMER WEATHER MAKING YOU ALL LOSE FOCUS?
S-SORRY, SENSEI.
THERE'S ANOTHER ONE!
HMPH. SLACKERS.
?!
HMM?
ROLL

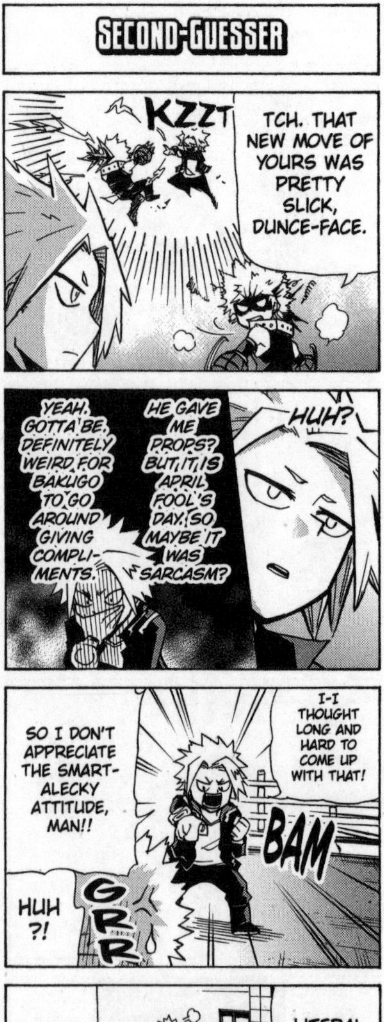
SECOND-GUESSER
TCH. THAT NEW MOVE OF YOURS WAS PRETTY SLICK, DUNCE-FACE.
KZZT
HUH?
HE GAVE ME PROPS? BUT IT IS APRIL FOOL'S DAY. SO MAYBE IT WAS SARCASM?
YEAH. GOTTA BE. DEFINITELY WEIRD FOR BAKUGO TO GO AROUND GIVING COMPLIMENTS.
I-I THOUGHT LONG AND HARD TO COME UP WITH THAT!
BAM
SO I DON'T APPRECIATE THE SMART-ALECKY ATTITUDE, MAN!!
GRR
HUH ?!
LITERAL INJURY TO INSULT.
FSSH
FSSH
THAT GUY'S A MONSTER.
HE SOUNDED GENUINE, THOUGH.

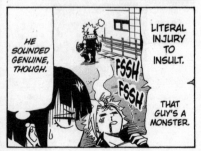

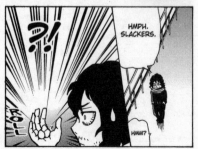

Poker Face Backfire

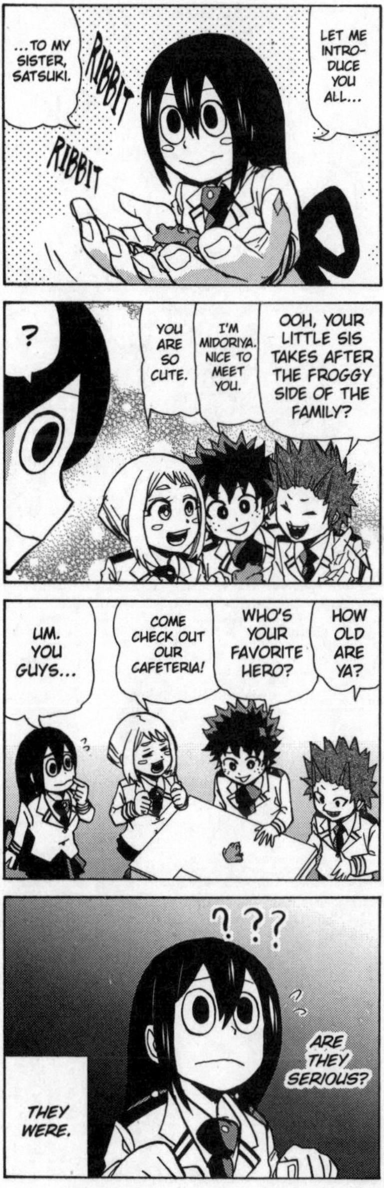
LET ME INTRODUCE YOU ALL...
RIBBIT
RIBBIT
...TO MY SISTER, SATSUKI.
OOH, YOUR LITTLE SIS TAKES AFTER THE FROGGY SIDE OF THE FAMILY?
I'M MIDORIYA. NICE TO MEET YOU.
YOU ARE SO CUTE.
?
HOW OLD ARE YA?
WHO'S YOUR FAVORITE HERO?
COME CHECK OUT OUR CAFETERIA!
UM. YOU GUYS...
???
ARE THEY SERIOUS?
THEY WERE.

Fair Use of Force

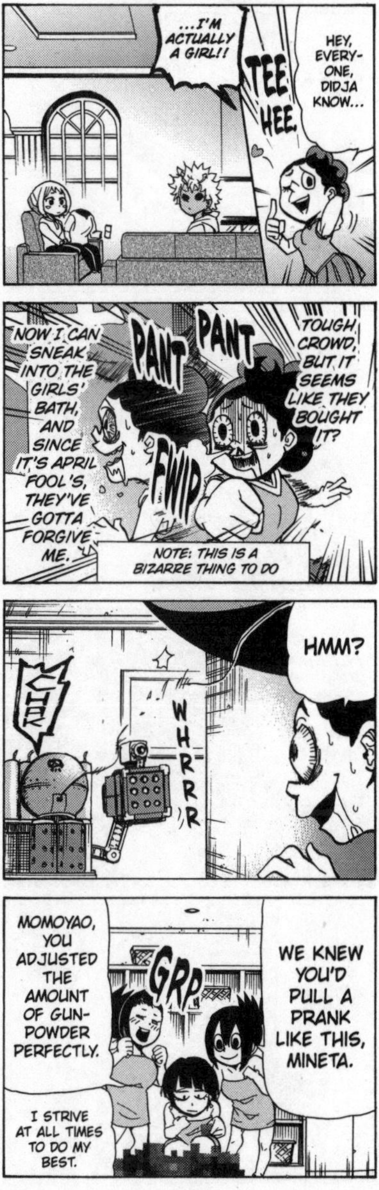
HEY, EVERYONE, DIDJA KNOW...
TEE HEE.
...I'M ACTUALLY A GIRL!!
TOUGH CROWD, BUT IT SEEMS LIKE THEY BOUGHT IT?
PANT
PANT
FWIP
NOW I CAN SNEAK INTO THE GIRLS' BATH, AND SINCE IT'S APRIL FOOL'S, THEY'VE GOTTA FORGIVE ME.
NOTE: THIS IS A BIZARRE THING TO DO
HMM?
WHRRR
CHAK
WE KNEW YOU'D PULL A PRANK LIKE THIS, MINETA.
GRP
MOMOYAO, YOU ADJUSTED THE AMOUNT OF GUNPOWDER PERFECTLY.
I STRIVE AT ALL TIMES TO DO MY BEST.

OUR PROTAGONIST

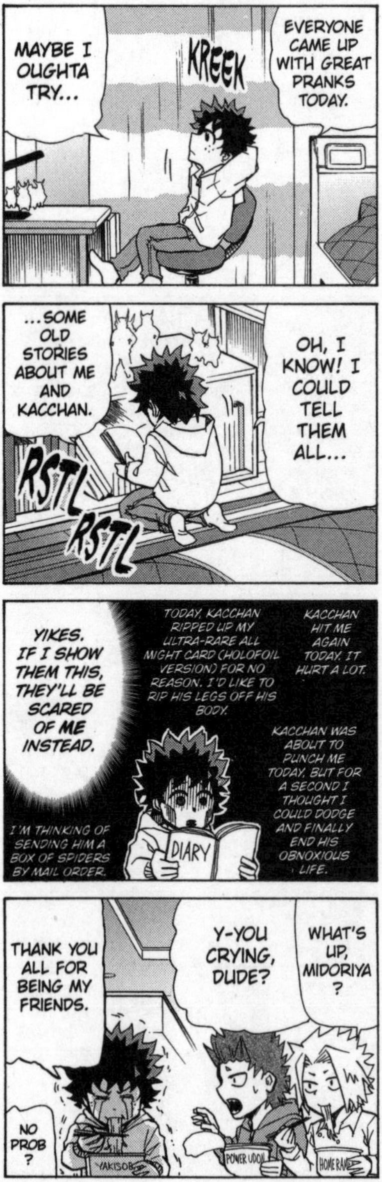
EVERYONE CAME UP WITH GREAT PRANKS TODAY.
KREEK
MAYBE I OUGHTA TRY...
OH, I KNOW! I COULD TELL THEM ALL...
...SOME OLD STORIES ABOUT ME AND KACCHAN.
RSTL
RSTL
KACCHAN HIT ME AGAIN TODAY. IT HURT A LOT.
TODAY, KACCHAN RIPPED UP MY ULTRA-RARE ALL MIGHT CARD (HOLOFOIL VERSION) FOR NO REASON. I'D LIKE TO RIP HIS LEGS OFF HIS BODY.
KACCHAN WAS ABOUT TO PUNCH ME TODAY, BUT FOR A SECOND I THOUGHT I COULD DODGE AND FINALLY END HIS OBNOXIOUS LIFE.
YIKES. IF I SHOW THEM THIS, THEY'LL BE SCARED OF ME INSTEAD.
I'M THINKING OF SENDING HIM A BOX OF SPIDERS BY MAIL ORDER.
DIARY
WHAT'S UP, MIDORIYA?
Y-YOU CRYING, DUDE?
THANK YOU ALL FOR BEING MY FRIENDS.
NO PROB?
POWER UDON

COMEDY GENIUS

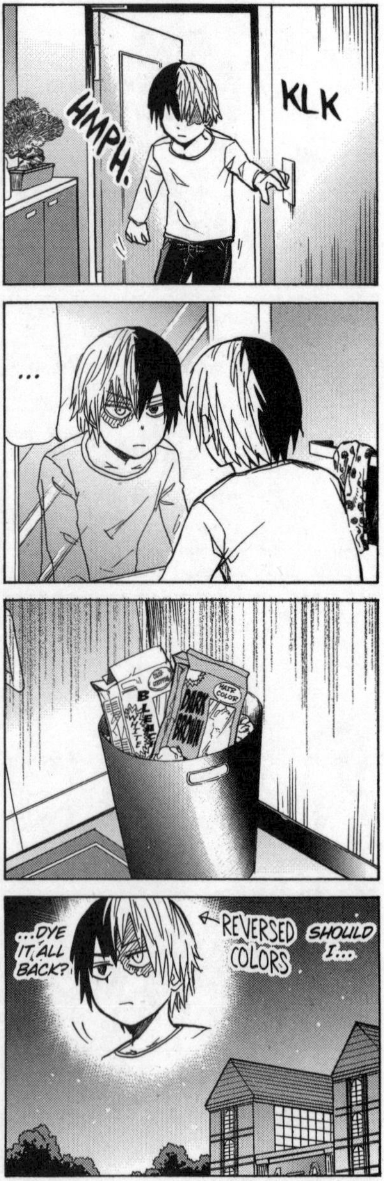
KLK
HMPH.
...
HAIR COLOR
DARK BROWN
BLEACH
WHITE
SHOULD I...
REVERSED COLORS
...DYE IT ALL BACK?

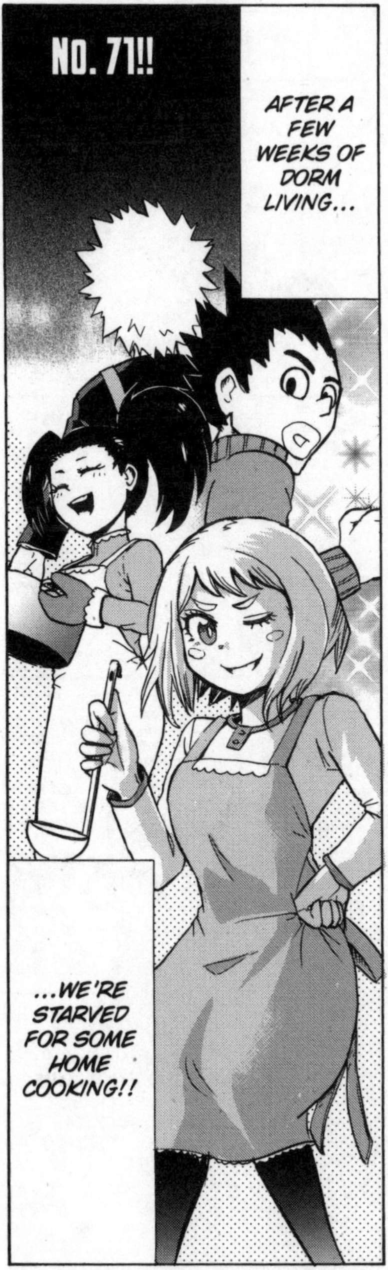
No. 71!!
AFTER A FEW WEEKS OF DORM LIVING...
...WE'RE STARVED FOR SOME HOME COOKING!!

PIGS TO THE SLAUGHTER

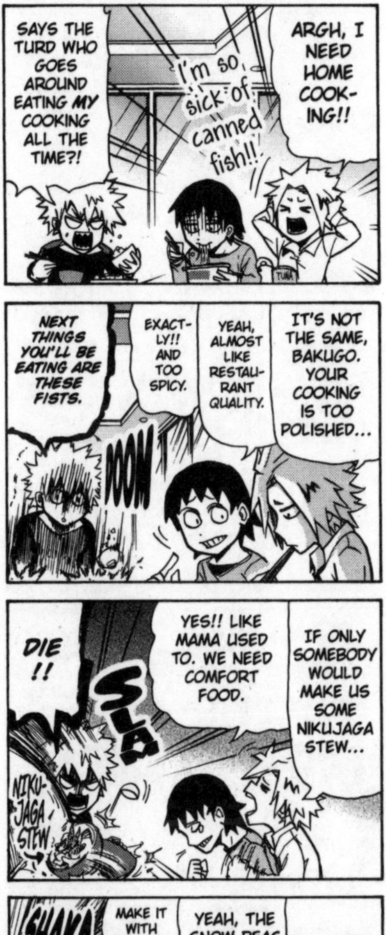
ARGH, I NEED HOME COOKING!!
I'm so sick of canned fish!!
SAYS THE TURD WHO GOES AROUND EATING MY COOKING ALL THE TIME?!
TUNA
IT'S NOT THE SAME, BAKUGO. YOUR COOKING IS TOO POLISHED...
YEAH, ALMOST LIKE RESTAURANT QUALITY.
EXACTLY!! AND TOO SPICY.
NEXT THINGS YOU'LL BE EATING ARE THESE FISTS.
DOOM
IF ONLY SOMEBODY WOULD MAKE US SOME NIKUJAGA STEW...
YES!! LIKE MAMA USED TO. WE NEED COMFORT FOOD.
DIE!!
SLAM
NIKUJAGA STEW
NAH, STILL TOO POLISHED...
YEAH, THE SNOW PEAS WERE TOTALLY UNNECESSARY...
MAKE IT WITH DISCOUNTED PORK NEXT TIME, BUD.
SHAKA
SHAKA
SHAKA

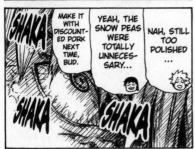

LOVE AND...CARE?

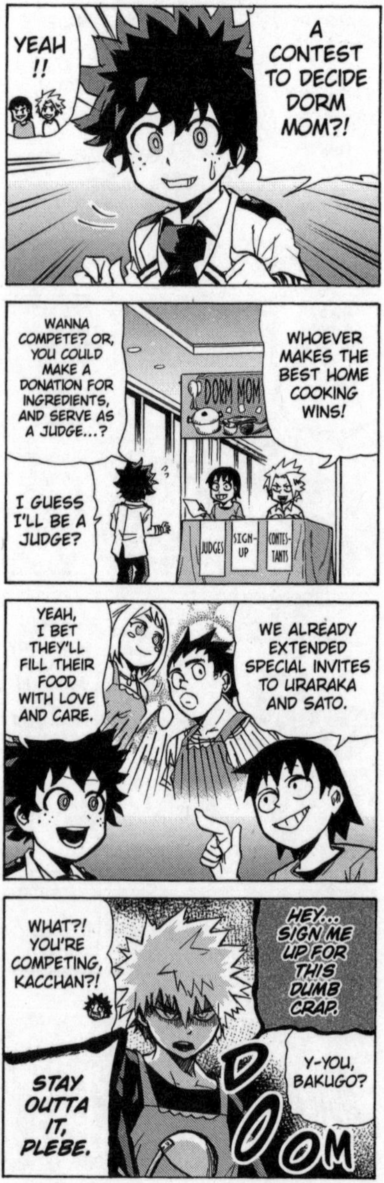
A CONTEST TO DECIDE DORM MOM?!
YEAH !!
WHOEVER MAKES THE BEST HOME COOKING WINS!
DORM MOM
WANNA COMPETE? OR, YOU COULD MAKE A DONATION FOR INGREDIENTS, AND SERVE AS A JUDGE...?
CONTES-TANTS
SIGN-UP
JUDGES
I GUESS I'LL BE A JUDGE?
WE ALREADY EXTENDED SPECIAL INVITES TO URARAKA AND SATO.
YEAH, I BET THEY'LL FILL THEIR FOOD WITH LOVE AND CARE.
HEY... SIGN ME UP FOR THIS DUMB CRAP.
WHAT?! YOU'RE COMPETING, KACCHAN?!
Y-YOU, BAKUGO?
DOOM
STAY OUTTA IT, PLEBE.

THE CONTESTANTS

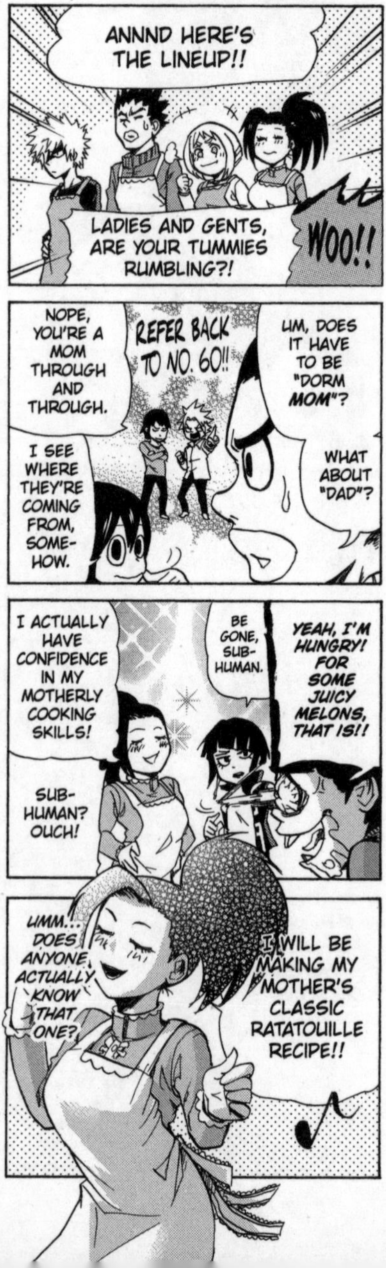
ANNND HERE'S THE LINEUP!!
WOO!!
LADIES AND GENTS, ARE YOUR TUMMIES RUMBLING?!
UM, DOES IT HAVE TO BE "DORM MOM"?
REFER BACK TO NO. 60!!
NOPE, YOU'RE A MOM THROUGH AND THROUGH.
WHAT ABOUT "DAD"?
I SEE WHERE THEY'RE COMING FROM, SOMEHOW.
YEAH, I'M HUNGRY! FOR SOME JUICY MELONS, THAT IS!!
BE GONE, SUBHUMAN.
I ACTUALLY HAVE CONFIDENCE IN MY MOTHERLY COOKING SKILLS!
SUB-HUMAN? OUCH!
I WILL BE MAKING MY MOTHER'S CLASSIC RATATOUILLE RECIPE!!
UMM... DOES ANYONE ACTUALLY KNOW THAT ONE?

Born in France (According to Him)

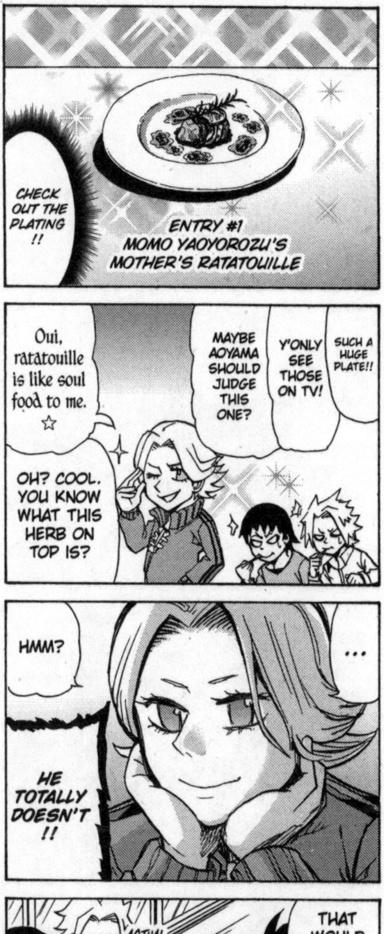
ENTRY #1 MOMO YAOYOROZU'S MOTHER'S RATATOUILLE
CHECK OUT THE PLATING!!
SUCH A HUGE PLATE!!
Y'ONLY SEE THOSE ON TV!
MAYBE AOYAMA SHOULD JUDGE THIS ONE?
Oui, ratatouille is like soul food to me. ☆
OH? COOL. YOU KNOW WHAT THIS HERB ON TOP IS?
...
HMM?
HE TOTALLY DOESN'T!!
THAT WOULD BE THYME.
ACTUAL ARISTOCRAT
But of course. Thyme is money, as we say. ☆
FAKE ARISTOCRAT
WHAT A SHADY CHARACTER.

Mom's Apple Pie

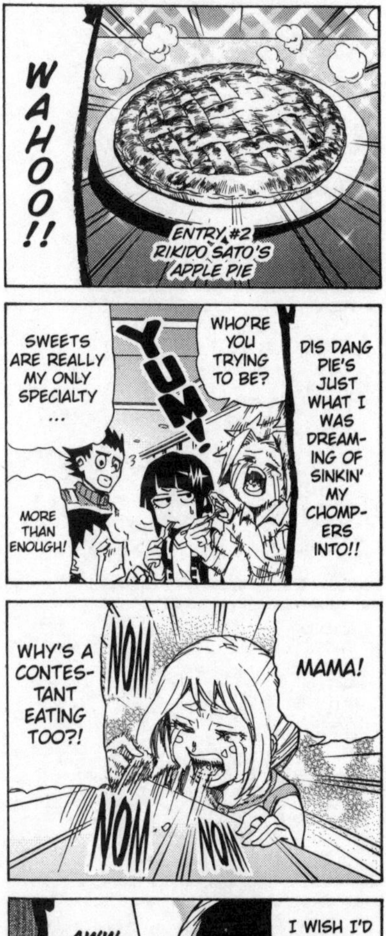
ENTRY #2 RIKIDO SATO'S APPLE PIE
WAHOO!!
DIS DANG PIE'S JUST WHAT I WAS DREAMING OF SINKIN' MY CHOMPERS INTO!!
WHO'RE YOU TRYING TO BE?
YUM!
SWEETS ARE REALLY MY ONLY SPECIALTY...
MORE THAN ENOUGH!
MAMA!
NOM
WHY'S A CONTESTANT EATING TOO?!
NOM NOM
I WISH I'D HAD A MOTHER WHO BAKED PIES... INSTEAD OF MY FACE.
AWW, TODOROKI!!
AH
OH... SORRY.

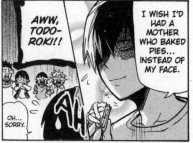

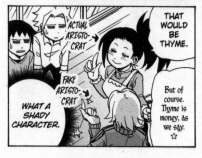

Dark Horse

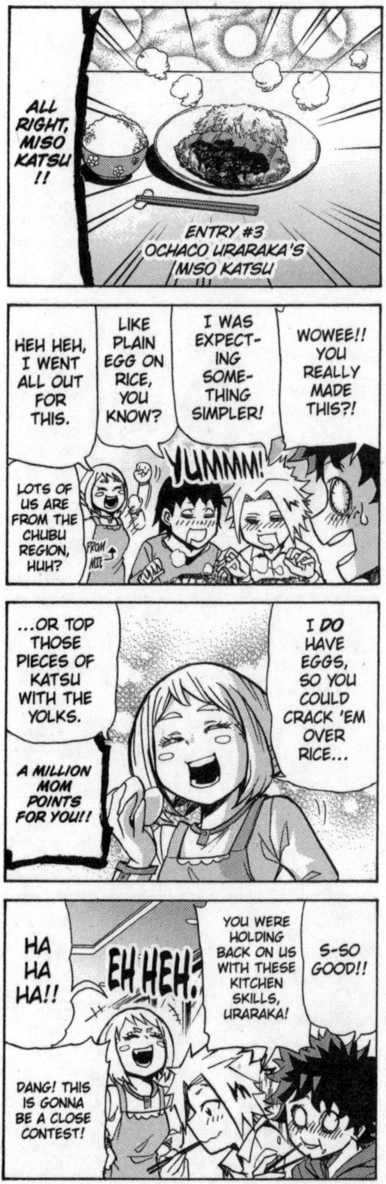
ALL RIGHT, MISO KATSU!!
ENTRY #3 OCHACO URARAKA'S MISO KATSU
WOWEE!! YOU REALLY MADE THIS?!
I WAS EXPECT-ING SOME-THING SIMPLER!
LIKE PLAIN EGG ON RICE, YOU KNOW?
HEH HEH, I WENT ALL OUT FOR THIS.
YUMMM!
LOTS OF US ARE FROM THE CHUBU REGION, HUH?
FROM MIE
I DO HAVE EGGS, SO YOU COULD CRACK 'EM OVER RICE...
...OR TOP THOSE PIECES OF KATSU WITH THE YOLKS.
A MILLION MOM POINTS FOR YOU!!
S-SO GOOD!!
YOU WERE HOLDING BACK ON US WITH THESE KITCHEN SKILLS, URARAKA!
EH HEH.
HA HA HA!!
DANG! THIS IS GONNA BE A CLOSE CONTEST!

Calm Before the Flavorstorm

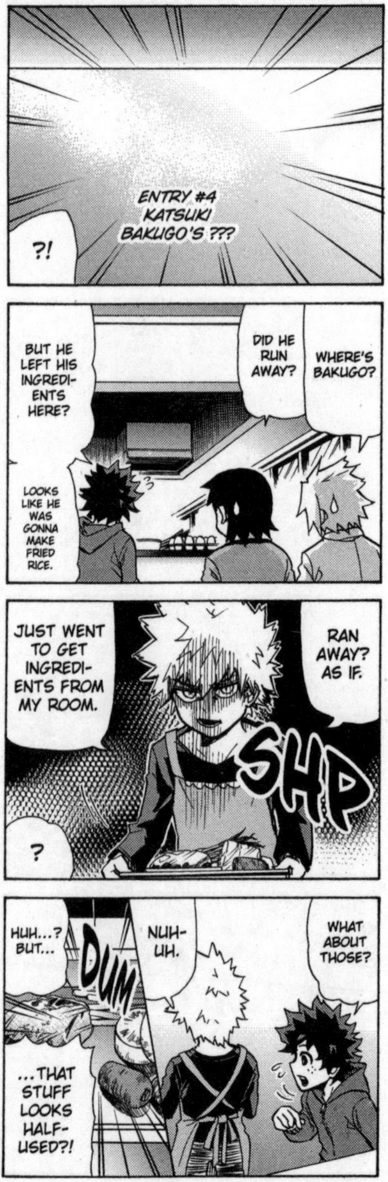
ENTRY #4 KATSUKI BAKUGO'S ???
?!
WHERE'S BAKUGO?
DID HE RUN AWAY?
BUT HE LEFT HIS INGREDI-ENTS HERE?
LOOKS LIKE HE WAS GONNA MAKE FRIED RICE.
RAN AWAY? AS IF.
JUST WENT TO GET INGREDI-ENTS FROM MY ROOM.
SHP
?
WHAT ABOUT THOSE?
NUH-UH.
HUH...? BUT...
DUM
...THAT STUFF LOOKS HALF-USED?!

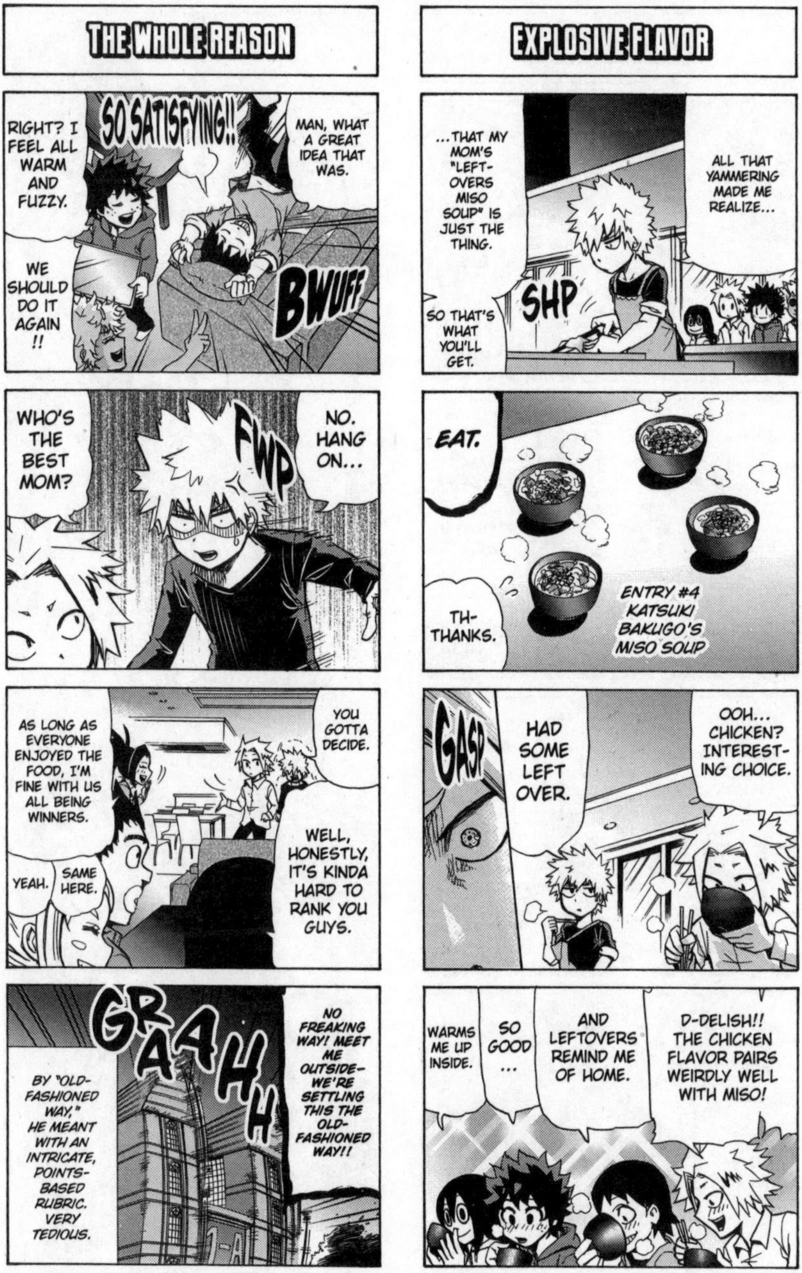
EXPLOSIVE FLAVOR
ALL THAT YAMMERING MADE ME REALIZE...
...THAT MY MOM'S "LEFT-OVERS MISO SOUP" IS JUST THE THING.
SHP
SO THAT'S WHAT YOU'LL GET.
EAT.
ENTRY #4 KATSUKI BAKUGO'S MISO SOUP
TH-THANKS.
OOH... CHICKEN? INTEREST-ING CHOICE.
HAD SOME LEFT OVER.
GASP
D-DELISH!! THE CHICKEN FLAVOR PAIRS WEIRDLY WELL WITH MISO!
AND LEFTOVERS REMIND ME OF HOME.
SO GOOD...
WARMS ME UP INSIDE.
THE WHOLE REASON
MAN, WHAT A GREAT IDEA THAT WAS.
SO SATISFYING!!
RIGHT? I FEEL ALL WARM AND FUZZY.
BWUFF
WE SHOULD DO IT AGAIN!!
NO. HANG ON...
FWP
WHO'S THE BEST MOM?
YOU GOTTA DECIDE.
AS LONG AS EVERYONE ENJOYED THE FOOD, I'M FINE WITH US ALL BEING WINNERS.
WELL, HONESTLY, IT'S KINDA HARD TO RANK YOU GUYS.
SAME HERE.
YEAH.
NO FREAKING WAY! MEET ME OUTSIDE-WE'RE SETTLING THIS THE OLD-FASHIONED WAY!!
GRAAHH
BY "OLD-FASHIONED WAY," HE MEANT WITH AN INTRICATE, POINTS-BASED RUBRIC. VERY TEDIOUS.
1-A

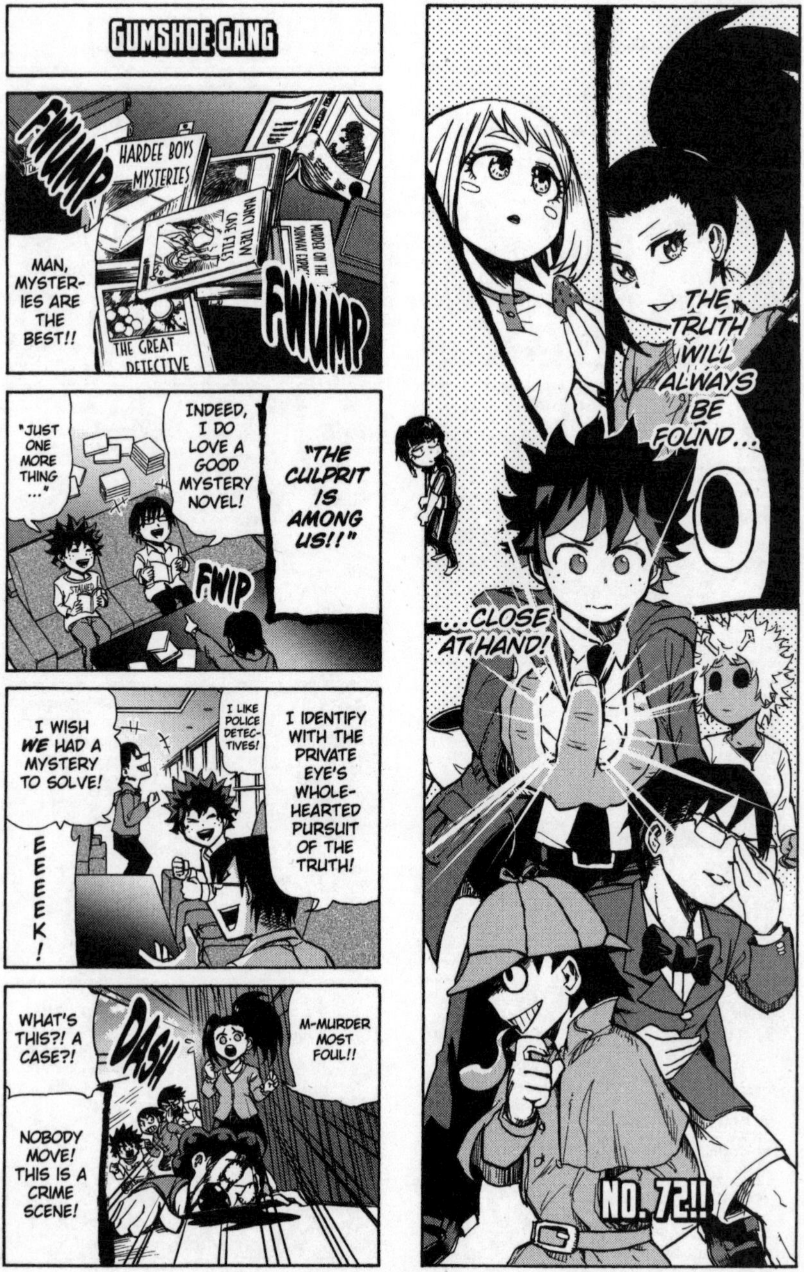
THE TRUTH WILL ALWAYS BE FOUND...
...CLOSE AT HAND!
NO. 72!!
GUMSHOE GANG
FWUMP
HARDEE BOYS MYSTERIES
THE GREAT DETECTIVE
FWUMP
MAN, MYSTER-IES ARE THE BEST!!
"THE CULPRIT IS AMONG US!!"
INDEED, I DO LOVE A GOOD MYSTERY NOVEL!
"JUST ONE MORE THING..."
FWIP
I IDENTIFY WITH THE PRIVATE EYE'S WHOLE-HEARTED PURSUIT OF THE TRUTH!
I LIKE POLICE DETEC-TIVES!
I WISH WE HAD A MYSTERY TO SOLVE!
EEEEEK!
M-MURDER MOST FOUL!!
DASH
WHAT'S THIS?! A CASE?!
NOBODY MOVE! THIS IS A CRIME SCENE!

THE CASE

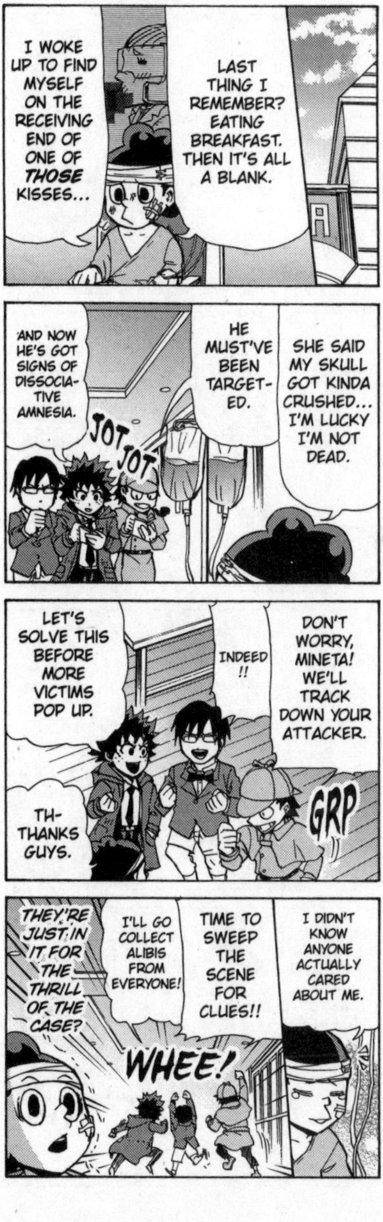
LAST THING I REMEMBER? EATING BREAKFAST. THEN IT'S ALL A BLANK.
I WOKE UP TO FIND MYSELF ON THE RECEIVING END OF ONE OF *THOSE* KISSES...
SHE SAID MY SKULL GOT KINDA CRUSHED... I'M LUCKY I'M NOT DEAD.
HE MUST'VE BEEN TARGETED.
AND NOW HE'S GOT SIGNS OF DISSOCIATIVE AMNESIA.
JOT JOT
DON'T WORRY, MINETA! WE'LL TRACK DOWN YOUR ATTACKER.
INDEED!!
LET'S SOLVE THIS BEFORE MORE VICTIMS POP UP.
GRP
TH-THANKS GUYS.
I DIDN'T KNOW ANYONE ACTUALLY CARED ABOUT ME.
TIME TO SWEEP THE SCENE FOR CLUES!!
I'LL GO COLLECT ALIBIS FROM EVERYONE!
THEY'RE JUST IN IT FOR THE THRILL OF THE CASE?
WHEE!

THREADS

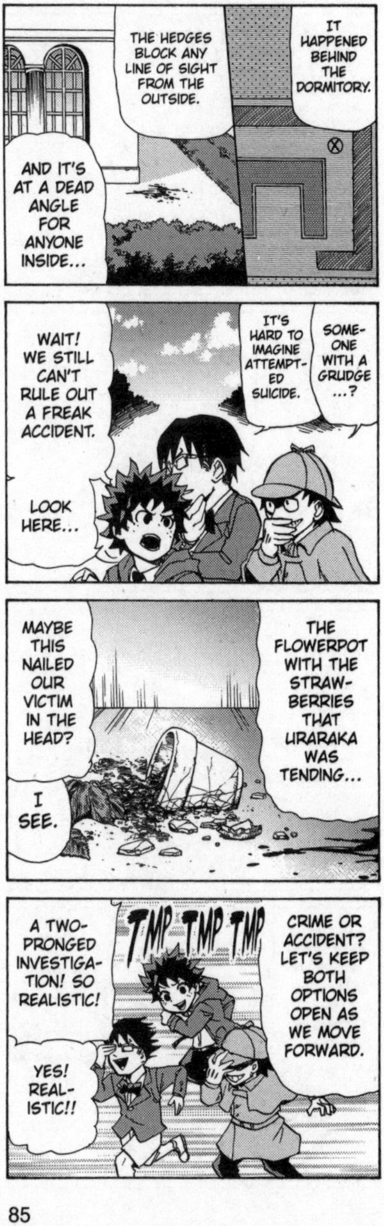
IT HAPPENED BEHIND THE DORMITORY.
THE HEDGES BLOCK ANY LINE OF SIGHT FROM THE OUTSIDE.
AND IT'S AT A DEAD ANGLE FOR ANYONE INSIDE...
SOMEONE WITH A GRUDGE...?
IT'S HARD TO IMAGINE ATTEMPTED SUICIDE.
WAIT! WE STILL CAN'T RULE OUT A FREAK ACCIDENT.
LOOK HERE...
THE FLOWERPOT WITH THE STRAWBERRIES THAT URARAKA WAS TENDING...
MAYBE THIS NAILED OUR VICTIM IN THE HEAD?
I SEE.
CRIME OR ACCIDENT? LET'S KEEP BOTH OPTIONS OPEN AS WE MOVE FORWARD.
TMP TMP TMP
A TWO-PRONGED INVESTIGATION! SO REALISTIC!
YES! REALISTIC!!

CSI: U.A.

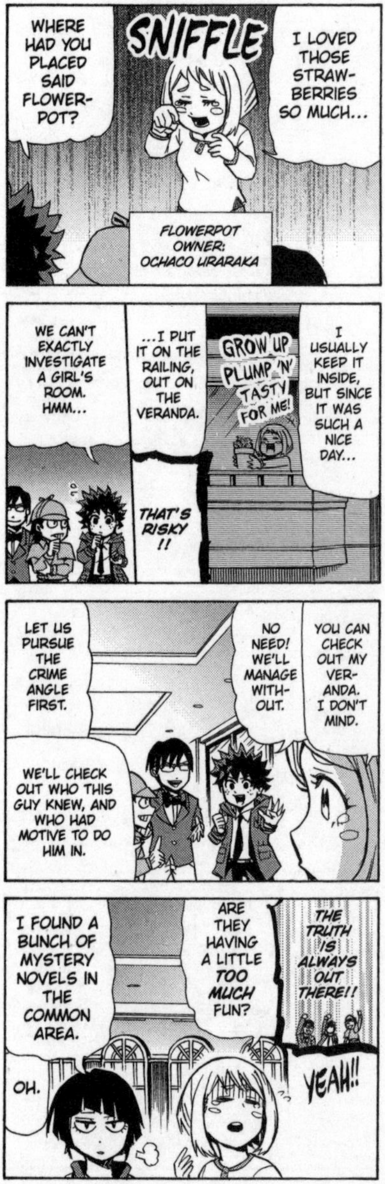
I LOVED THOSE STRAW-BERRIES SO MUCH…
SNIFFLE
WHERE HAD YOU PLACED SAID FLOWER-POT?
FLOWERPOT OWNER: OCHACO URARAKA
I USUALLY KEEP IT INSIDE, BUT SINCE IT WAS SUCH A NICE DAY…
GROW UP PLUMP 'N' TASTY FOR ME!
…I PUT IT ON THE RAILING, OUT ON THE VERANDA.
WE CAN'T EXACTLY INVESTIGATE A GIRL'S ROOM. HMM…
THAT'S RISKY!!
YOU CAN CHECK OUT MY VER-ANDA. I DON'T MIND.
NO NEED! WE'LL MANAGE WITH-OUT.
LET US PURSUE THE CRIME ANGLE FIRST.
WE'LL CHECK OUT WHO THIS GUY KNEW, AND WHO HAD MOTIVE TO DO HIM IN.
THE TRUTH IS ALWAYS OUT THERE!!
YEAH!!
ARE THEY HAVING A LITTLE TOO MUCH FUN?
I FOUND A BUNCH OF MYSTERY NOVELS IN THE COMMON AREA.
OH.

MOTIVE

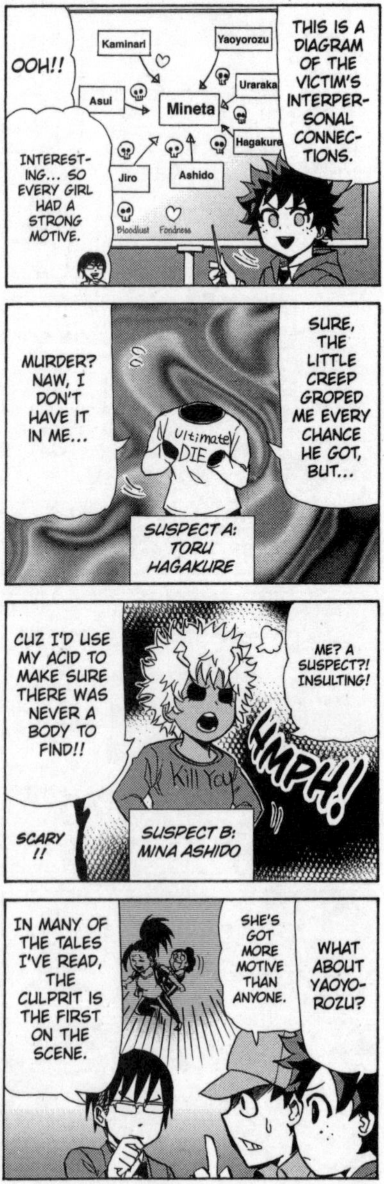
THIS IS A DIAGRAM OF THE VICTIM'S INTERPER-SONAL CONNEC-TIONS.
Yaoyorozu
Kaminari
Uraraka
Mineta
Asui
Hagakure
Jiro
Ashido
Bloodlust
Fondness
OOH!!
INTEREST-ING… SO EVERY GIRL HAD A STRONG MOTIVE.
SURE, THE LITTLE CREEP GROPED ME EVERY CHANCE HE GOT, BUT…
Ultimate DIE
MURDER? NAW, I DON'T HAVE IT IN ME…
SUSPECT A: TORU HAGAKURE
ME? A SUSPECT?! INSULTING!
HMPH!
Kill You
CUZ I'D USE MY ACID TO MAKE SURE THERE WAS NEVER A BODY TO FIND!!
SUSPECT B: MINA ASHIDO
SCARY!!
WHAT ABOUT YAOYO-ROZU?
SHE'S GOT MORE MOTIVE THAN ANYONE.
IN MANY OF THE TALES I'VE READ, THE CULPRIT IS THE FIRST ON THE SCENE.

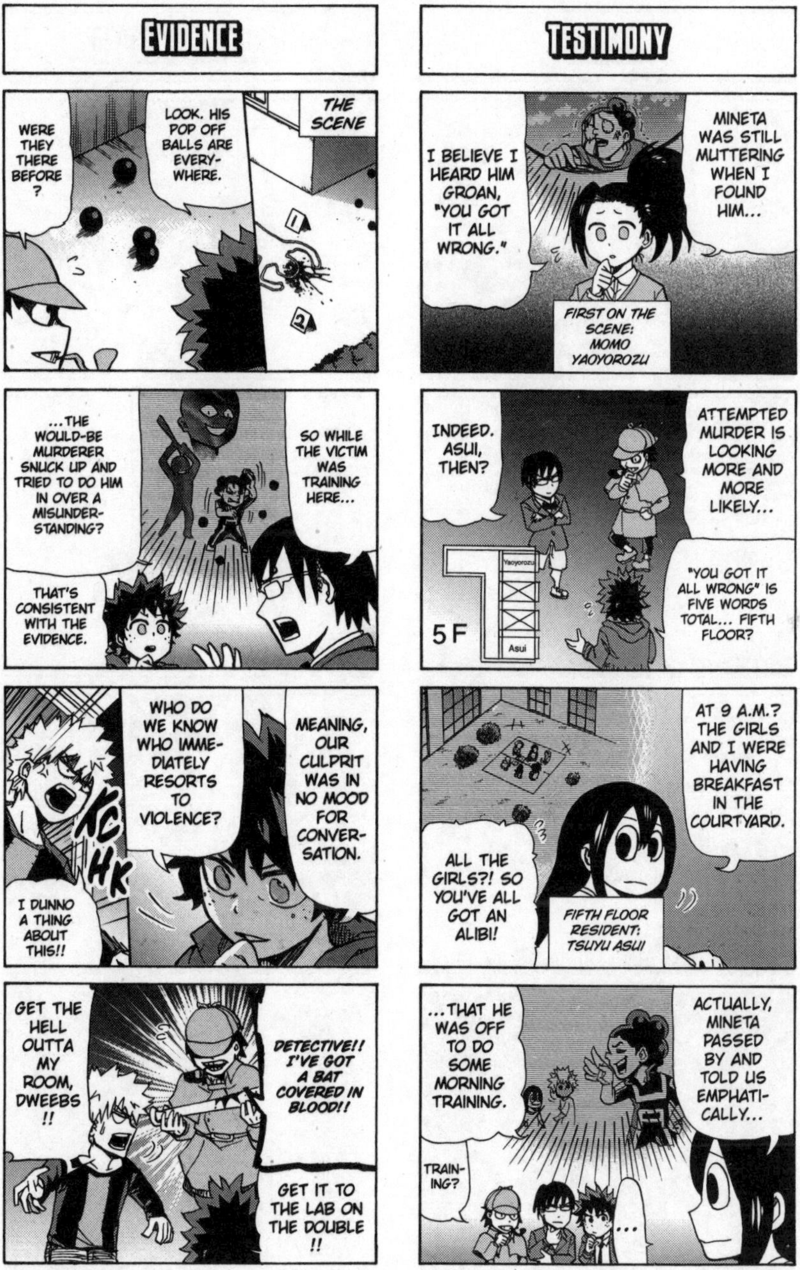
TESTIMONY
MINETA WAS STILL MUTTERING WHEN I FOUND HIM...
I BELIEVE I HEARD HIM GROAN, "YOU GOT IT ALL WRONG."
FIRST ON THE SCENE: MOMO YAOYOROZU
ATTEMPTED MURDER IS LOOKING MORE AND MORE LIKELY...
INDEED. ASUI, THEN?
"YOU GOT IT ALL WRONG" IS FIVE WORDS TOTAL... FIFTH FLOOR?
Yaoyorozu
Asui
5 F
AT 9 A.M.? THE GIRLS AND I WERE HAVING BREAKFAST IN THE COURTYARD.
ALL THE GIRLS?! SO YOU'VE ALL GOT AN ALIBI!
FIFTH FLOOR RESIDENT: TSUYU ASUI
ACTUALLY, MINETA PASSED BY AND TOLD US EMPHATICALLY...
...THAT HE WAS OFF TO DO SOME MORNING TRAINING.
...
TRAINING?
EVIDENCE
THE SCENE
LOOK. HIS POP OFF BALLS ARE EVERYWHERE.
WERE THEY THERE BEFORE?
1
2
SO WHILE THE VICTIM WAS TRAINING HERE...
...THE WOULD-BE MURDERER SNUCK UP AND TRIED TO DO HIM IN OVER A MISUNDERSTANDING?
THAT'S CONSISTENT WITH THE EVIDENCE.
MEANING, OUR CULPRIT WAS IN NO MOOD FOR CONVERSATION.
WHO DO WE KNOW WHO IMMEDIATELY RESORTS TO VIOLENCE?
KCHK
I DUNNO A THING ABOUT THIS!!
DETECTIVE!! I'VE GOT A BAT COVERED IN BLOOD!!
GET THE HELL OUTTA MY ROOM, DWEEBS!!
GET IT TO THE LAB ON THE DOUBLE!!

COUNTEREVIDENCE

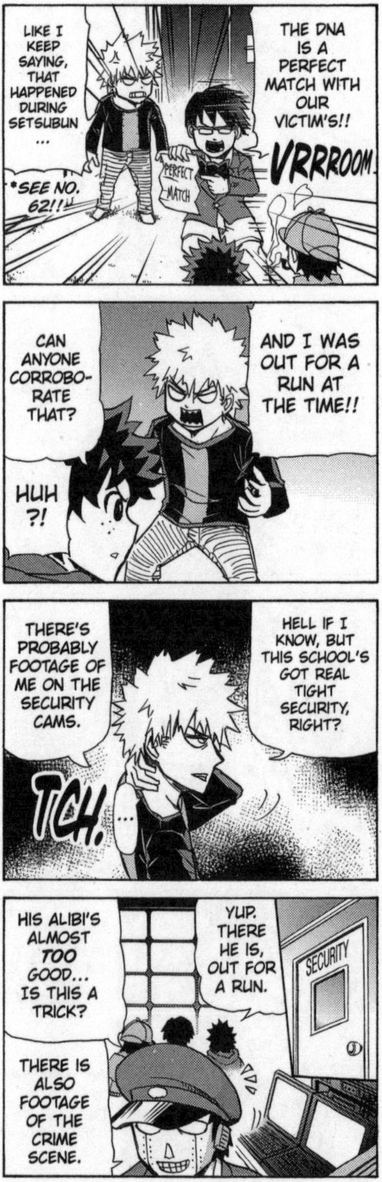
THE DNA IS A PERFECT MATCH WITH OUR VICTIM'S!!
VRRROOM
PERFECT MATCH
LIKE I KEEP SAYING, THAT HAPPENED DURING SETSUBUN...
*SEE NO. 62!!
AND I WAS OUT FOR A RUN AT THE TIME!!
CAN ANYONE CORROBORATE THAT?
HUH?!
HELL IF I KNOW, BUT THIS SCHOOL'S GOT REAL TIGHT SECURITY, RIGHT?
THERE'S PROBABLY FOOTAGE OF ME ON THE SECURITY CAMS.
TCH.
...
YUP. THERE HE IS, OUT FOR A RUN.
SECURITY
HIS ALIBI'S ALMOST TOO GOOD... IS THIS A TRICK?
THERE IS ALSO FOOTAGE OF THE CRIME SCENE.

TRUTH

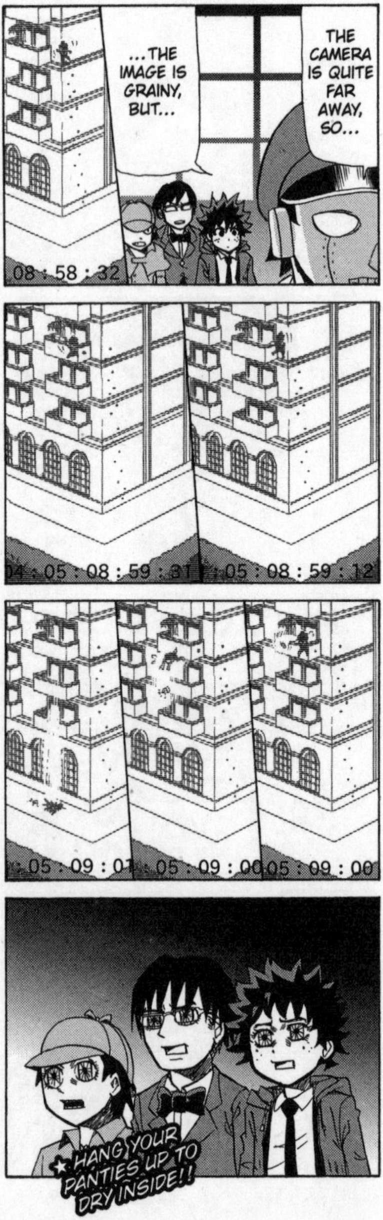
THE CAMERA IS QUITE FAR AWAY, SO...
...THE IMAGE IS GRAINY, BUT...
08 : 58 : 32
05 : 08 : 59 : 12
05 : 09 : 00
★HANG YOUR PANTIES UP TO DRY INSIDE!!

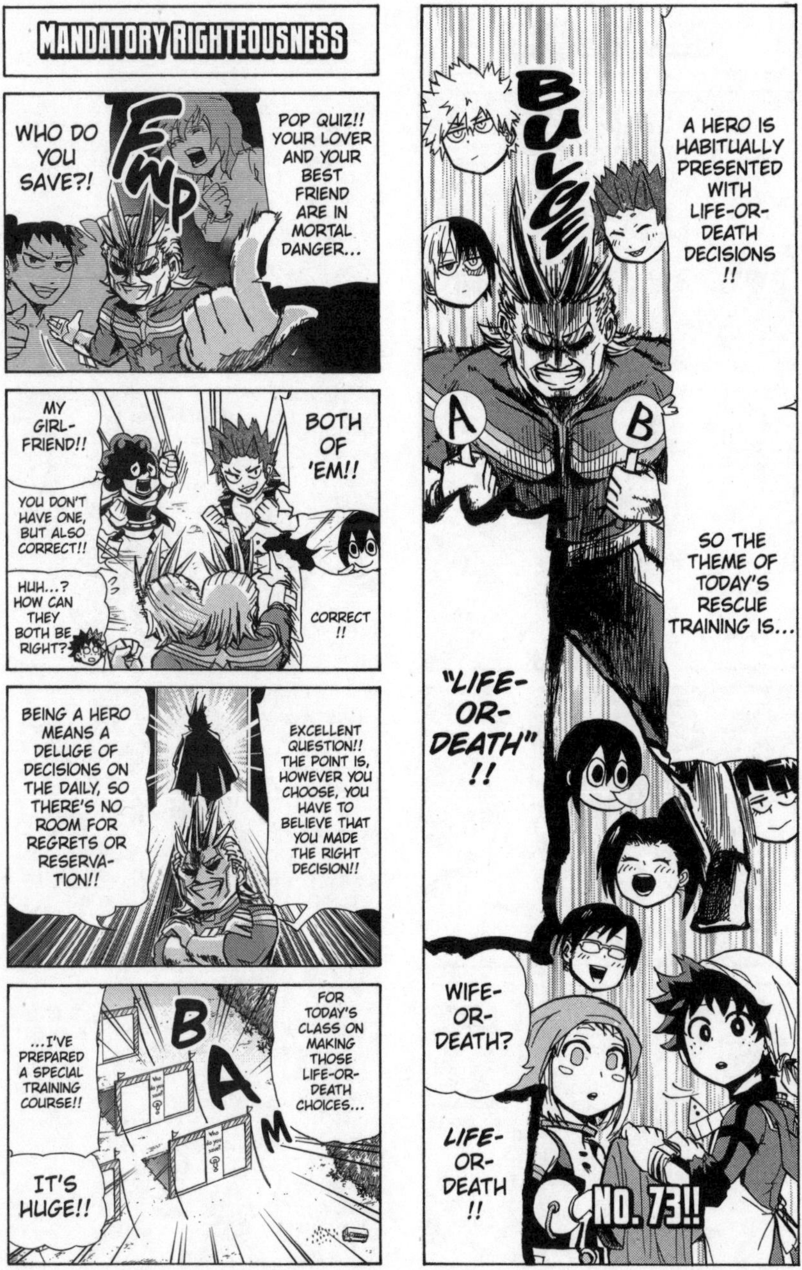
BULGE
A HERO IS HABITUALLY PRESENTED WITH LIFE-OR-DEATH DECISIONS!!
A
B
SO THE THEME OF TODAY'S RESCUE TRAINING IS...
"LIFE-OR-DEATH"!!
WIFE-OR-DEATH?
LIFE-OR-DEATH!!
NO. 73!!
MANDATORY RIGHTEOUSNESS
POP QUIZ!! YOUR LOVER AND YOUR BEST FRIEND ARE IN MORTAL DANGER...
FWP
WHO DO YOU SAVE?!
BOTH OF 'EM!!
MY GIRL-FRIEND!!
YOU DON'T HAVE ONE, BUT ALSO CORRECT!!
CORRECT!!
HUH...? HOW CAN THEY BOTH BE RIGHT?
EXCELLENT QUESTION!! THE POINT IS, HOWEVER YOU CHOOSE, YOU HAVE TO BELIEVE THAT YOU MADE THE RIGHT DECISION!!
BEING A HERO MEANS A DELUGE OF DECISIONS ON THE DAILY, SO THERE'S NO ROOM FOR REGRETS OR RESERVA-TION!!
FOR TODAY'S CLASS ON MAKING THOSE LIFE-OR-DEATH CHOICES...
BAM
...I'VE PREPARED A SPECIAL TRAINING COURSE!!
Who do you save?
IT'S HUGE!!

ALIGNMENT SYSTEM

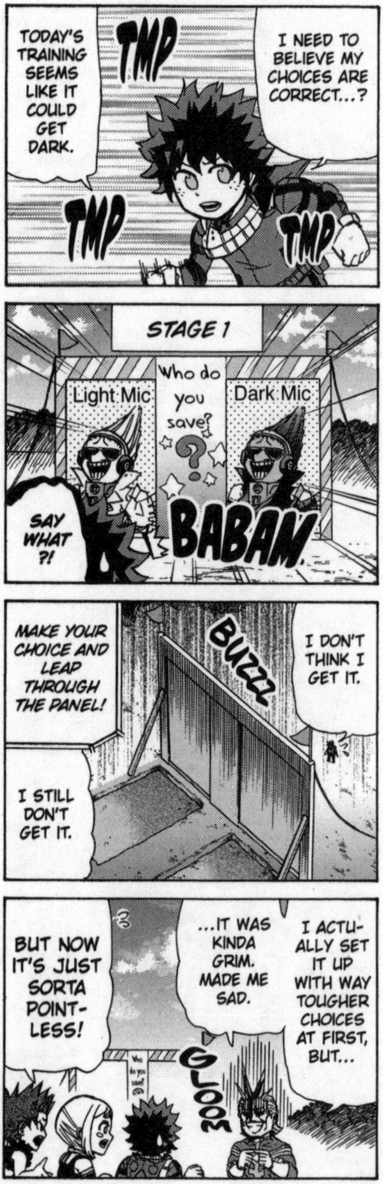

I NEED TO BELIEVE MY CHOICES ARE CORRECT...?
TMP
TODAY'S TRAINING SEEMS LIKE IT COULD GET DARK.
TMP
TMP
STAGE 1
Dark Mic
Who do you save?
Light Mic
BABAM
SAY WHAT ?!
I DON'T THINK I GET IT.
BUZZZ
MAKE YOUR CHOICE AND LEAP THROUGH THE PANEL!
I STILL DON'T GET IT.
I ACTU-ALLY SET IT UP WITH WAY TOUGHER CHOICES AT FIRST, BUT...
...IT WAS KINDA GRIM. MADE ME SAD.
BUT NOW IT'S JUST SORTA POINT-LESS!
GLOOM

BEYOND THE CHOICE

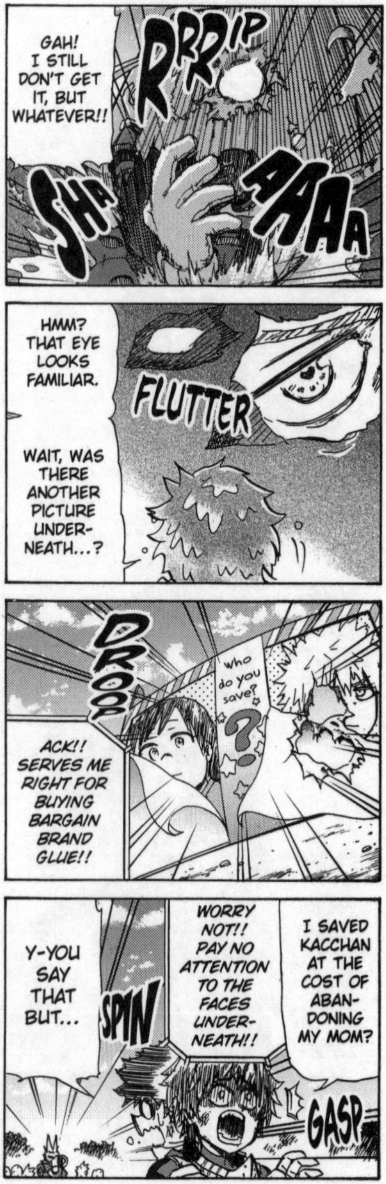

RRRIP
GAH! I STILL DON'T GET IT, BUT WHATEVER!!
AAAA
SHA
FLUTTER
HMM? THAT EYE LOOKS FAMILIAR.
WAIT, WAS THERE ANOTHER PICTURE UNDER-NEATH...?
Who do you save?
DROOP
ACK!! SERVES ME RIGHT FOR BUYING BARGAIN BRAND GLUE!!
I SAVED KACCHAN AT THE COST OF ABAN-DONING MY MOM?
WORRY NOT!! PAY NO ATTENTION TO THE FACES UNDER-NEATH!!
GASP
SPIN
Y-YOU SAY THAT BUT...

Psych!

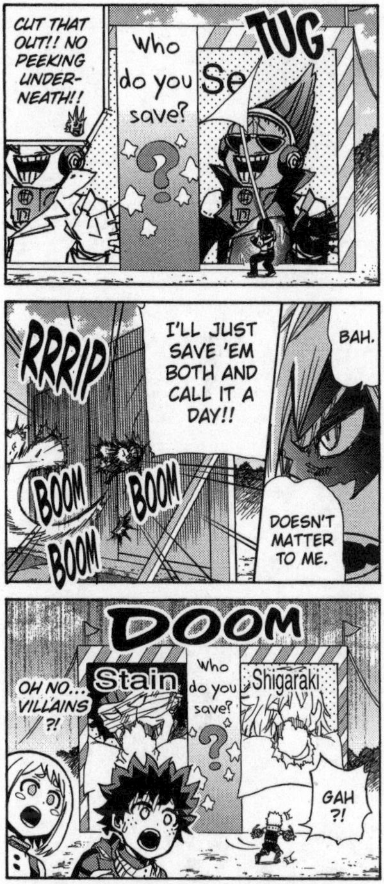
TUG
Se
Who do you save?
CUT THAT OUT!! NO PEEKING UNDERNEATH!!
BAH.
I'LL JUST SAVE 'EM BOTH AND CALL IT A DAY!!
RRRIP
DOESN'T MATTER TO ME.
BOOM
BOOM
BOOM
DOOM
Shigaraki
Who do you save?
Stain
OH NO... VILLAINS?!
GAH?!
Fuyumi To
Who do you save?
Enji Todoroki
YOU WEREN'T KIDDING ABOUT THIS TRAINING BEING GRIM!!
S-SORRY. DIDN'T MEAN FOR IT TO GO THIS WAY.

Crappy Options

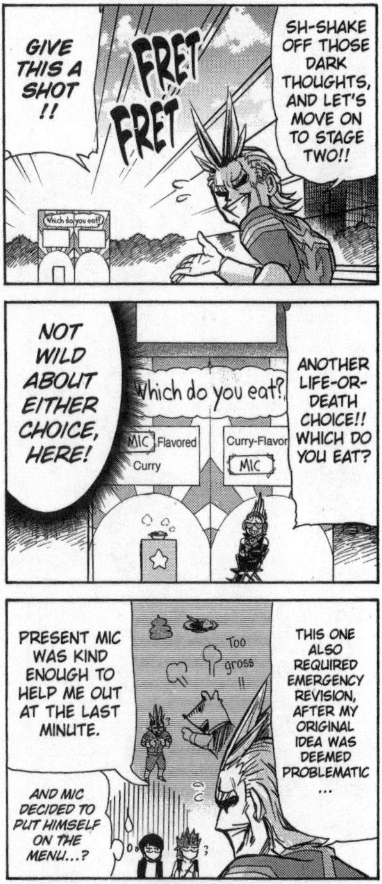
SH-SHAKE OFF THOSE DARK THOUGHTS, AND LET'S MOVE ON TO STAGE TWO!!
FRET
FRET
GIVE THIS A SHOT!!
Which do you eat?
ANOTHER LIFE-OR-DEATH CHOICE!! WHICH DO YOU EAT?
Which do you eat?
Curry-Flavor MIC
MIC Flavored Curry
NOT WILD ABOUT EITHER CHOICE, HERE!
THIS ONE ALSO REQUIRED EMERGENCY REVISION, AFTER MY ORIGINAL IDEA WAS DEEMED PROBLEMATIC...
Too gross!!
PRESENT MIC WAS KIND ENOUGH TO HELP ME OUT AT THE LAST MINUTE.
AND MIC DECIDED TO PUT HIMSELF ON THE MENU...?
HANG ON?! THAT'S NOT THE USUAL HEAVY INK OUTLINING HIS EYES TODAY! THOSE ARE JUST DARK CIRCLES!!
I RARELY SLEEP AFTER LESSON PLANNING.
SAVING PEOPLE'S SUPPOSED TO BE YOUR SPECIALTY!!

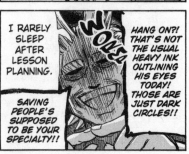

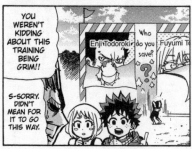

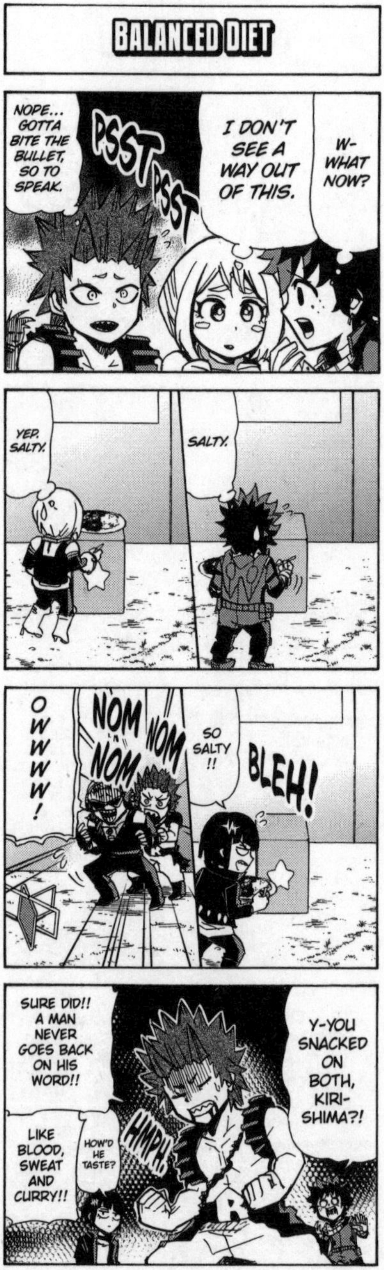
BALANCED DIET
W-WHAT NOW?
I DON'T SEE A WAY OUT OF THIS.
PSST PSST
NOPE... GOTTA BITE THE BULLET, SO TO SPEAK.
SALTY.
YEP. SALTY.
BLEH!
SO SALTY!!
NOM NOM NOM
OWWWWW!
Y-YOU SNACKED ON BOTH, KIRI-SHIMA?!
HMPH!
SURE DID!! A MAN NEVER GOES BACK ON HIS WORD!!
HOW'D HE TASTE?
LIKE BLOOD, SWEAT AND CURRY!!

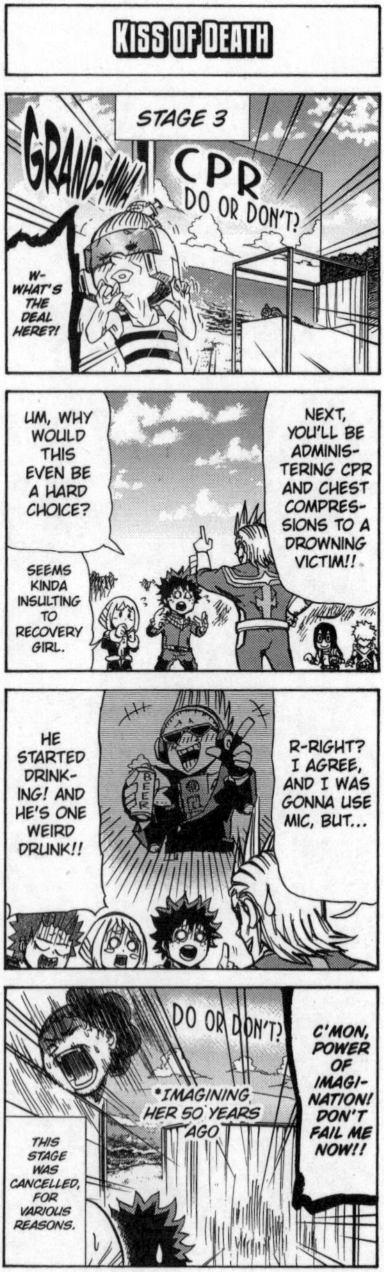
KISS OF DEATH
STAGE 3
CPR DO OR DON'T?
GRAND-MWA
W-WHAT'S THE DEAL HERE?!
NEXT, YOU'LL BE ADMINIS-TERING CPR AND CHEST COMPRES-SIONS TO A DROWNING VICTIM!!
UM, WHY WOULD THIS EVEN BE A HARD CHOICE?
SEEMS KINDA INSULTING TO RECOVERY GIRL.
R-RIGHT? I AGREE, AND I WAS GONNA USE MIC, BUT...
BEER
HE STARTED DRINK-ING! AND HE'S ONE WEIRD DRUNK!!
C'MON, POWER OF IMAGI-NATION! DON'T FAIL ME NOW!!
DO OR DON'T?
*IMAGINING HER 50 YEARS AGO
THIS STAGE WAS CANCELLED, FOR VARIOUS REASONS.

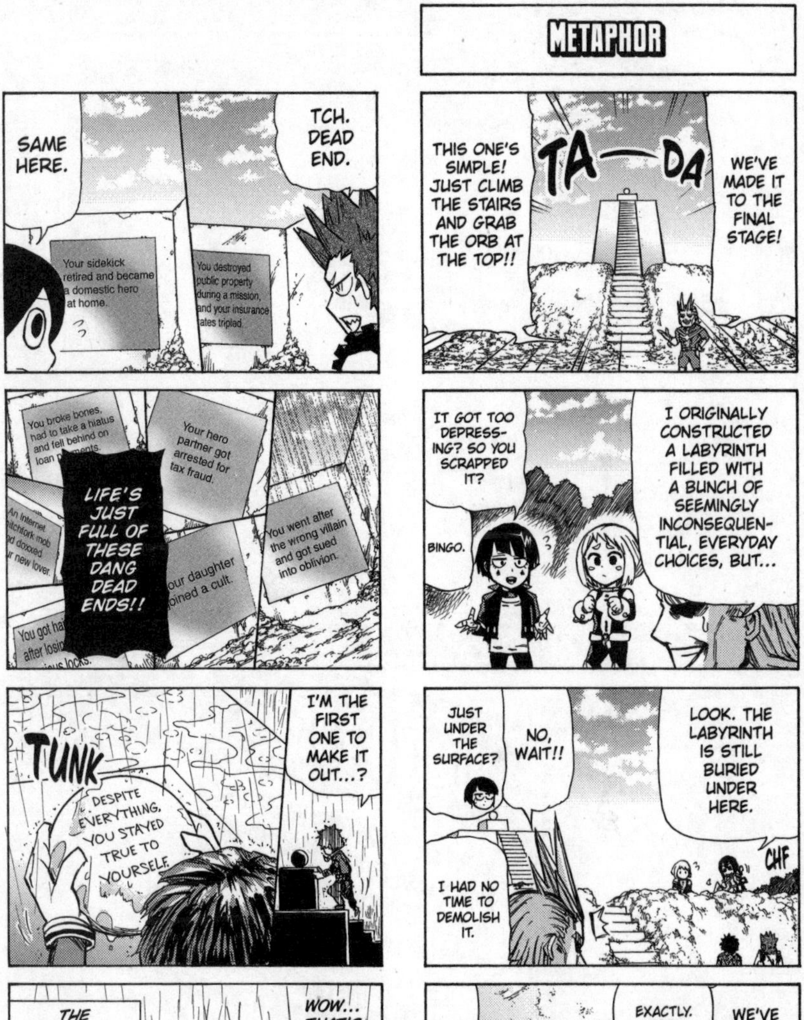
METAPHOR
WE'VE MADE IT TO THE FINAL STAGE!
TA—DA
THIS ONE'S SIMPLE! JUST CLIMB THE STAIRS AND GRAB THE ORB AT THE TOP!!
I ORIGINALLY CONSTRUCTED A LABYRINTH FILLED WITH A BUNCH OF SEEMINGLY INCONSEQUENTIAL, EVERYDAY CHOICES, BUT...
IT GOT TOO DEPRESSING? SO YOU SCRAPPED IT?
BINGO.
LOOK. THE LABYRINTH IS STILL BURIED UNDER HERE.
CHF
NO, WAIT!!
JUST UNDER THE SURFACE?
I HAD NO TIME TO DEMOLISH IT.
WE'VE COME THIS FAR. LET'S FINISH THIS RIGHT.
EXACTLY. WE'RE PREPARED FOR WHATEVER!!
OH NO...
Uh-huh!
Totally!
TCH. DEAD END.
You destroyed public property during a mission, and your insurance rates tripled.
SAME HERE.
Your sidekick retired and became a domestic hero at home.
You went after the wrong villain and got sued into oblivion.
Your hero partner got arrested for tax fraud.
You broke bones, had to take a hiatus and fell behind on
LIFE'S JUST FULL OF THESE DANG DEAD ENDS!!
I'M THE FIRST ONE TO MAKE IT OUT...?
TUNK
DESPITE EVERYTHING, YOU STAYED TRUE TO YOURSELF.
WOW... THAT'S ACTUALLY KINDA POWERFUL...
THE LESSON WAS A TOTAL BUST, BUT WE STILL SOMEHOW LEARNED ABOUT THE IMPORTANCE OF EVERYDAY CHOICES.

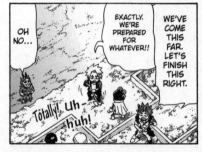

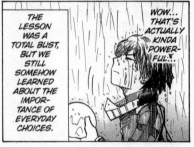

DABI

WHAT LIES BEYOND THOSE COLD, COLD EYES?

THIS COOLER-THAN-ICE DUDE TENDS NOT TO GET CLOSE TO OTHERS, SO IN *SMASH!!*, HE'S BASICALLY A KITTY!! HE'S NOT USED TO NONSENSICAL ANTICS, SO WHEN HIS FELLOW VILLAINS TURN UP THE WACKY DIAL, HE STILL TAKES A SERIOUS APPROACH AND REACTS LIKE HE'S NEVER READ A GAG MANGA BEFORE!!

THE *SMASH!!* VERSION OF SHIGARAKI IS BEYOND BULLHEADED, SO HE AND DABI CAN'T HELP BUT SQUABBLE LIKE AN OLD MARRIED COUPLE. BUT DON'T GET WORN DOWN, DABI! JUST BE YOURSELF!!

HIMIKO TOGA

NOBODY SEES THE WORLD QUITE THE WAY TOGA DOES. IN OTHER WORDS, SHE'S ONE BAD GIRL! CAPABLE OF CONSISTENTLY CATCHING EVEN HER FELLOW LEAGUE OF VILLAINS CHUMS OFF-GUARD.

I TEND TO THINK SHE DIDN'T HAVE A GREAT HOME LIFE... STILL, SHE ALWAYS JOINS THE LEAGUE IN THEIR MISADVENTURES, SO SOMETHING ABOUT THEM MUST APPEAL TO HER. BY THE WAY, I HAVE NO IDEA HOW THOSE HAIR BUNS ARE HELD TOGETHER.

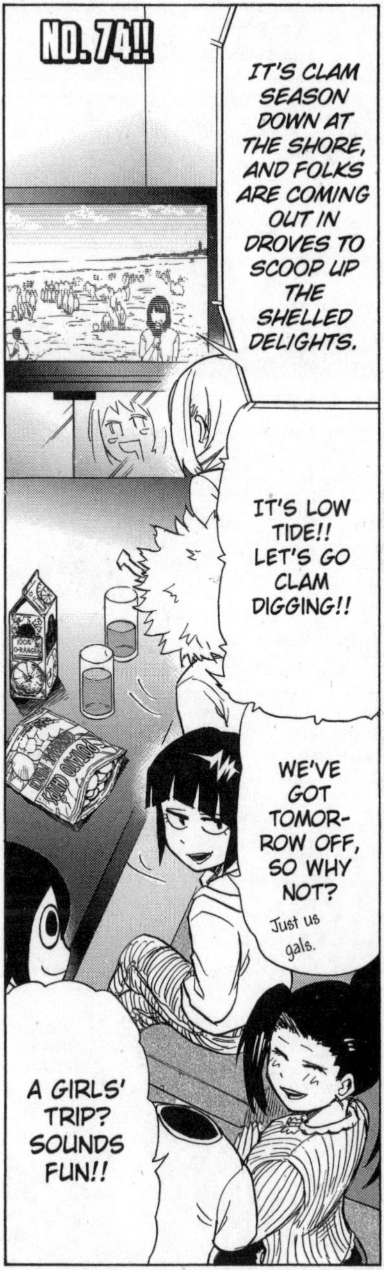
No. 74!!
IT'S CLAM SEASON DOWN AT THE SHORE, AND FOLKS ARE COMING OUT IN DROVES TO SCOOP UP THE SHELLED DELIGHTS.
IT'S LOW TIDE!! LET'S GO CLAM DIGGING!!
100% ORANGE
WE'VE GOT TOMORROW OFF, SO WHY NOT?
Just us gals.
A GIRLS' TRIP? SOUNDS FUN!!

HAVES AND HAVE-NOTS

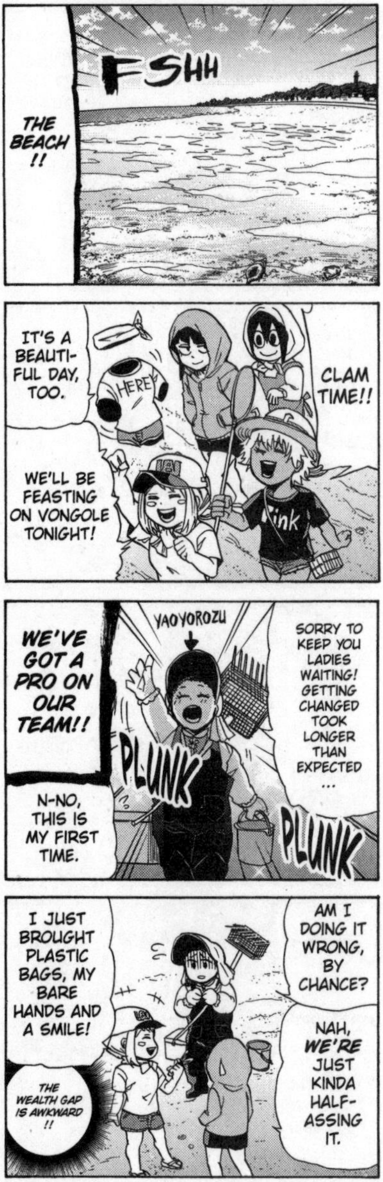
FSHH
THE BEACH!!
CLAM TIME!!
IT'S A BEAUTIFUL DAY, TOO.
HERE
Fink
WE'LL BE FEASTING ON VONGOLE TONIGHT!
SORRY TO KEEP YOU LADIES WAITING! GETTING CHANGED TOOK LONGER THAN EXPECTED...
YAOYOROZU
WE'VE GOT A PRO ON OUR TEAM!!
PLUNK
PLUNK
N-NO, THIS IS MY FIRST TIME.
AM I DOING IT WRONG, BY CHANCE?
NAH, WE'RE JUST KINDA HALF-ASSING IT.
I JUST BROUGHT PLASTIC BAGS, MY BARE HANDS AND A SMILE!
THE WEALTH GAP IS AWKWARD!!

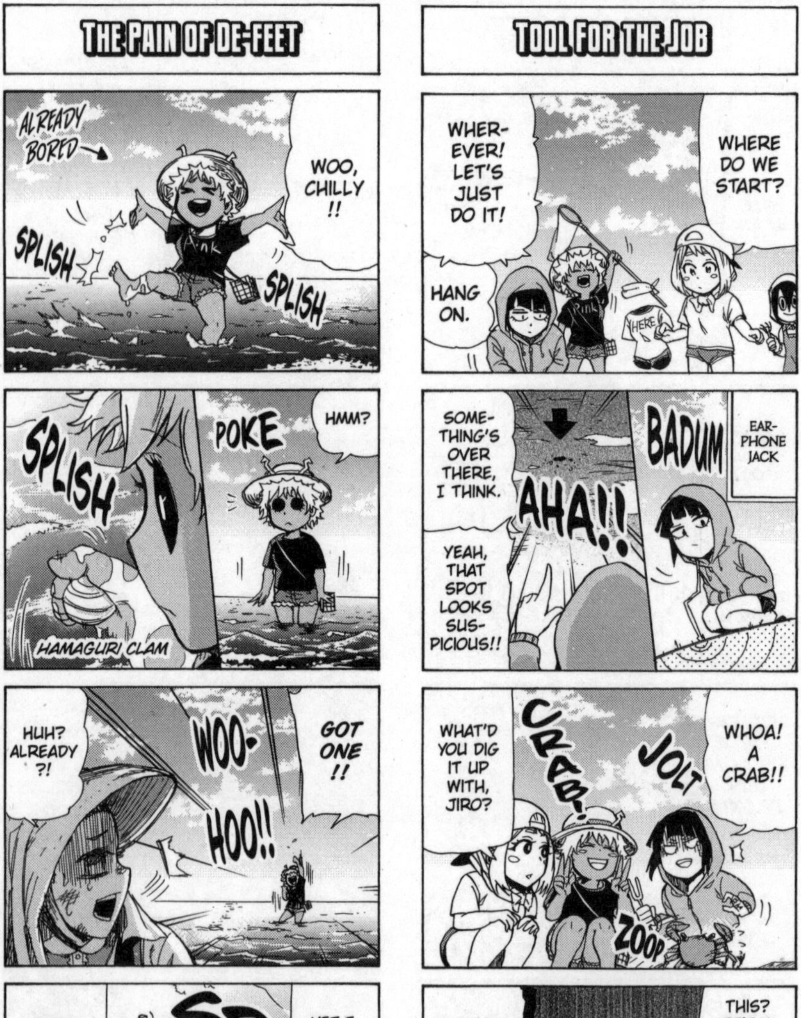
TOOL FOR THE JOB
WHERE DO WE START?
WHER-EVER! LET'S JUST DO IT!
HANG ON.
HERE
EAR-PHONE JACK
BADUM
SOME-THING'S OVER THERE, I THINK.
AHA!!
YEAH, THAT SPOT LOOKS SUS-PICIOUS!!
WHOA! A CRAB!!
JOLT
CRAB!
WHAT'D YOU DIG IT UP WITH, JIRO?
ZOOP
THIS? IT'S A TUNING FORK.
WEIRD!!
IT'S ALL I HAD AT HOME.
THE PAIN OF DE-FEET
WOO, CHILLY!!
ALREADY BORED
SPLISH
SPLISH
HMM?
POKE
SPLISH
HAMAGURI CLAM
GOT ONE!!
WOO-HOO!!
HUH? ALREADY?!
YET I, WITH MY SPECIAL-IZED TOOLS...
SPLASH
...HAVE ONLY CAUGHT SEAWEED AND DEAD JELLYFISH.
PLUNK
Her toes are beating me?

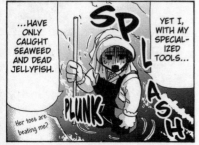

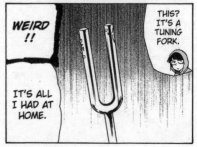

MOMO WOE

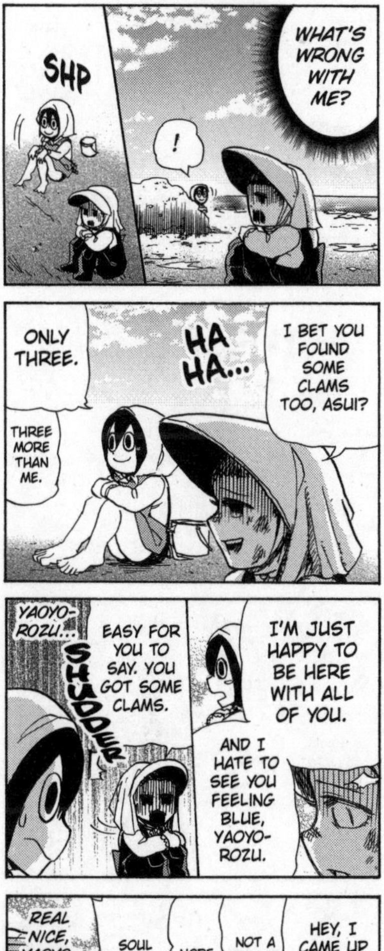
WHAT'S WRONG WITH ME?
!
SHP
I BET YOU FOUND SOME CLAMS TOO, ASUI?
HA HA...
ONLY THREE.
THREE MORE THAN ME.
I'M JUST HAPPY TO BE HERE WITH ALL OF YOU.
AND I HATE TO SEE YOU FEELING BLUE, YAOYOROZU.
EASY FOR YOU TO SAY. YOU GOT SOME CLAMS.
SHUDDER
YAOYOROZU...
HEY, I CAME UP WITH NOTHING TOO.
NOT A THING?
NOPE.
SOUL SISTER!!
REAL NICE, YAOYOROZU...
HERE
At last, a true friend!!

MONETIZATION

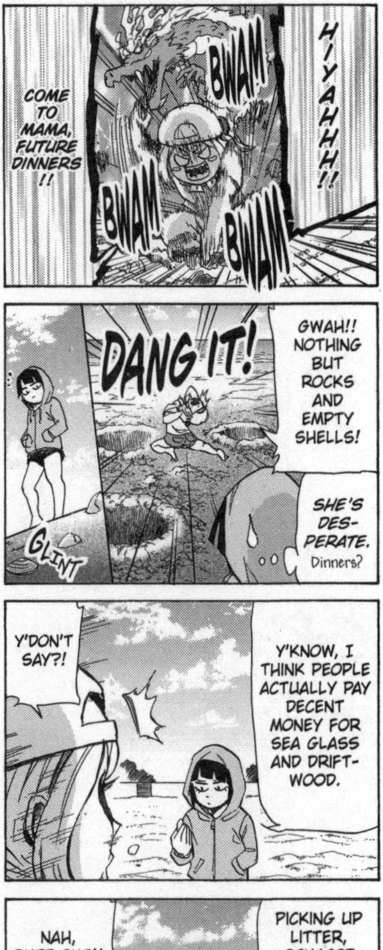
HIYAHHH!!
BWAM
BWAM
COME TO MAMA, FUTURE DINNERS!!
BWAM
BWAM
GWAH!! NOTHING BUT ROCKS AND EMPTY SHELLS!
DANG IT!
SHE'S DESPERATE.
Dinners?
GLINT
Y'KNOW, I THINK PEOPLE ACTUALLY PAY DECENT MONEY FOR SEA GLASS AND DRIFTWOOD.
Y'DON'T SAY?!
PICKING UP LITTER, OCHACO? SUCH A GOOD CITIZEN! LEMME HELP!!
FWP
NAH, BUTT OUT!! THIS IS MY TERRITORY, SEE?
UM?

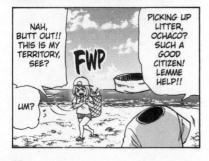

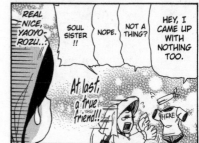

Spiriting Away

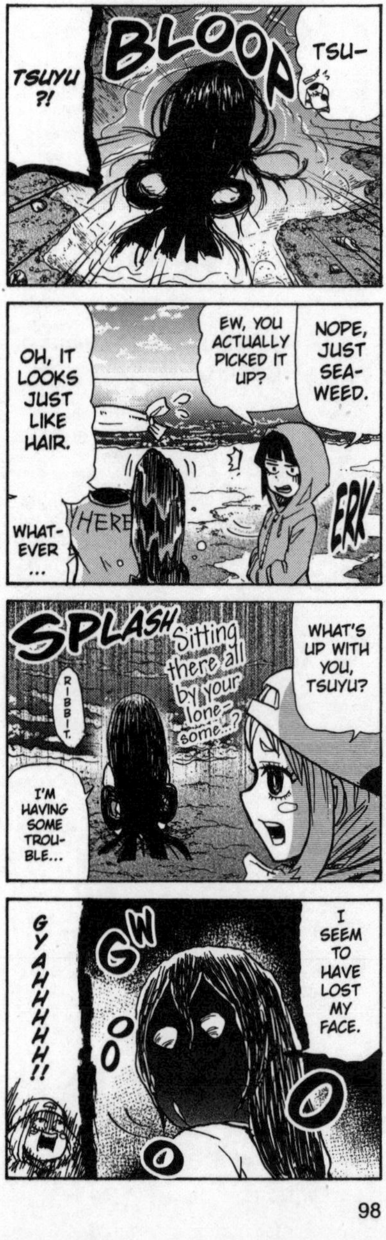
TSU-
BLOOP
TSUYU?!
NOPE, JUST SEA-WEED.
EW, YOU ACTUALLY PICKED IT UP?
OH, IT LOOKS JUST LIKE HAIR.
ERK
HERE
WHAT-EVER...
WHAT'S UP WITH YOU, TSUYU?
Sitting there all by your lone-some...?
SPLASH
RIBBIT.
I'M HAVING SOME TROU-BLE...
I SEEM TO HAVE LOST MY FACE.
GW
GYAHHHHH!!

The Circle of Life

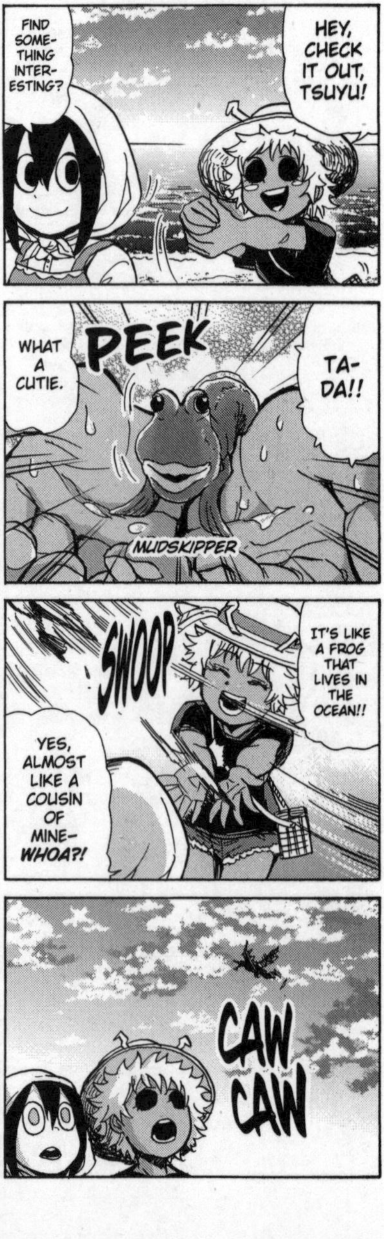
HEY, CHECK IT OUT, TSUYU!
FIND SOME-THING INTER-ESTING?
TA-DA!!
PEEK
WHAT A CUTIE.
MUDSKIPPER
IT'S LIKE A FROG THAT LIVES IN THE OCEAN!!
SWOOP
YES, ALMOST LIKE A COUSIN OF MINE-WHOA?!
CAW CAW

BY HER GRACE

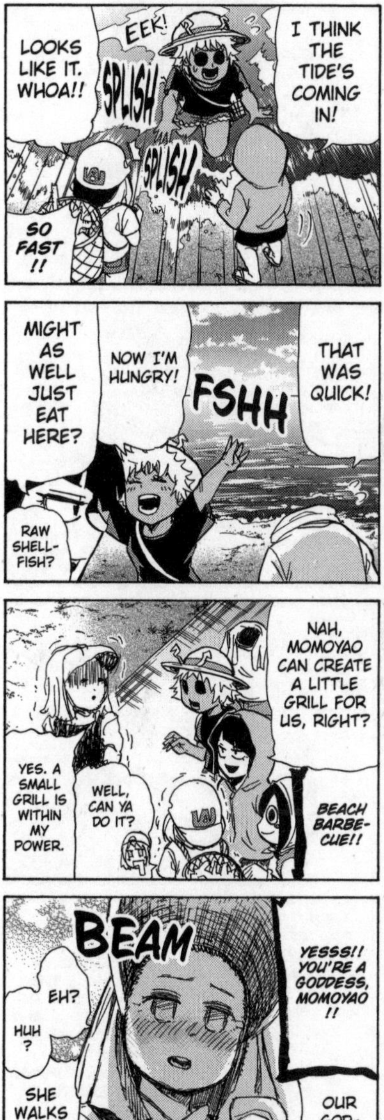
I THINK THE TIDE'S COMING IN!
EEK!
SPLISH
LOOKS LIKE IT. WHOA!!
SPLISH
SO FAST!!
THAT WAS QUICK!
FSHH
NOW I'M HUNGRY!
MIGHT AS WELL JUST EAT HERE?
RAW SHELLFISH?
NAH, MOMOYAO CAN CREATE A LITTLE GRILL FOR US, RIGHT?
BEACH BARBECUE!!
WELL, CAN YA DO IT?
YES. A SMALL GRILL IS WITHIN MY POWER.
YESSS!! YOU'RE A GODDESS, MOMOYAO!!
BEAM
EH?
HUH?
OUR GODDESS!
SHE WALKS AMONG US!
THIS CHEERED HER UP.

ONE SIZE FITS...ALL?

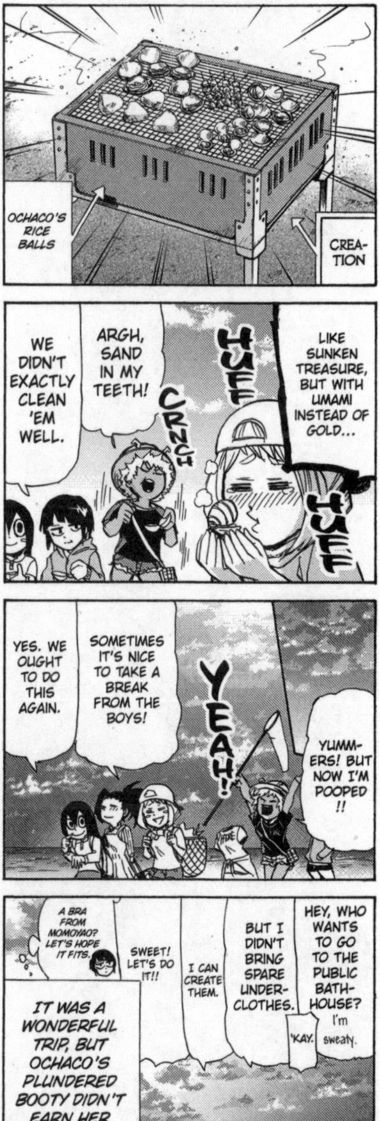
CREATION
OCHACO'S RICE BALLS
LIKE SUNKEN TREASURE, BUT WITH UMAMI INSTEAD OF GOLD...
HUFF
ARGH, SAND IN MY TEETH!
CRNCH
WE DIDN'T EXACTLY CLEAN 'EM WELL.
HUFF
YUMMERS! BUT NOW I'M POOPED!!
YEAH!
SOMETIMES IT'S NICE TO TAKE A BREAK FROM THE BOYS!
YES. WE OUGHT TO DO THIS AGAIN.
HEY, WHO WANTS TO GO TO THE PUBLIC BATHHOUSE?
I'm sweaty.
'KAY.
BUT I DIDN'T BRING SPARE UNDERCLOTHES.
I CAN CREATE THEM.
SWEET! LET'S DO IT!!
A BRA FROM MOMOYAO? LET'S HOPE IT FITS.
IT WAS A WONDERFUL TRIP, BUT OCHACO'S PLUNDERED BOOTY DIDN'T EARN HER A CENT.

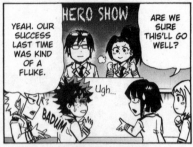

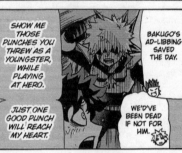

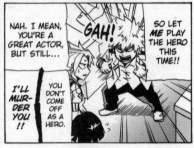

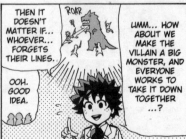

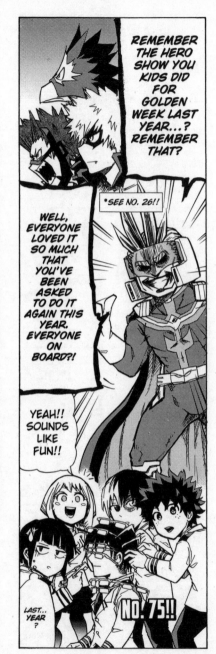

REMEMBER THE HERO SHOW YOU KIDS DID FOR GOLDEN WEEK LAST YEAR...? REMEMBER THAT?
*SEE NO. 26!!
WELL, EVERYONE LOVED IT SO MUCH THAT YOU'VE BEEN ASKED TO DO IT AGAIN THIS YEAR. EVERYONE ON BOARD?!
YEAH!! SOUNDS LIKE FUN!!
NO. 75!!
LAST... YEAR?

AUTOPSY
HERO SHOW
ARE WE SURE THIS'LL GO WELL?
YEAH. OUR SUCCESS LAST TIME WAS KIND OF A FLUKE.
Ugh...
BADUM
BAKUGO'S AD-LIBBING SAVED THE DAY.
SHOW ME THOSE PUNCHES YOU THREW AS A YOUNGSTER, WHILE PLAYING AT HERO.
WE'D'VE BEEN DEAD IF NOT FOR HIM.
JUST ONE GOOD PUNCH WILL REACH MY HEART.
SO LET ME PLAY THE HERO THIS TIME!!
GAH!
NAH. I MEAN, YOU'RE A GREAT ACTOR, BUT STILL...
YOU DON'T COME OFF AS A HERO.
I'LL MURDER YOU!!
UMM... HOW ABOUT WE MAKE THE VILLAIN A BIG MONSTER, AND EVERYONE WORKS TO TAKE IT DOWN TOGETHER...?
ROAR
THEN IT DOESN'T MATTER IF... WHOEVER... FORGETS THEIR LINES.
OOH. GOOD IDEA.

TYPECASTING

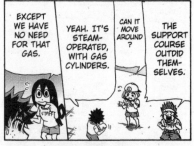

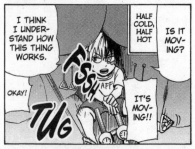

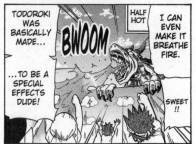

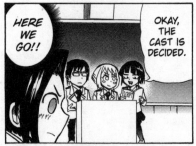

OKAY, THE CAST IS DECIDED.
HERE WE GO!!
EVER SINCE THE LAST SHOW, I'VE BEEN TOILING AWAY WITH ACTING LESSONS.
WHATEVER JUICY ROLE THEY GIVE ME, I'LL BE ABLE TO HANDLE IT!
KATSUKI BAKUGO WILL BE THE LEAD...
HELL YEAH!!
...BUT HIS STANDARD COSTUME IS TOO EDGY, SO WE'LL HAVE TO CHANGE IT.
WHAT?!
THE REST OF YOU, PLEASE CHECK THE SCRIPT FOR YOUR ROLES.
Momo Yaoyorozu – Tree in background No dialogue; just sway back and forth a little.
Minoru Mineta – Bait for the monster Just try to control yourself
Script

INDUSTRIAL LIGHT, MAGIC, FIRE, ICE

DAY OF THE SHOW
RAWWWR
WOWWWW!!
THE SUPPORT COURSE OUTDID THEMSELVES.
CAN IT MOVE AROUND?
YEAH. IT'S STEAM-OPERATED, WITH GAS CYLINDERS.
EXCEPT WE HAVE NO NEED FOR THAT GAS.
IS IT MOVING?
HALF COLD, HALF HOT
I THINK I UNDERSTAND HOW THIS THING WORKS.
FSSH
IT'S MOVING!!
OKAY!
TUG
I CAN EVEN MAKE IT BREATHE FIRE.
HALF HOT
BWOOM
TODOROKI WAS BASICALLY MADE...
SWEET!!
...TO BE A SPECIAL EFFECTS DUDE!

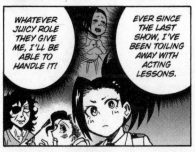

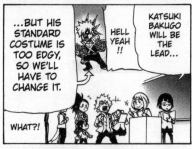

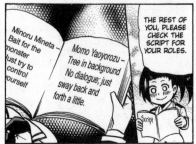

Auteur Ochaco

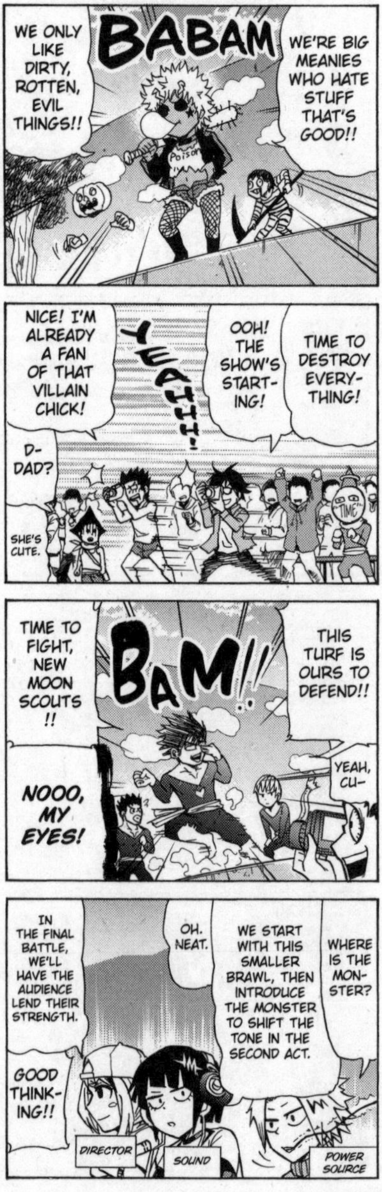
WE'RE BIG MEANIES WHO HATE STUFF THAT'S GOOD!!
BABAM
WE ONLY LIKE DIRTY, ROTTEN, EVIL THINGS!!
TIME TO DESTROY EVERYTHING!
OOH! THE SHOW'S STARTING!
YEAHHH!
NICE! I'M ALREADY A FAN OF THAT VILLAIN CHICK!
D-DAD?
SHE'S CUTE.
THIS TURF IS OURS TO DEFEND!!
BAM!!
TIME TO FIGHT, NEW MOON SCOUTS!!
YEAH, CU-
NOOO, MY EYES!
WHERE IS THE MONSTER?
WE START WITH THIS SMALLER BRAWL, THEN INTRODUCE THE MONSTER TO SHIFT THE TONE IN THE SECOND ACT.
OH. NEAT.
IN THE FINAL BATTLE, WE'LL HAVE THE AUDIENCE LEND THEIR STRENGTH.
GOOD THINKING!!
POWER SOURCE
SOUND
DIRECTOR

Smile

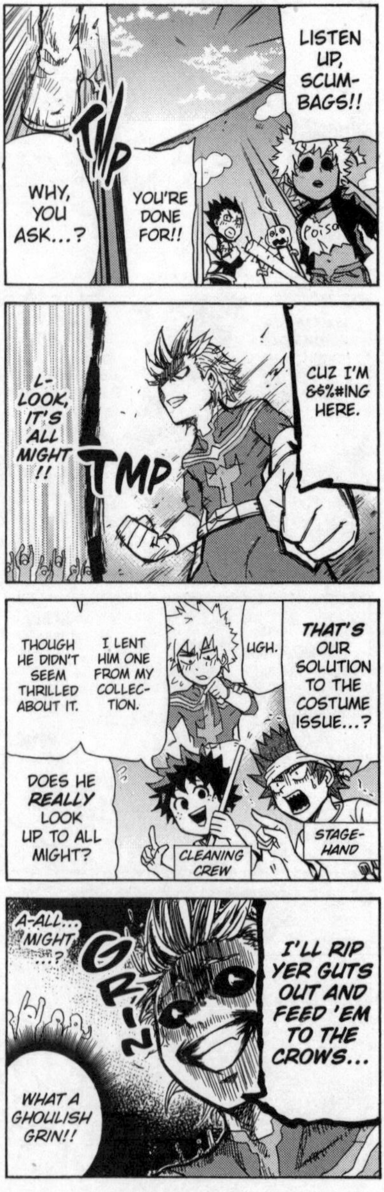
LISTEN UP, SCUM-BAGS!!
TMP
YOU'RE DONE FOR!!
WHY, YOU ASK...?
CUZ I'M &$%#ING HERE.
TMP
L-LOOK, IT'S ALL MIGHT!!
THAT'S OUR SOLUTION TO THE COSTUME ISSUE...?
UGH.
I LENT HIM ONE FROM MY COLLECTION.
THOUGH HE DIDN'T SEEM THRILLED ABOUT IT.
STAGE-HAND
DOES HE REALLY LOOK UP TO ALL MIGHT?
CLEANING CREW
I'LL RIP YER GUTS OUT AND FEED 'EM TO THE CROWS...
GRIN
A-ALL... MIGHT...?
WHAT A GHOULISH GRIN!!

New Threat on the Horizon

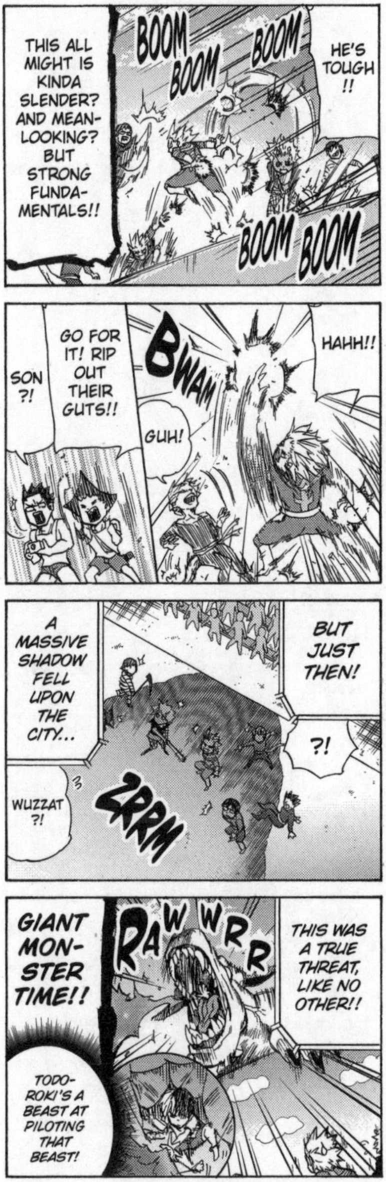
HE'S TOUGH!!
BOOM BOOM BOOM
BOOM BOOM
THIS ALL MIGHT IS KINDA SLENDER? AND MEAN-LOOKING? BUT STRONG FUNDAMENTALS!!
HAHH!!
BWAM
GUH!
GO FOR IT! RIP OUT THEIR GUTS!!
SON?!
BUT JUST THEN!
?!
A MASSIVE SHADOW FELL UPON THE CITY...
ZRRM
WUZZAT?!
THIS WAS A TRUE THREAT, LIKE NO OTHER!!
RAWWRR
GIANT MONSTER TIME!!
TODOROKI'S A BEAST AT PILOTING THAT BEAST!

Win By Saving

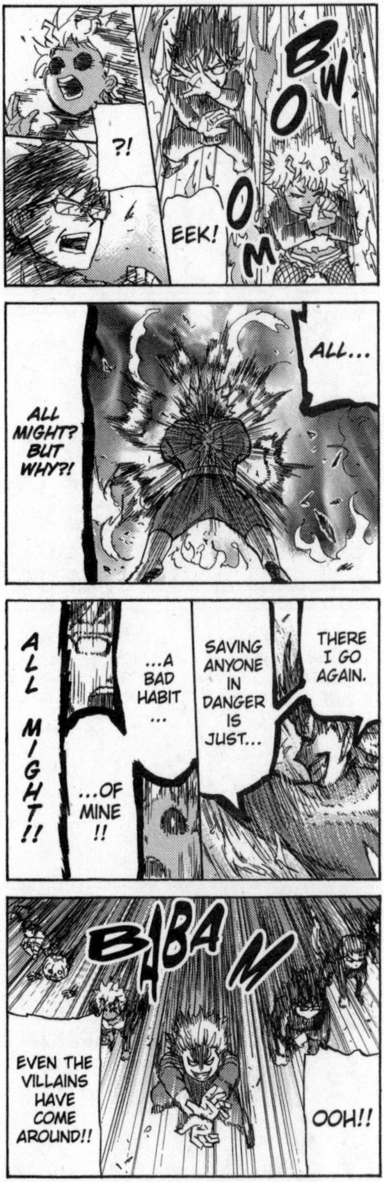
BWOOOM
EEK!
?!
ALL...
ALL MIGHT? BUT WHY?!
THERE I GO AGAIN.
SAVING ANYONE IN DANGER IS JUST...
...A BAD HABIT...
...OF MINE!!
ALL MIGHT!!
OOH!!
BABAM
EVEN THE VILLAINS HAVE COME AROUND!!

SPIRIT BALLER

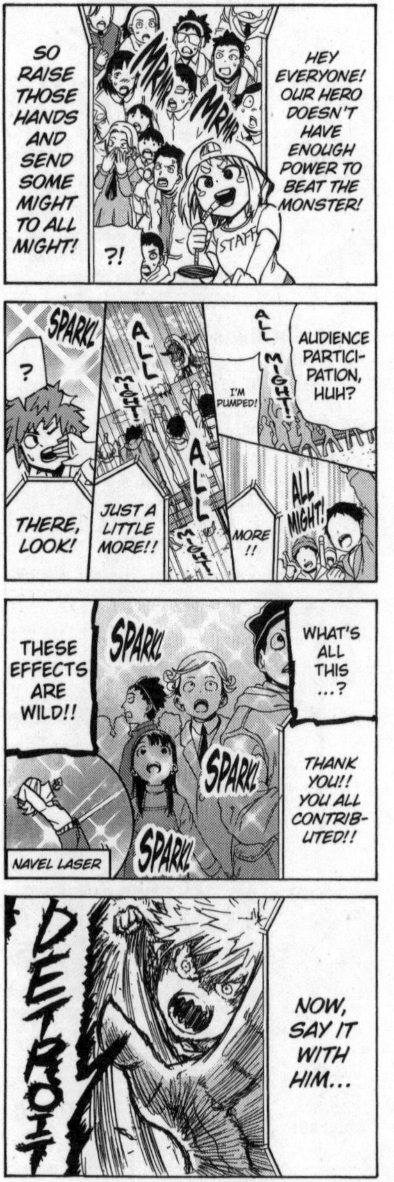
HEY EVERYONE! OUR HERO DOESN'T HAVE ENOUGH POWER TO BEAT THE MONSTER!
MRMR
MRMR
?!
SO RAISE THOSE HANDS AND SEND SOME MIGHT TO ALL MIGHT!
AUDIENCE PARTICI-PATION, HUH?
ALL MIGHT!
I'M PUMPED!
ALL MIGHT!
MORE!!
ALL MIGHT!
ALL MIGHT!
JUST A LITTLE MORE!!
ALL MIGHT!
SPARKL
?
THERE, LOOK!
WHAT'S ALL THIS ...?
SPARKL
THANK YOU!! YOU ALL CONTRIB-UTED!!
SPARKL
SPARKL
THESE EFFECTS ARE WILD!!
NAVEL LASER
NOW, SAY IT WITH HIM...
DETROIT

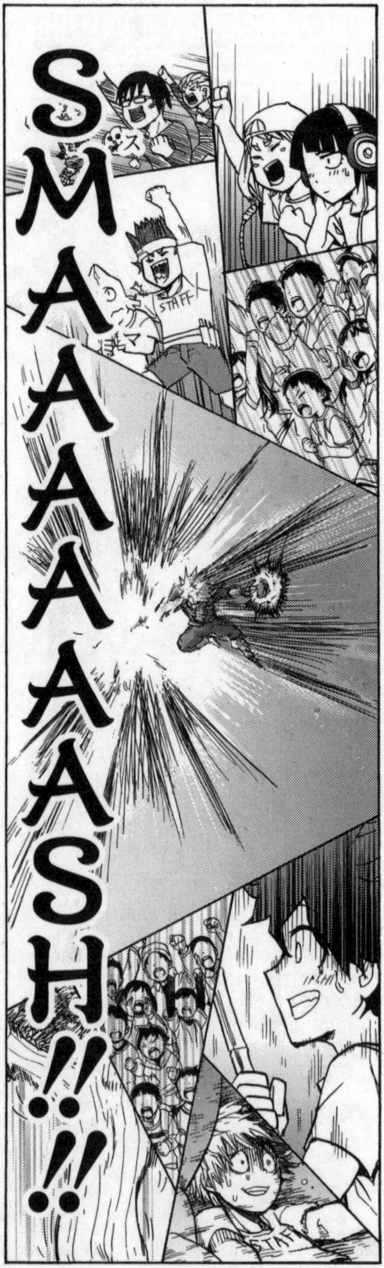
SMAAAAAASH!!!!

BRAVO

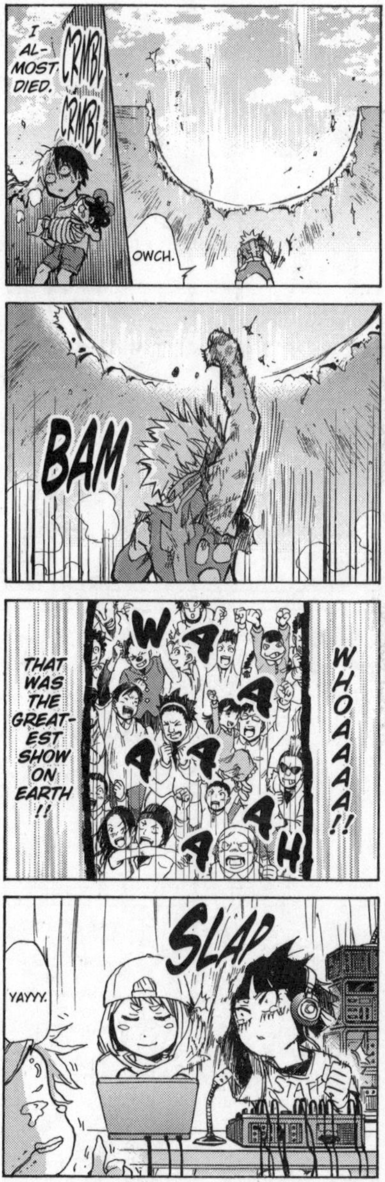
I ALMOST DIED.
CRMBL CRMBL
OWCH.
BAM
WHOAAAAA!!
WAAAAAH
THAT WAS THE GREATEST SHOW ON EARTH!!
SLAP
YAYYY.

PRIORITIES

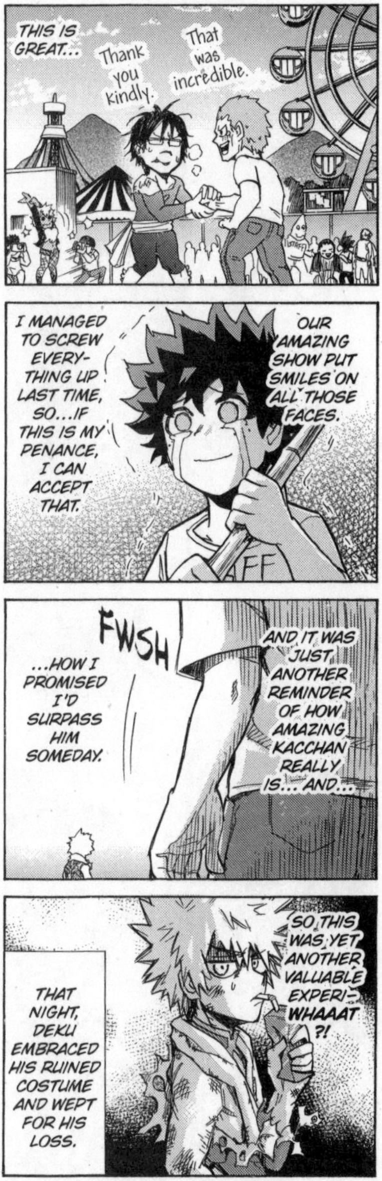
That was incredible.
Thank you kindly.
THIS IS GREAT...
OUR AMAZING SHOW PUT SMILES ON ALL THOSE FACES.
I MANAGED TO SCREW EVERYTHING UP LAST TIME, SO...IF THIS IS MY PENANCE, I CAN ACCEPT THAT.
FWSH
AND IT WAS JUST ANOTHER REMINDER OF HOW AMAZING KACCHAN REALLY IS... AND...
...HOW I PROMISED I'D SURPASS HIM SOMEDAY.
SO THIS WAS YET ANOTHER VALUABLE EXPERI- WHAAAT?!
THAT NIGHT, DEKU EMBRACED HIS RUINED COSTUME AND WEPT FOR HIS LOSS.

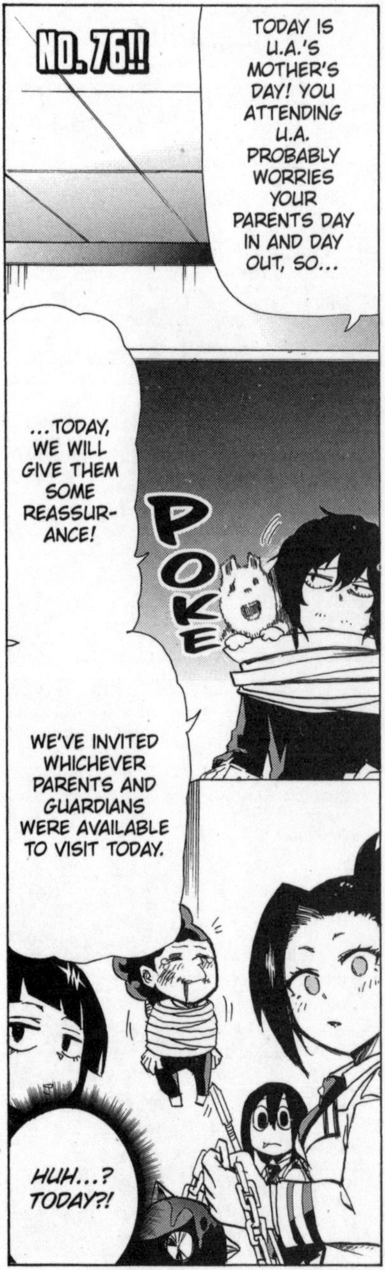
No. 76!!
TODAY IS U.A.'S MOTHER'S DAY! YOU ATTENDING U.A. PROBABLY WORRIES YOUR PARENTS DAY IN AND DAY OUT, SO...
...TODAY, WE WILL GIVE THEM SOME REASSURANCE!
POKE
WE'VE INVITED WHICHEVER PARENTS AND GUARDIANS WERE AVAILABLE TO VISIT TODAY.
HUH...? TODAY?!

MR. MOM

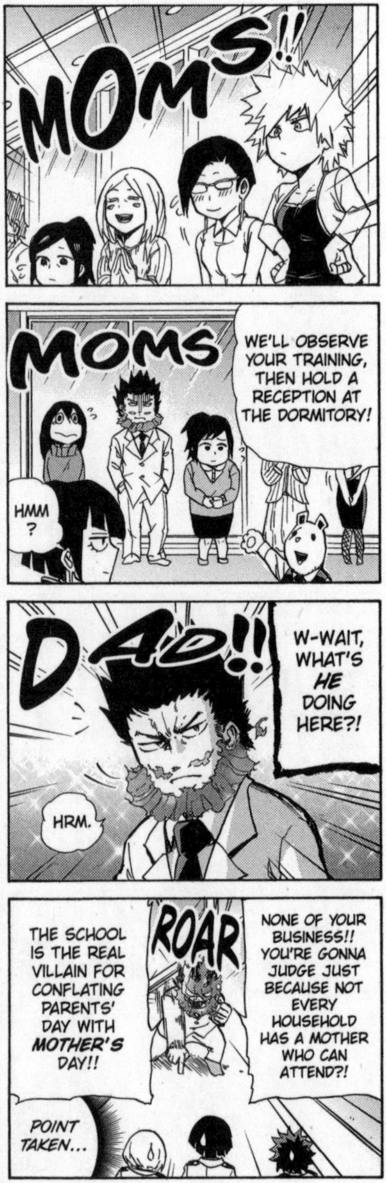
MOMS!!
MOMS
WE'LL OBSERVE YOUR TRAINING, THEN HOLD A RECEPTION AT THE DORMITORY!
HMM ?
DAD!!
W-WAIT, WHAT'S *HE* DOING HERE?!
HRM.
NONE OF YOUR BUSINESS!! YOU'RE GONNA JUDGE JUST BECAUSE NOT EVERY HOUSEHOLD HAS A MOTHER WHO CAN ATTEND?!
ROAR
THE SCHOOL IS THE REAL VILLAIN FOR CONFLATING PARENTS' DAY WITH *MOTHER'S* DAY!!
POINT TAKEN...

GEEZ, MOMMMM

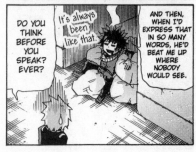

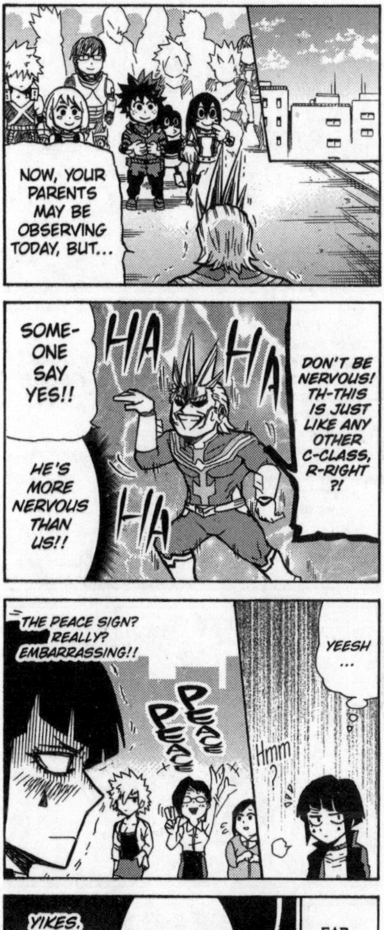
NOW, YOUR PARENTS MAY BE OBSERVING TODAY, BUT...
DON'T BE NERVOUS! TH-THIS IS JUST LIKE ANY OTHER C-CLASS, R-RIGHT?!
HA HA HA
SOME-ONE SAY YES!!
HE'S MORE NERVOUS THAN US!!
YEESH ...
THE PEACE SIGN? REALLY? EMBARRASSING!!
PEACE PEACE
Hmm ?
EAR-PHONE JACK (MOM)
AND STOP EAVES-DROPPING LIKE THAT!
YIKES. TODAY'S GONNA GIVE ME A HEAD-ACHE.

THOSE WHO DON'T LEARN FROM HISTORY

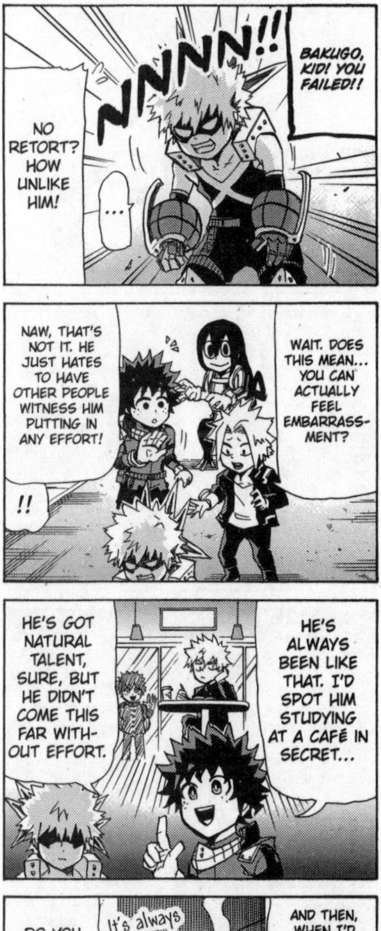
BAKUGO, KID! YOU FAILED!!
NNNN!!
NO RETORT? HOW UNLIKE HIM!
...
WAIT. DOES THIS MEAN... YOU CAN ACTUALLY FEEL EMBARRASS-MENT?
NAW, THAT'S NOT IT. HE JUST HATES TO HAVE OTHER PEOPLE WITNESS HIM PUTTING IN ANY EFFORT!
!!
HE'S ALWAYS BEEN LIKE THAT. I'D SPOT HIM STUDYING AT A CAFÉ IN SECRET...
HE'S GOT NATURAL TALENT, SURE, BUT HE DIDN'T COME THIS FAR WITH-OUT EFFORT.
AND THEN, WHEN I'D EXPRESS THAT IN SO MANY WORDS, HE'D BEAT ME UP WHERE NOBODY WOULD SEE.
It's always been like that.
DO YOU THINK BEFORE YOU SPEAK? EVER?

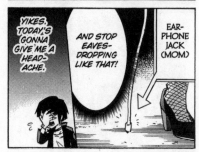

STAR APPEAL

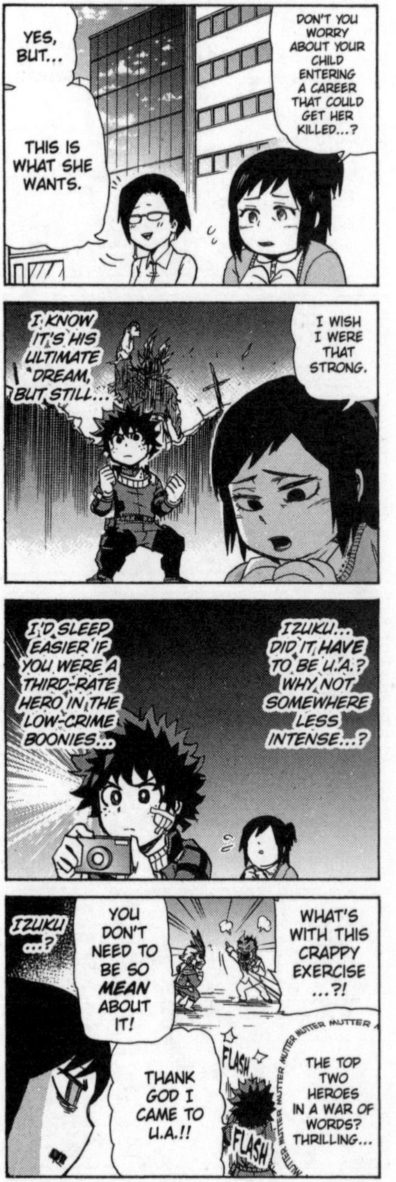
DON'T YOU WORRY ABOUT YOUR CHILD ENTERING A CAREER THAT COULD GET HER KILLED...?
YES, BUT...
THIS IS WHAT SHE WANTS.
I WISH I WERE THAT STRONG.
I KNOW IT'S HIS ULTIMATE DREAM, BUT STILL...
IZUKU... DID IT HAVE TO BE U.A.? WHY NOT SOMEWHERE LESS INTENSE...?
I'D SLEEP EASIER IF YOU WERE A THIRD-RATE HERO IN THE LOW-CRIME BOONIES...
WHAT'S WITH THIS CRAPPY EXERCISE ...?!
YOU DON'T NEED TO BE SO MEAN ABOUT IT!
IZUKU ...?
MUTTER MUTTER MUTTER MUTTER
THE TOP TWO HEROES IN A WAR OF WORDS? THRILLING...
FLASH
FLASH
THANK GOD I CAME TO U.A.!!

GEEZ, DAAAAAD

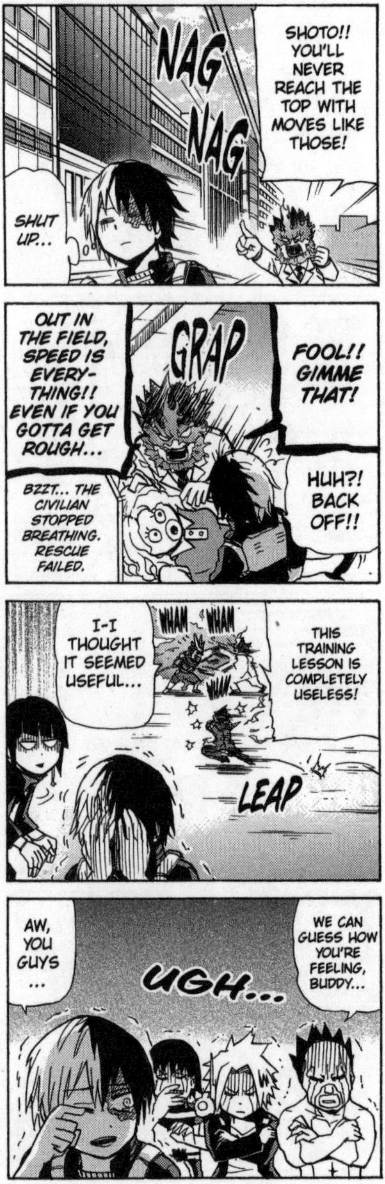
SHOTO!! YOU'LL NEVER REACH THE TOP WITH MOVES LIKE THOSE!
NAG NAG
SHUT UP...
FOOL!! GIMME THAT!
GRAP
OUT IN THE FIELD, SPEED IS EVERY-THING!! EVEN IF YOU GOTTA GET ROUGH...
HUH?! BACK OFF!!
BZZT... THE CIVILIAN STOPPED BREATHING. RESCUE FAILED.
THIS TRAINING LESSON IS COMPLETELY USELESS!
WHAM WHAM
WHAM
I-I THOUGHT IT SEEMED USEFUL...
LEAP
WE CAN GUESS HOW YOU'RE FEELING, BUDDY...
UGH...
AW, YOU GUYS ...

Networking

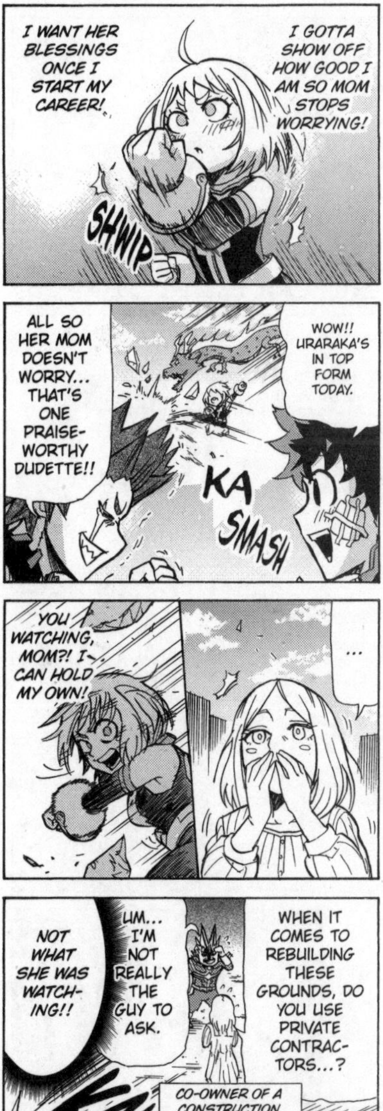
I GOTTA SHOW OFF HOW GOOD I AM SO MOM STOPS WORRYING!
I WANT HER BLESSINGS ONCE I START MY CAREER!
SHWIP
WOW!! URARAKA'S IN TOP FORM TODAY.
ALL SO HER MOM DOESN'T WORRY... THAT'S ONE PRAISE-WORTHY DUDETTE!!
KA SMASH
...
YOU WATCHING, MOM?! I CAN HOLD MY OWN!
WHEN IT COMES TO REBUILDING THESE GROUNDS, DO YOU USE PRIVATE CONTRAC-TORS...?
UM... I'M NOT REALLY THE GUY TO ASK.
NOT WHAT SHE WAS WATCH-ING!!
CO-OWNER OF A CONSTRUCTION BUSINESS

Monsters Are Made

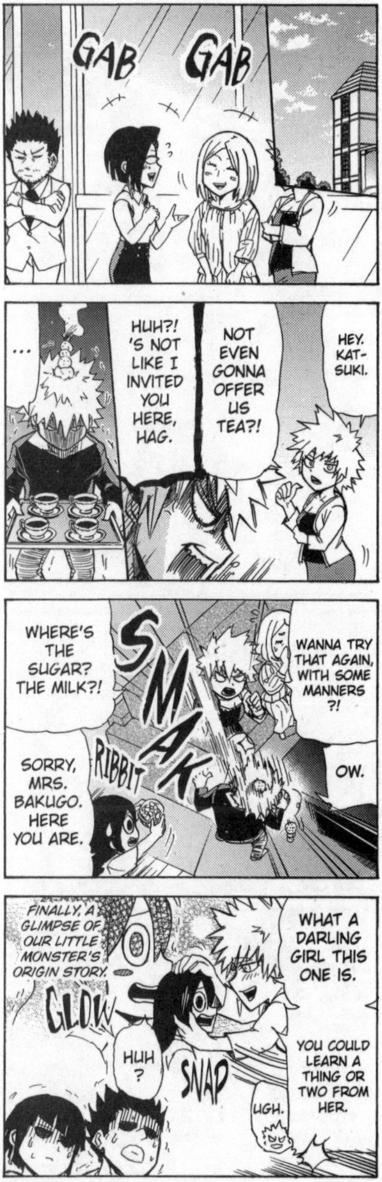
GAB
GAB
HEY. KAT-SUKI.
NOT EVEN GONNA OFFER US TEA?!
HUH?! 'S NOT LIKE I INVITED YOU HERE, HAG.
...
WANNA TRY THAT AGAIN, WITH SOME MANNERS ?!
SMAK
WHERE'S THE SUGAR? THE MILK?!
OW.
RIBBIT
SORRY, MRS. BAKUGO. HERE YOU ARE.
WHAT A DARLING GIRL THIS ONE IS.
FINALLY, A GLIMPSE OF OUR LITTLE MONSTER'S ORIGIN STORY.
GLOW
SNAP
YOU COULD LEARN A THING OR TWO FROM HER.
HUH ?
UGH.

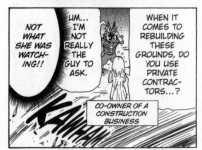

SWEET THANG

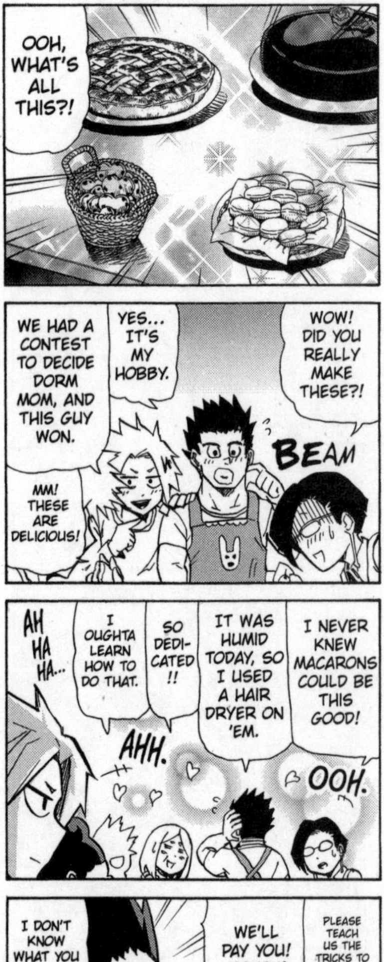
OOH, WHAT'S ALL THIS?!
WOW! DID YOU REALLY MAKE THESE?!
BEAM
YES... IT'S MY HOBBY.
WE HAD A CONTEST TO DECIDE DORM MOM, AND THIS GUY WON.
MM! THESE ARE DELICIOUS!
I NEVER KNEW MACARONS COULD BE THIS GOOD!
IT WAS HUMID TODAY, SO I USED A HAIR DRYER ON 'EM.
SO DEDICATED!!
I OUGHTA LEARN HOW TO DO THAT.
AH HA HA...
OOH.
AHH.
PLEASE TEACH US THE TRICKS TO SEDUCTION, PROFESSOR LOVE!!
WE'LL PAY YOU! MONEY! FAVORS!
I DON'T KNOW WHAT YOU GUYS ARE TALKING ABOUT!
HE ENDED UP HOLDING WEEKLY COOKING CLASSES.
BAM

WIN-WIN

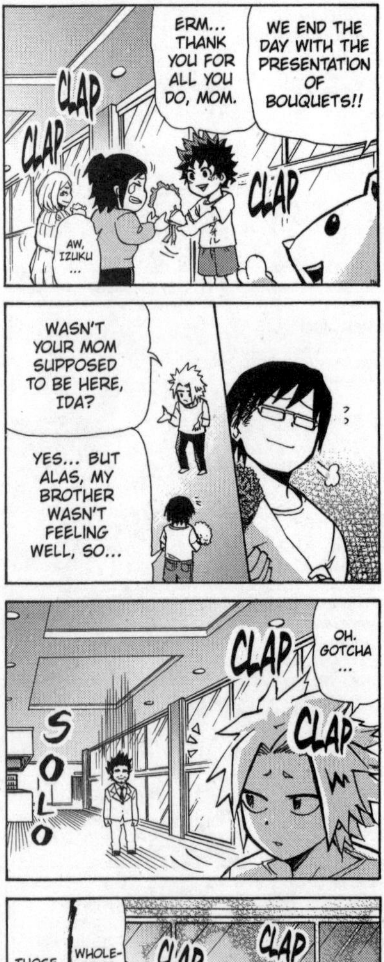
WE END THE DAY WITH THE PRESENTATION OF BOUQUETS!!
ERM... THANK YOU FOR ALL YOU DO, MOM.
CLAP
CLAP
CLAP
AW, IZUKU ...
WASN'T YOUR MOM SUPPOSED TO BE HERE, IDA?
YES... BUT ALAS, MY BROTHER WASN'T FEELING WELL, SO...
OH. GOTCHA ...
CLAP
CLAP
SOLO
CLAP
CLAP
CLAP
WHOLESOME, HUH?
THOSE TWO? WHY? WHO CARES?

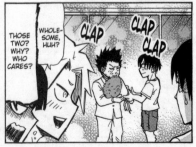

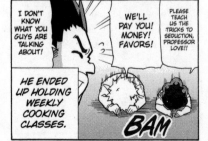

GOOFING OFF IN *SHONEN JUMP*!!

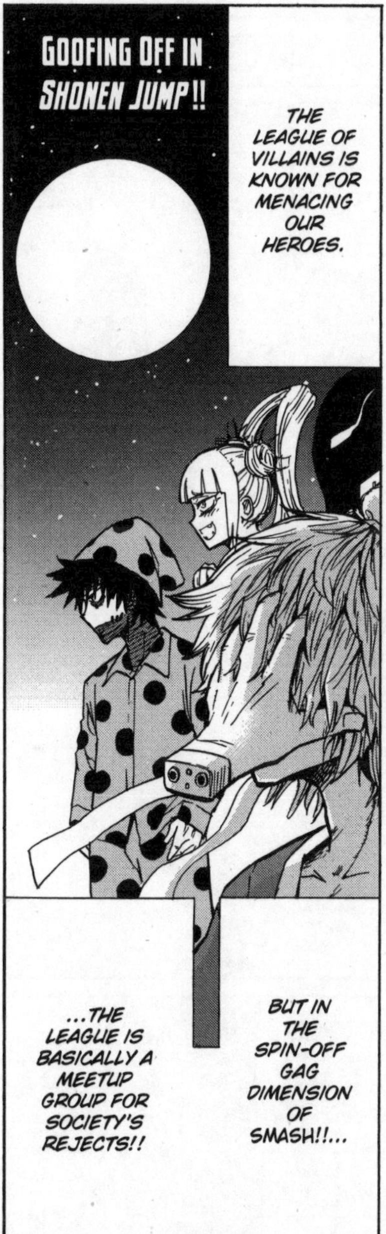
THE LEAGUE OF VILLAINS IS KNOWN FOR MENACING OUR HEROES.
BUT IN THE SPIN-OFF GAG DIMENSION OF SMASH!!...
...THE LEAGUE IS BASICALLY A MEETUP GROUP FOR SOCIETY'S REJECTS!!

*SMASH!! IS SERIALIZED IN JUMP+, BUT THIS CHAPTER RAN IN SHONEN JUMP!!

TANABATA HOLIDAY

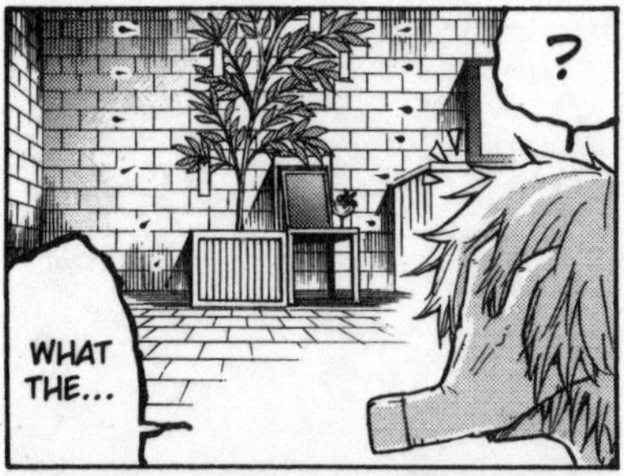
?
WHAT THE...

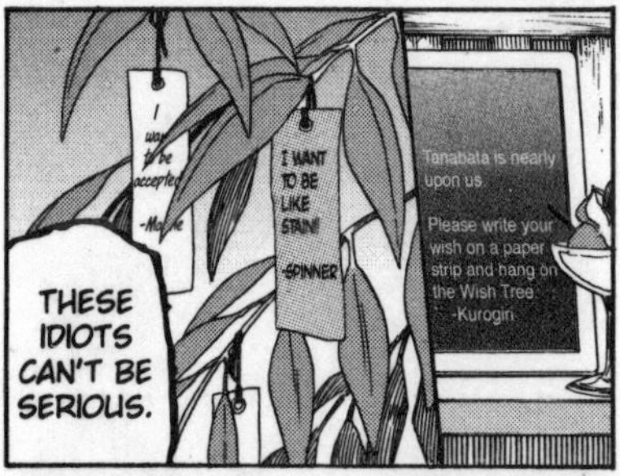
Tanabata is nearly upon us.
Please write your wish on a paper strip and hang on the Wish Tree. -Kurogiri
I WANT TO BE LIKE STAIN!! -SPINNER
I want to be accepted
THESE IDIOTS CAN'T BE SERIOUS.

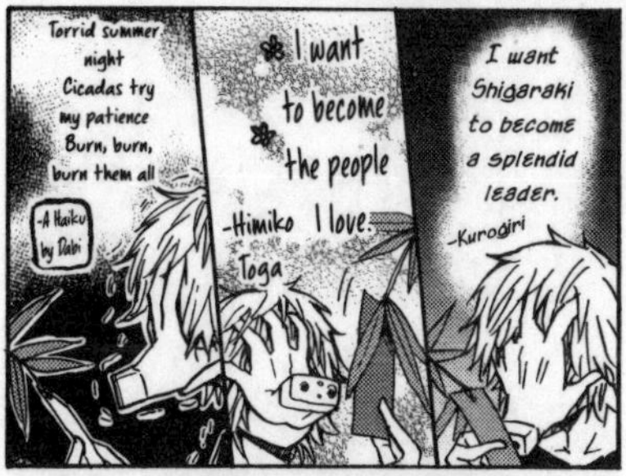
I want Shigaraki to become a splendid leader. -Kurogiri
I want to become the people I love. -Himiko Toga
Torrid summer night Cicadas try my patience Burn, burn, burn them all
-A Haiku by Dabi

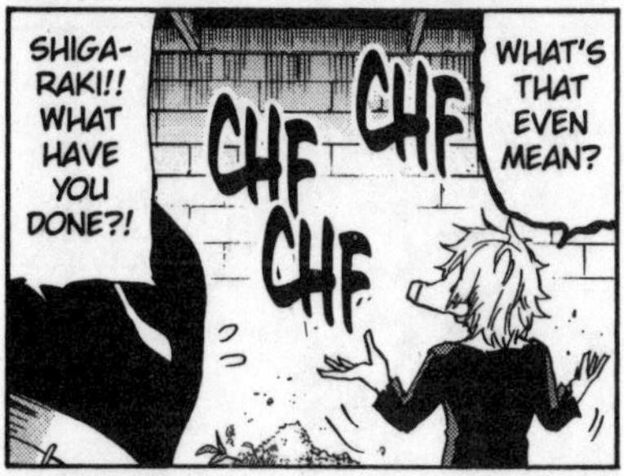
WHAT'S THAT EVEN MEAN?
CHF
CHF
CHF
SHIGA-RAKI!! WHAT HAVE YOU DONE?!

F.O.M.O.

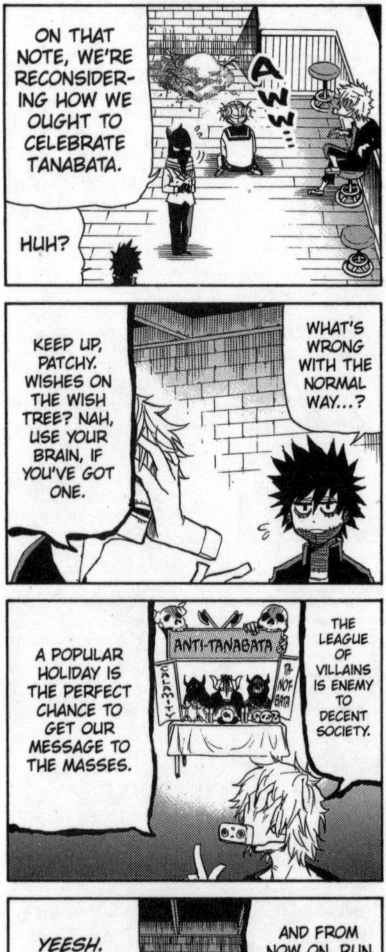

AWW...
ON THAT NOTE, WE'RE RECONSIDERING HOW WE OUGHT TO CELEBRATE TANABATA.
HUH?
WHAT'S WRONG WITH THE NORMAL WAY...?
KEEP UP, PATCHY. WISHES ON THE WISH TREE? NAH, USE YOUR BRAIN, IF YOU'VE GOT ONE.
THE LEAGUE OF VILLAINS IS ENEMY TO DECENT SOCIETY.
ANTI-TANABATA
TA-NOT-BATA
CALAMITY
A POPULAR HOLIDAY IS THE PERFECT CHANCE TO GET OUR MESSAGE TO THE MASSES.
AND FROM NOW ON, RUN EVERYTHING BY ME. NO HAVING FUN UNLESS I'M INVOLVED.
Apologies.
YEESH. HE JUST HATES BEING LEFT OUT!

MY RED VALENTINE

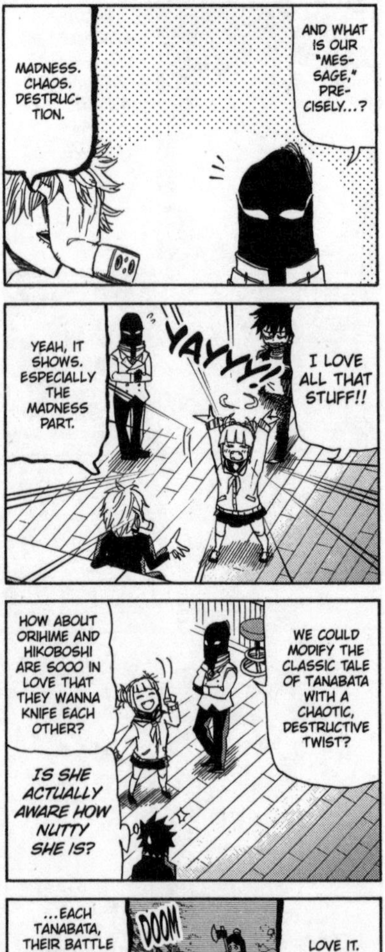

AND WHAT IS OUR "MESSAGE," PRECISELY...?
MADNESS. CHAOS. DESTRUCTION.
I LOVE ALL THAT STUFF!!
YAYYY!!
YEAH, IT SHOWS. ESPECIALLY THE MADNESS PART.
WE COULD MODIFY THE CLASSIC TALE OF TANABATA WITH A CHAOTIC, DESTRUCTIVE TWIST?
HOW ABOUT ORIHIME AND HIKOBOSHI ARE SOOO IN LOVE THAT THEY WANNA KNIFE EACH OTHER?
IS SHE ACTUALLY AWARE HOW NUTTY SHE IS?
LOVE IT. HOW ABOUT, THE CELESTIAL RIVER USUALLY HOLDS THEM BACK, BUT...
DOOM
DOOM
DOOM
...EACH TANABATA, THEIR BATTLE BEGINS ANEW, AND THE DRY RIVERBED IS ONCE AGAIN STAINED WITH BLOOD.
YEAH. LET'S GO WITH THAT.
YAY!

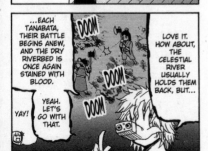

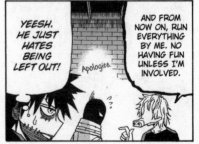

DARK AU

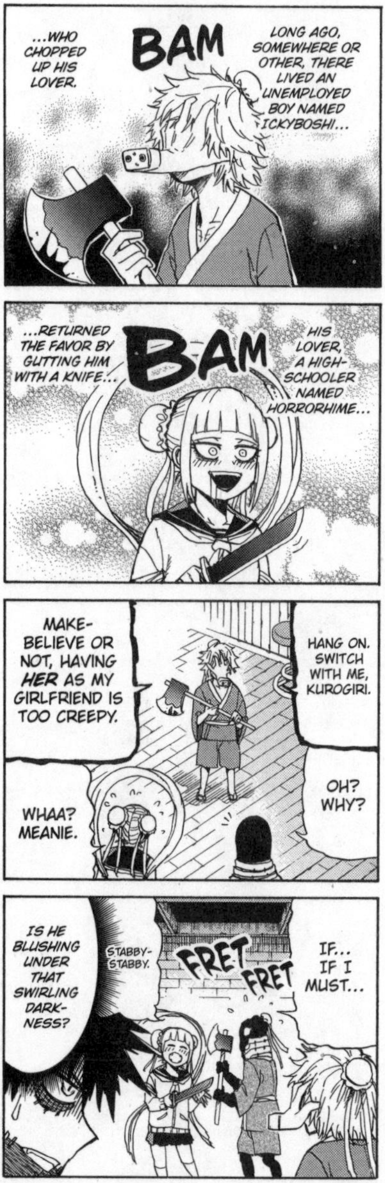
LONG AGO, SOMEWHERE OR OTHER, THERE LIVED AN UNEMPLOYED BOY NAMED ICKYBOSHI...
BAM
...WHO CHOPPED UP HIS LOVER.
HIS LOVER, A HIGH-SCHOOLER NAMED HORRORHIME...
BAM
...RETURNED THE FAVOR BY GUTTING HIM WITH A KNIFE...
HANG ON. SWITCH WITH ME, KUROGIRI.
MAKE-BELIEVE OR NOT, HAVING HER AS MY GIRLFRIEND IS TOO CREEPY.
OH? WHY?
WHAA? MEANIE.
IF... IF I MUST...
FRET FRET
STABBY-STABBY.
IS HE BLUSHING UNDER THAT SWIRLING DARKNESS?

METHOD ACTING

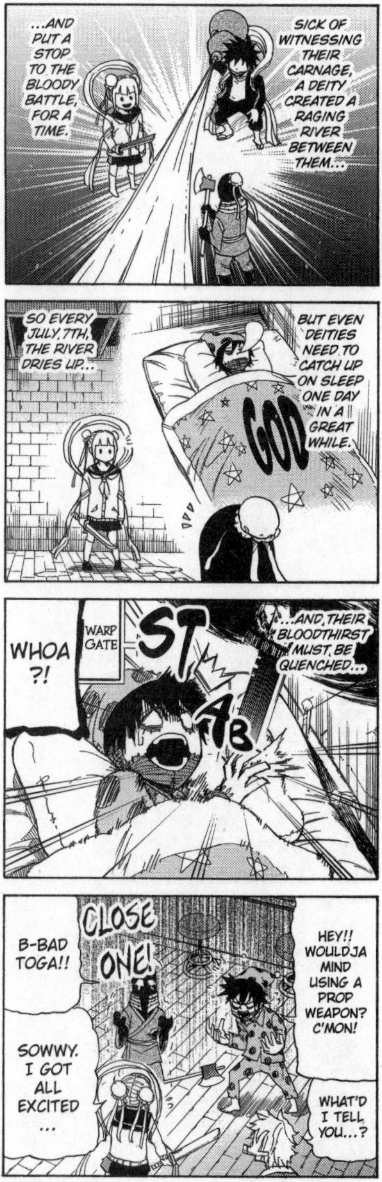
SICK OF WITNESSING THEIR CARNAGE, A DEITY CREATED A RAGING RIVER BETWEEN THEM...
...AND PUT A STOP TO THE BLOODY BATTLE, FOR A TIME.
BUT EVEN DEITIES NEED TO CATCH UP ON SLEEP ONE DAY IN A GREAT WHILE.
GOD
SO EVERY JULY 7TH, THE RIVER DRIES UP...
...AND THEIR BLOODTHIRST MUST BE QUENCHED...
STAB
WARP GATE
WHOA?!
HEY!! WOULDJA MIND USING A PROP WEAPON? C'MON!
WHAT'D I TELL YOU...?
CLOSE ONE!
B-BAD TOGA!!
SOWWY. I GOT ALL EXCITED ...

Join the Dark Side

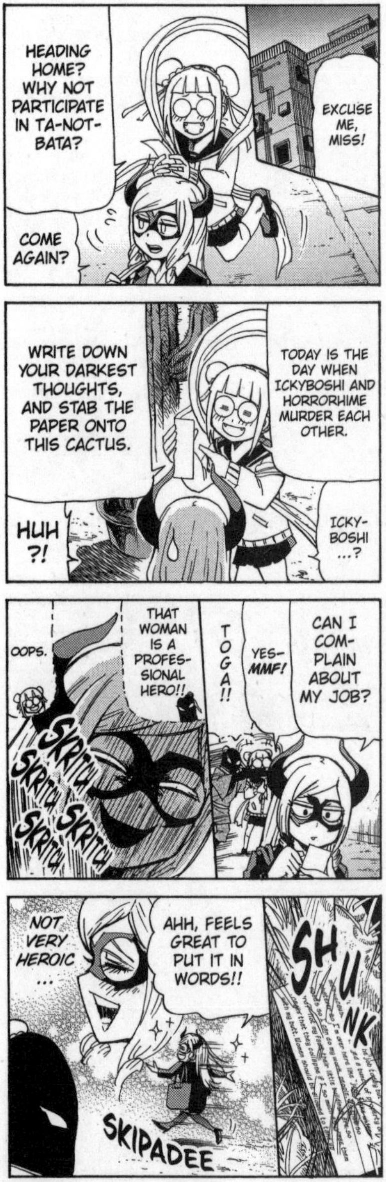
EXCUSE ME, MISS!
HEADING HOME? WHY NOT PARTICIPATE IN TA-NOT-BATA?
COME AGAIN?
TODAY IS THE DAY WHEN ICKYBOSHI AND HORRORHIME MURDER EACH OTHER.
WRITE DOWN YOUR DARKEST THOUGHTS, AND STAB THE PAPER ONTO THIS CACTUS.
ICKYBOSHI...?
HUH?!
CAN I COMPLAIN ABOUT MY JOB?
YES-MMF!
TOGA!!
THAT WOMAN IS A PROFESSIONAL HERO!!
OOPS.
SKRITCH SKRITCH SKRITCH SKRITCH
SHUNK
AHH, FEELS GREAT TO PUT IT IN WORDS!!
NOT VERY HEROIC...
SKIPADEE

Healthy Venting

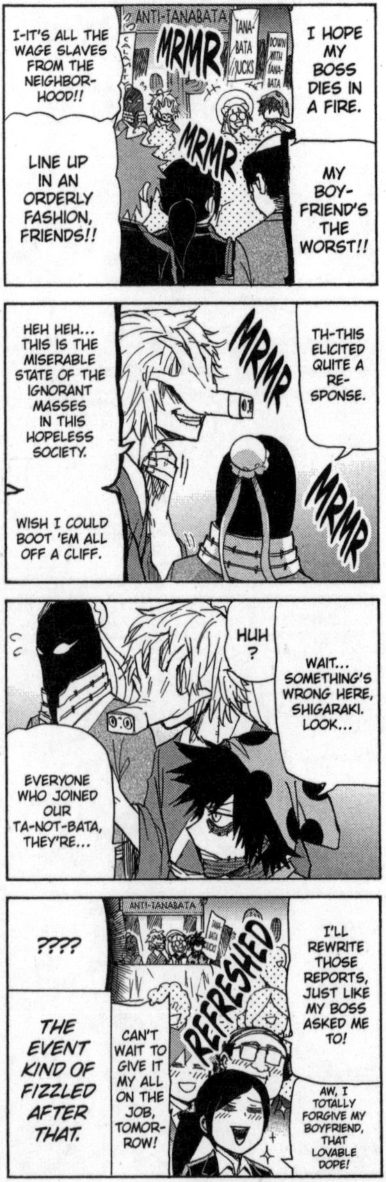
I HOPE MY BOSS DIES IN A FIRE.
ANTI-TANABATA
TANABATA SUCKS
DOWN WITH TANABATA
MRMR
I-IT'S ALL THE WAGE SLAVES FROM THE NEIGHBORHOOD!!
MRMR
MY BOYFRIEND'S THE WORST!!
LINE UP IN AN ORDERLY FASHION, FRIENDS!!
TH-THIS ELICITED QUITE A RESPONSE.
MRMR
HEH HEH... THIS IS THE MISERABLE STATE OF THE IGNORANT MASSES IN THIS HOPELESS SOCIETY.
MRMR
WISH I COULD BOOT 'EM ALL OFF A CLIFF.
HUH?
WAIT... SOMETHING'S WRONG HERE, SHIGARAKI. LOOK...
EVERYONE WHO JOINED OUR TA-NOT-BATA, THEY'RE...
I'LL REWRITE THOSE REPORTS, JUST LIKE MY BOSS ASKED ME TO!
REFRESHED
ANTI-TANABATA
TANABATA SUCKS
????
AW, I TOTALLY FORGIVE MY BOYFRIEND, THAT LOVABLE DOPE!
CAN'T WAIT TO GIVE IT MY ALL ON THE JOB, TOMORROW!
THE EVENT KIND OF FIZZLED AFTER THAT.

THE BONUS CONTENT STARTS HERE!! DON'T MISS HORIKOSHI'S AMAZING CONTRIBUTION!!

IT'S GOT ME FLOATING ON CLOUD NINE... OWW! DANG IT, OCHACO!!

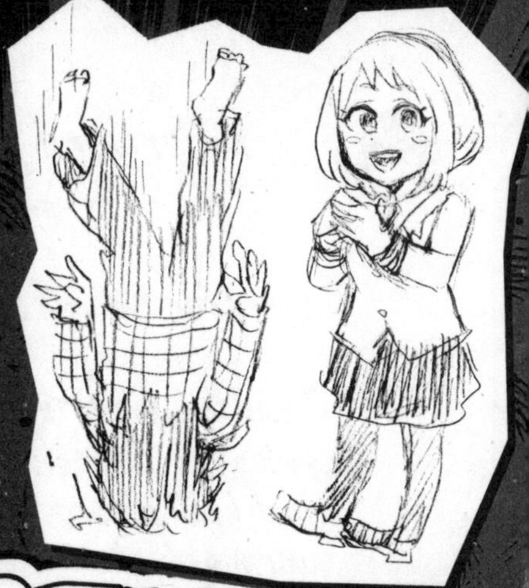

BONUS STUFF!!

MY HERO ACADEMIA SMASH

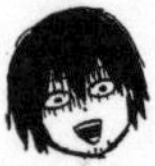

Afterword in Advance

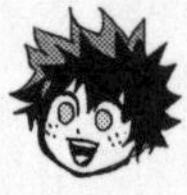

Sorry for the weirdly placed afterword again!

I say this every time, but thanks a ton for picking up Smash!! It's thanks to you people that I can afford to eat food, sleep in a warm bed, etc.

Also, thank you to Horikoshi himself and my editor Koike, who watch over me and give me guidance. I express my appreciation to them often (about once every two hours)!!

Anyway, the bonus bits start on the next page!! We'll talk again in volume 5!! See ya!!

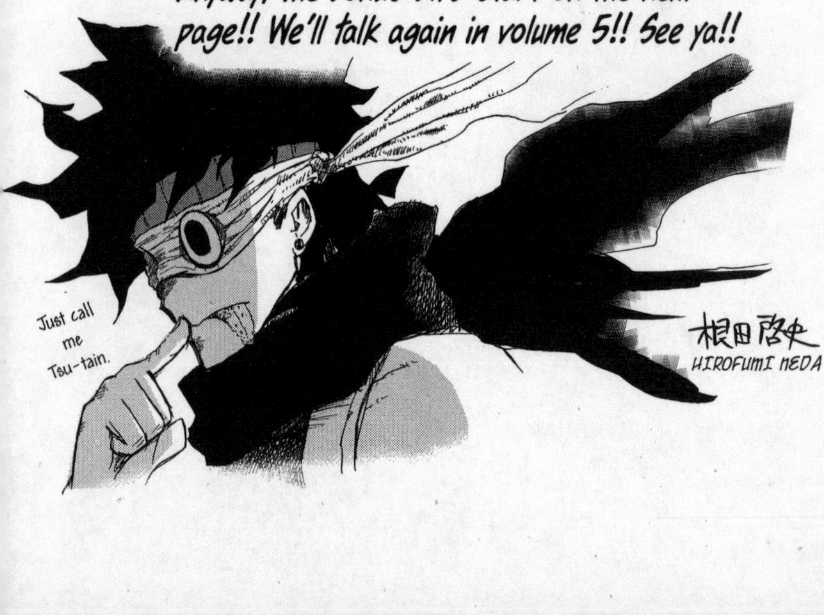
Just call me Tsu-tain.
根田啓史
HIROFUMI NEDA

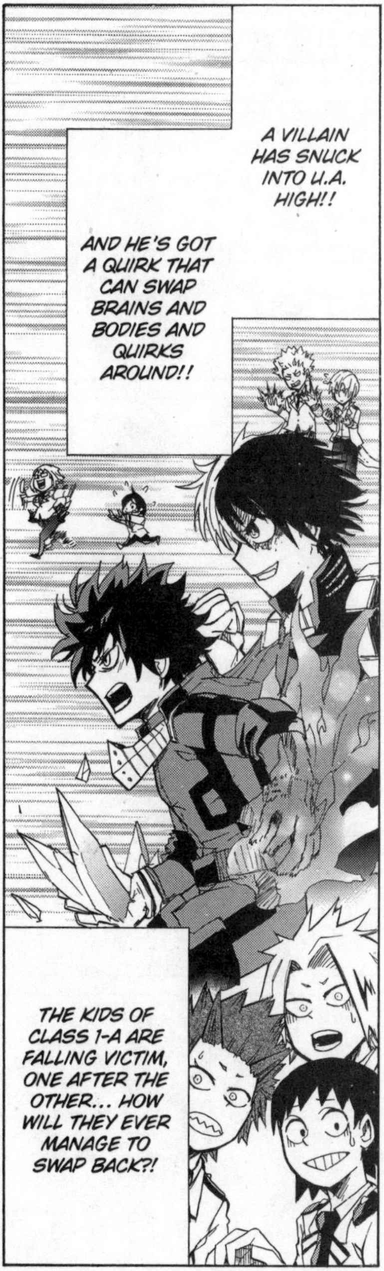
A VILLAIN HAS SNUCK INTO U.A. HIGH!!
AND HE'S GOT A QUIRK THAT CAN SWAP BRAINS AND BODIES AND QUIRKS AROUND!!
THE KIDS OF CLASS 1-A ARE FALLING VICTIM, ONE AFTER THE OTHER... HOW WILL THEY EVER MANAGE TO SWAP BACK?!

FREAKY THURSDAY

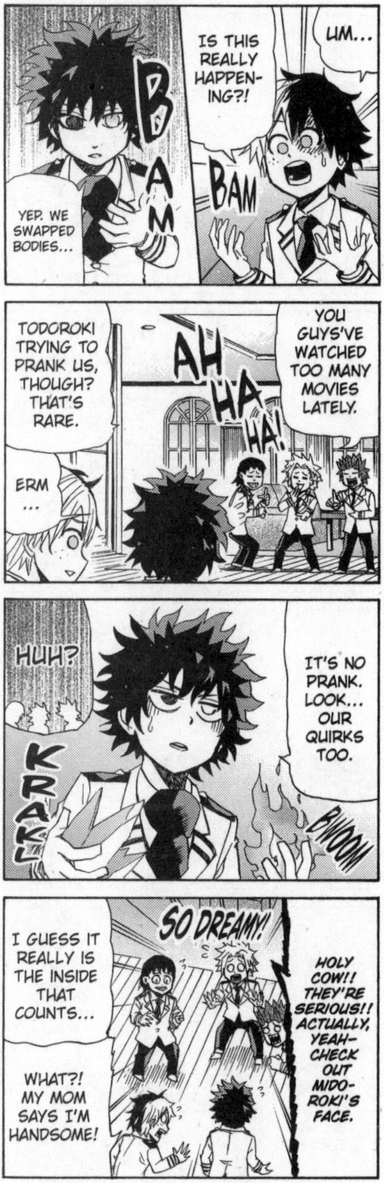
UM...
IS THIS REALLY HAPPEN-ING?!
BAM
BAM
YEP. WE SWAPPED BODIES...
YOU GUYS'VE WATCHED TOO MANY MOVIES LATELY.
AH HA HA!
TODOROKI TRYING TO PRANK US, THOUGH? THAT'S RARE.
ERM ...
IT'S NO PRANK. LOOK... OUR QUIRKS TOO.
BWOOM
HUH?
KRAK
HOLY COW!! THEY'RE SERIOUS!! ACTUALLY, YEAH-CHECK OUT MIDO-ROKI'S FACE.
SO DREAMY!
I GUESS IT REALLY IS THE INSIDE THAT COUNTS...
WHAT?! MY MOM SAYS I'M HANDSOME!

FROM DRAB TO FAB

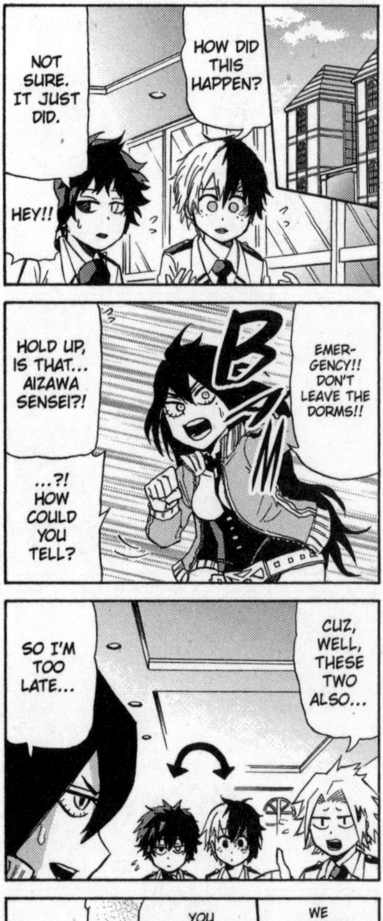
HOW DID THIS HAPPEN?
NOT SURE. IT JUST DID.
HEY!!
EMERGENCY!! DON'T LEAVE THE DORMS!!
BAM
HOLD UP, IS THAT... AIZAWA SENSEI?!
...?! HOW COULD YOU TELL?
CUZ, WELL, THESE TWO ALSO...
SO I'M TOO LATE...
WE TEACHERS ARE TRYING TO GET A HANDLE ON THE SITUATION, SO...
YOU WOULDN'T THINK IT, BUT THAT'S ACTUALLY A NICE, FRESH LOOK.
DON'T BE DISGUSTING!!
JOLT
WHAT IS IT?
For Midnight...
STOP STARING AND GO TELL THE OTHERS!!

DOWNSIDES AND UPSIDES TO CUP SIZE

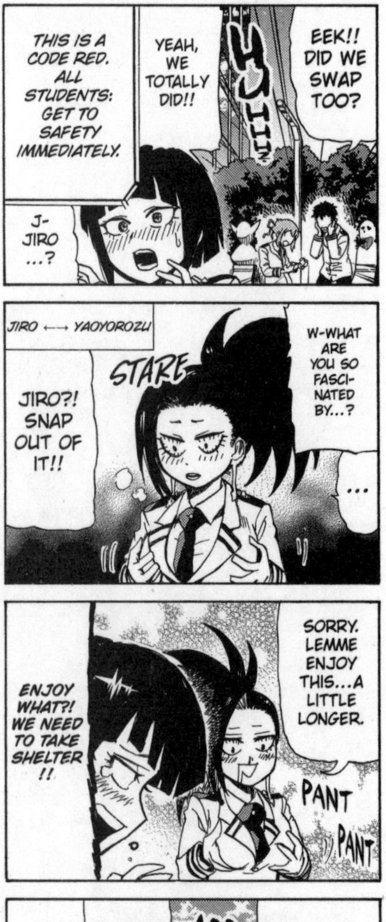
EEK!! DID WE SWAP TOO?
YEAH, WE TOTALLY DID!!
THIS IS A CODE RED. ALL STUDENTS: GET TO SAFETY IMMEDIATELY.
J-JIRO...?
W-WHAT ARE YOU SO FASCINATED BY...?
STARE
JIRO ←→ YAOYOROZU
JIRO?! SNAP OUT OF IT!!
...
SORRY. LEMME ENJOY THIS...A LITTLE LONGER.
PANT PANT
ENJOY WHAT?! WE NEED TO TAKE SHELTER!!
AH, AND HERE COMES THE BACKACHE I'VE HEARD SO MUCH ABOUT!!
GRP
LEMME GIVE YOU A MASSAGE ONCE WE SWITCH BACK, OKAY?
EHH?! IF YOU INSIST? TH-THANK YOU?
OH DEAR
...

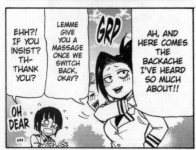

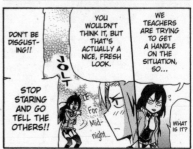

The Tail of Kacchan

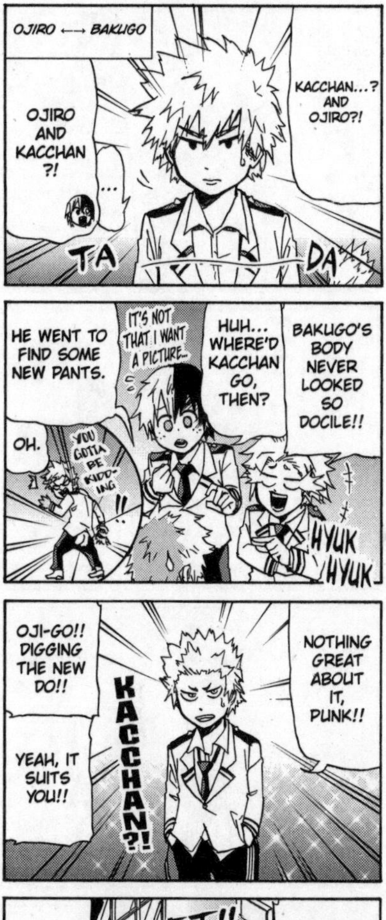
KACCHAN...? AND OJIRO?!
OJIRO ⟷ BAKUGO
OJIRO AND KACCHAN ?!
...
DA
TA
BAKUGO'S BODY NEVER LOOKED SO DOCILE!!
HUH... WHERE'D KACCHAN GO, THEN?
IT'S NOT THAT I WANT A PICTURE...
HE WENT TO FIND SOME NEW PANTS.
OH.
YOU GOTTA BE KIDDING !!
HYUK HYUK
NOTHING GREAT ABOUT IT, PUNK!!
KACCHAN?!
OJI-GO!! DIGGING THE NEW DO!!
YEAH, IT SUITS YOU!!
GYA HA HA!! SEEING 'EM LINED UP LIKE THAT, THOUGH... GYA HA HA!!
PFFFT!!
WHAT'S SO FUNNY?!
UM... EVERYTHING?
YOU'RE ALL DEAD!!

Abandon Ship

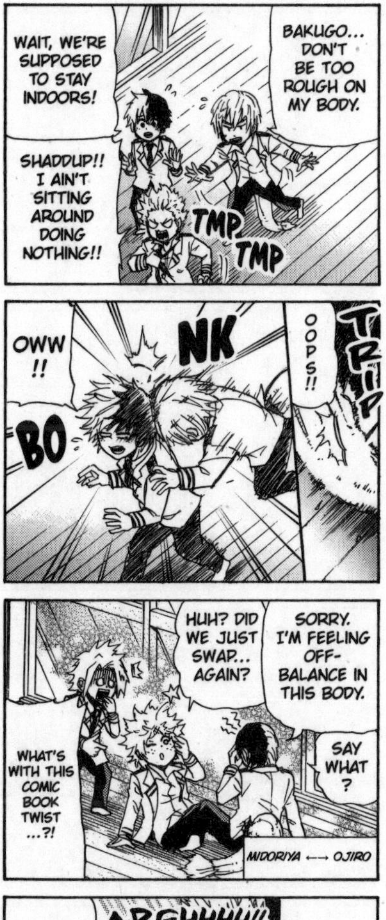
BAKUGO... DON'T BE TOO ROUGH ON MY BODY.
WAIT, WE'RE SUPPOSED TO STAY INDOORS!
SHADDUP!! I AIN'T SITTING AROUND DOING NOTHING!!
TMP TMP
TRIP
OOPS!!
NK
OWW !!
BO
SORRY. I'M FEELING OFF-BALANCE IN THIS BODY.
HUH? DID WE JUST SWAP... AGAIN?
SAY WHAT?
WHAT'S WITH THIS COMIC BOOK TWIST ...?!
MIDORIYA ⟷ OJIRO
N-NO. NO FREAKING WAY!! OUTTA MY BODY, NOW!!
ARGHHHH!!
I DUNNO HOW TO UNDO THIS THOUGH...
SCREW IT!! MY BODY'S ALREADY TAINTED! I DON'T NEED IT ANYMORE!! PREPARE TO DIE!!
NO, NO... WAIT !!

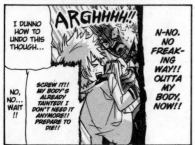

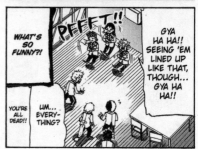

QUALITY TIME

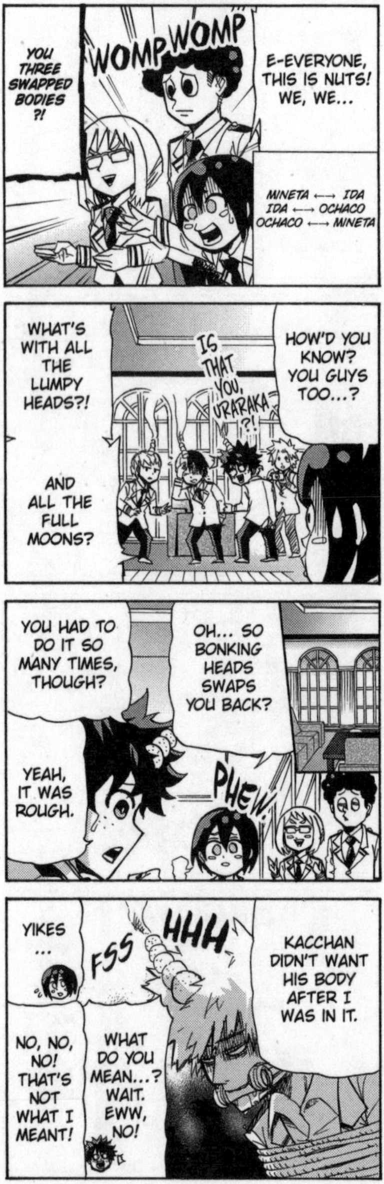
E-EVERYONE, THIS IS NUTS! WE, WE...
WOMP WOMP
YOU THREE SWAPPED BODIES ?!
MINETA ←→ IDA
IDA ←→ OCHACO
OCHACO ←→ MINETA
HOW'D YOU KNOW? YOU GUYS TOO...?
IS THAT YOU, URARAKA ?!
WHAT'S WITH ALL THE LUMPY HEADS?!
AND ALL THE FULL MOONS?
OH... SO BONKING HEADS SWAPS YOU BACK?
YOU HAD TO DO IT SO MANY TIMES, THOUGH?
PHEW
YEAH, IT WAS ROUGH.
KACCHAN DIDN'T WANT HIS BODY AFTER I WAS IN IT.
HHH
FSS
YIKES ...
WHAT DO YOU MEAN...? WAIT. EWW, NO!
NO, NO, NO! THAT'S NOT WHAT I MEANT!

FORBIDDEN FRUIT

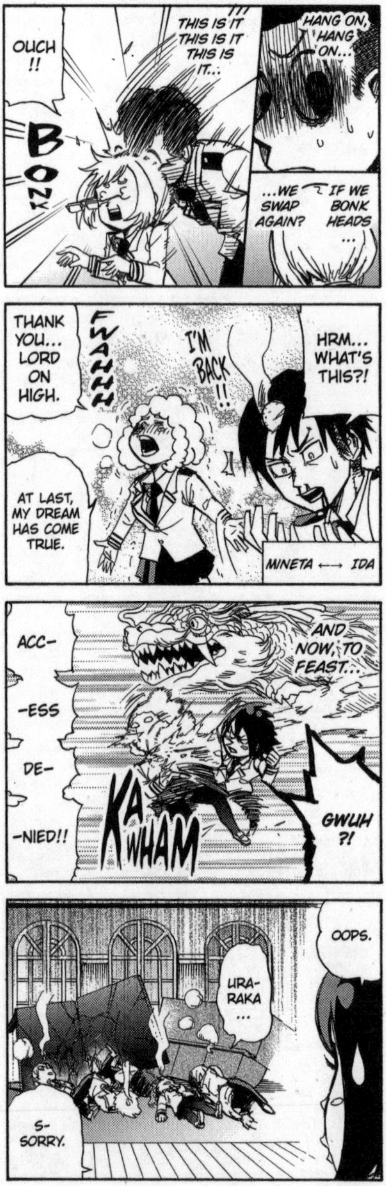
HANG ON, HANG ON...
THIS IS IT THIS IS IT THIS IS IT...
OUCH !!
IF WE BONK HEADS ...
...WE SWAP AGAIN?
BONK
HRM... WHAT'S THIS?!
I'M BACK !!
FWAHHH
THANK YOU... LORD ON HIGH.
AT LAST, MY DREAM HAS COME TRUE.
MINETA ←→ IDA
AND NOW, TO FEAST...
ACC-
-ESS
DE-
-NIED!!
GWUH ?!
KA WHAM
OOPS.
URA-RAKA ...
S-SORRY.

SUICIDE BOMBER

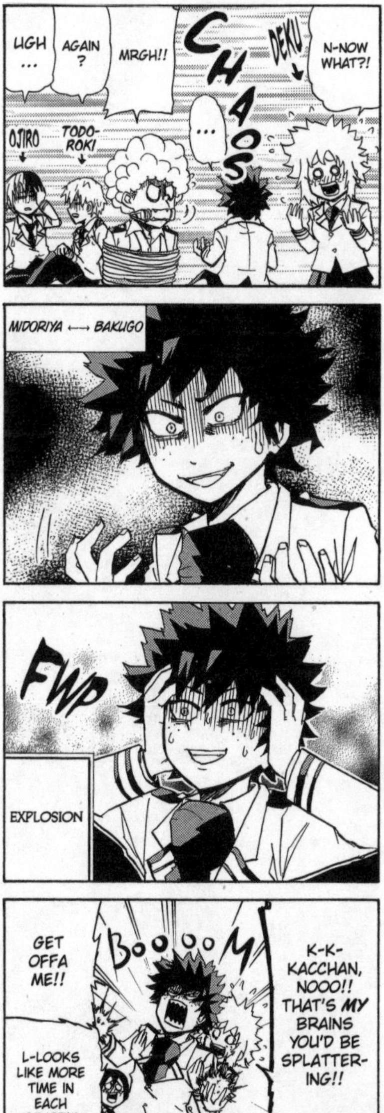
N-NOW WHAT?!
DEKU
CHAOS
MRGH!!
AGAIN ?
UGH ...
...
TODO-ROKI
OJIRO
MIDORIYA ⟷ BAKUGO
FWP
EXPLOSION
K-K-KACCHAN, NOOO!! THAT'S MY BRAINS YOU'D BE SPLATTERING!!
BOOOOM
GET OFFA ME!!
L-LOOKS LIKE MORE TIME IN EACH OTHER'S BODIES, DEKU...?

STRANGEREST THINGS

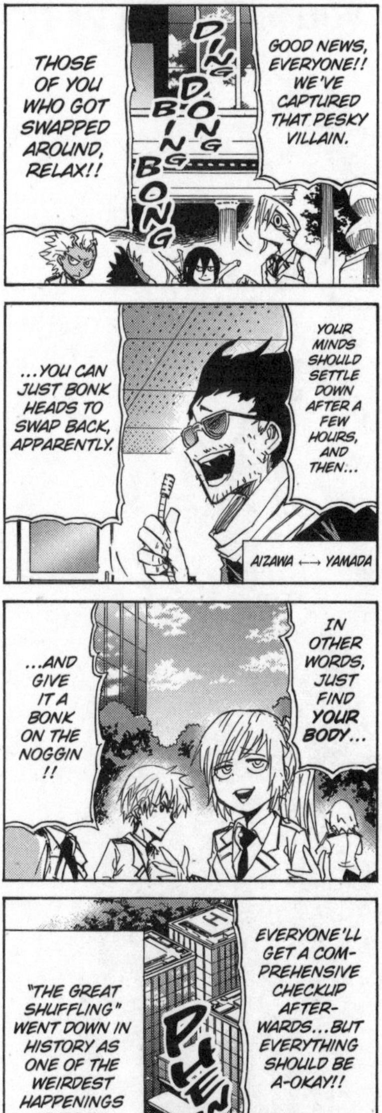
GOOD NEWS, EVERYONE!! WE'VE CAPTURED THAT PESKY VILLAIN.
DING DONG BING BONG
THOSE OF YOU WHO GOT SWAPPED AROUND, RELAX!!
YOUR MINDS SHOULD SETTLE DOWN AFTER A FEW HOURS, AND THEN...
...YOU CAN JUST BONK HEADS TO SWAP BACK, APPARENTLY.
AIZAWA ⟷ YAMADA
IN OTHER WORDS, JUST FIND YOUR BODY...
...AND GIVE IT A BONK ON THE NOGGIN!!
EVERYONE'LL GET A COMPREHENSIVE CHECKUP AFTERWARDS...BUT EVERYTHING SHOULD BE A-OKAY!!
PJEW
"THE GREAT SHUFFLING" WENT DOWN IN HISTORY AS ONE OF THE WEIRDEST HAPPENINGS EVER AT U.A....

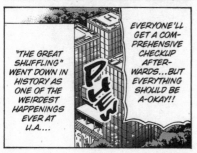

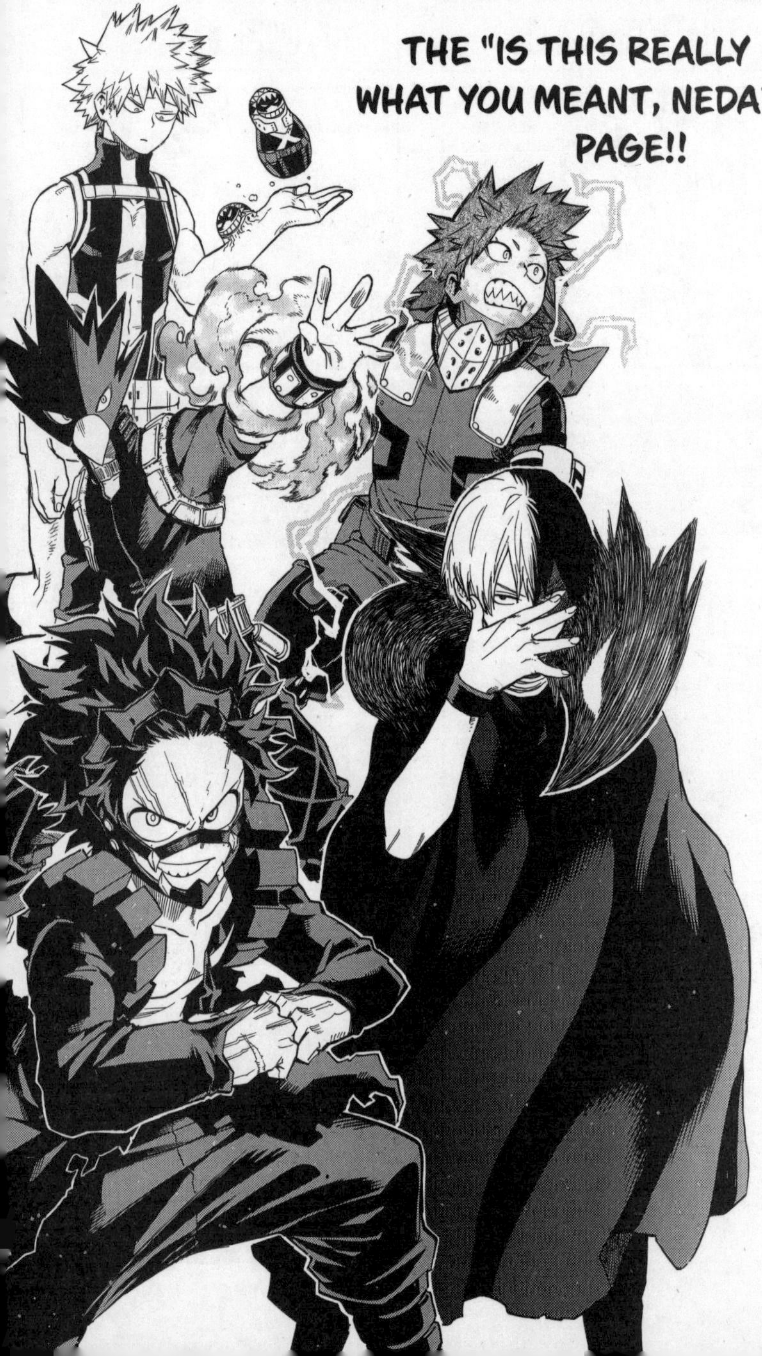
THE "IS THIS REALLY WHAT YOU MEANT, NEDA?" PAGE!!

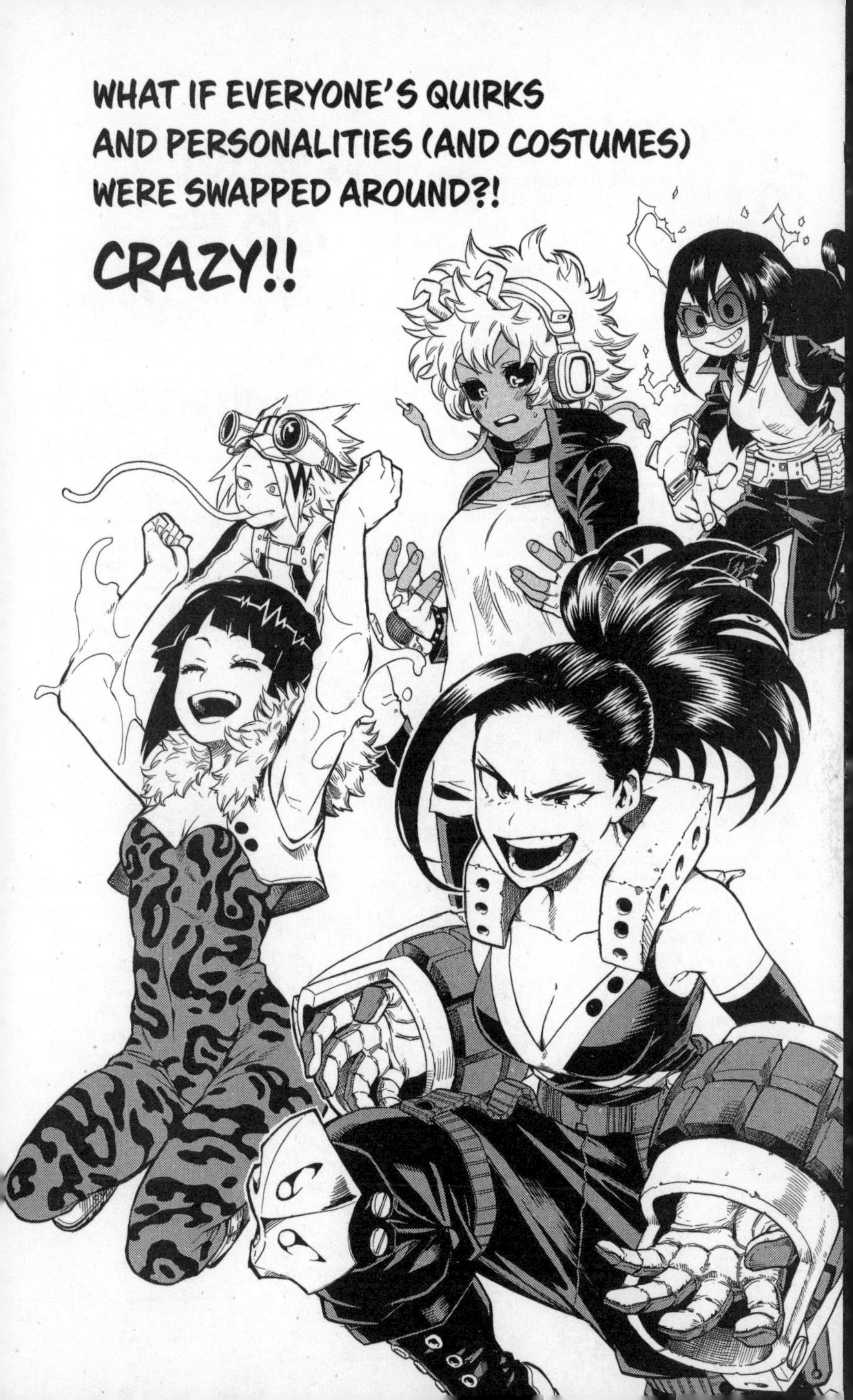
WHAT IF EVERYONE'S QUIRKS
AND PERSONALITIES (AND COSTUMES)
WERE SWAPPED AROUND?!
CRAZY!!

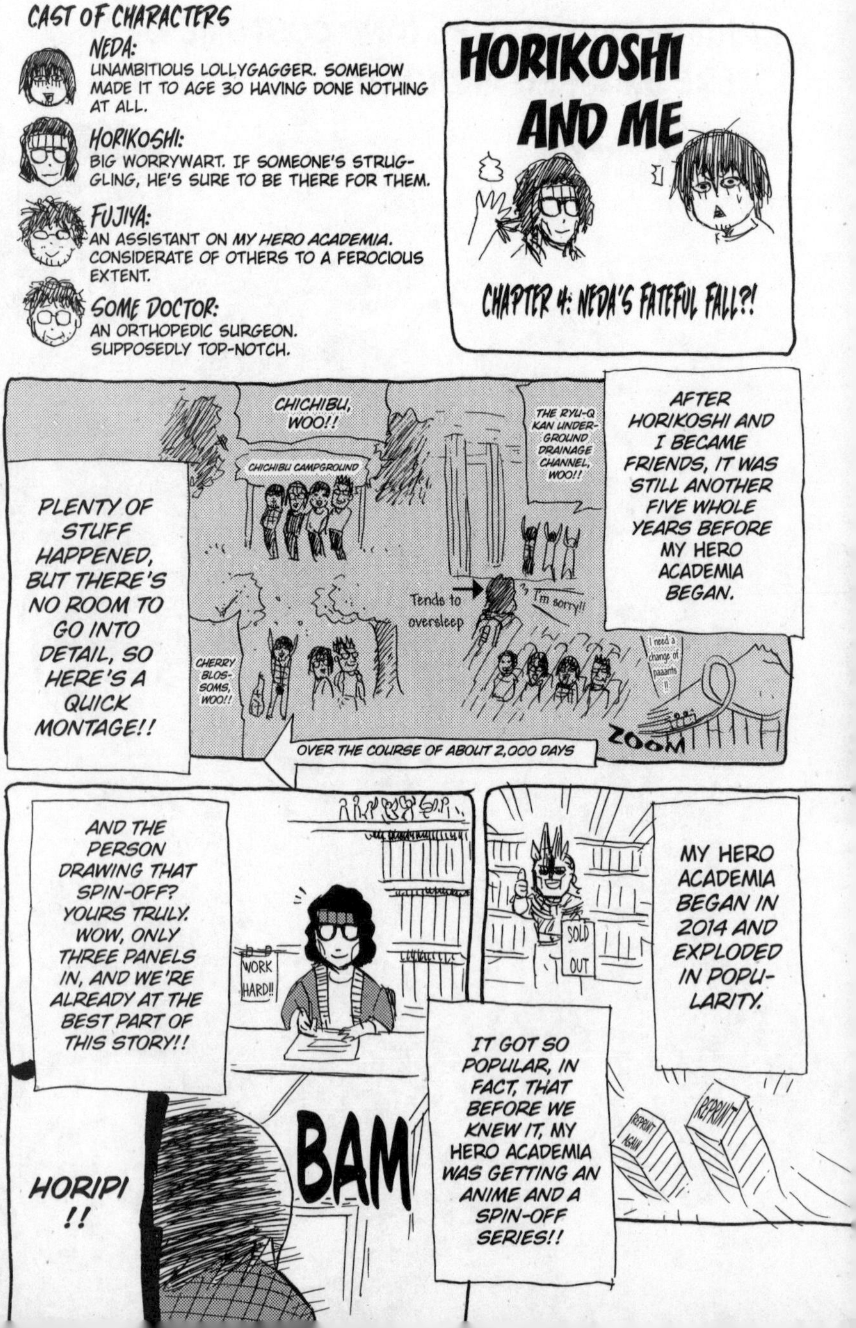
HORIKOSHI AND ME
CHAPTER 4: NEDA'S FATEFUL FALL?!
CAST OF CHARACTERS
NEDA:
UNAMBITIOUS LOLLYGAGGER. SOMEHOW MADE IT TO AGE 30 HAVING DONE NOTHING AT ALL.
HORIKOSHI:
BIG WORRYWART. IF SOMEONE'S STRUGGLING, HE'S SURE TO BE THERE FOR THEM.
FUJIYA:
AN ASSISTANT ON MY HERO ACADEMIA. CONSIDERATE OF OTHERS TO A FEROCIOUS EXTENT.
SOME DOCTOR:
AN ORTHOPEDIC SURGEON. SUPPOSEDLY TOP-NOTCH.
AFTER HORIKOSHI AND I BECAME FRIENDS, IT WAS STILL ANOTHER FIVE WHOLE YEARS BEFORE MY HERO ACADEMIA BEGAN.
THE RYU-Q KAN UNDERGROUND DRAINAGE CHANNEL, WOO!!
CHICHIBU, WOO!!
CHICHIBU CAMPGROUND
I'm sorry!!
Tends to oversleep
I need a change of paaaants!!
ZOOM
CHERRY BLOSSOMS, WOO!!
PLENTY OF STUFF HAPPENED, BUT THERE'S NO ROOM TO GO INTO DETAIL, SO HERE'S A QUICK MONTAGE!!
OVER THE COURSE OF ABOUT 2,000 DAYS
MY HERO ACADEMIA BEGAN IN 2014 AND EXPLODED IN POPULARITY.
SOLD OUT
REPRINT
REPRINT AGAIN
IT GOT SO POPULAR, IN FACT, THAT BEFORE WE KNEW IT, MY HERO ACADEMIA WAS GETTING AN ANIME AND A SPIN-OFF SERIES!!
AND THE PERSON DRAWING THAT SPIN-OFF? YOURS TRULY. WOW, ONLY THREE PANELS IN, AND WE'RE ALREADY AT THE BEST PART OF THIS STORY!!
WORK HARD!!
BAM
HORIPI!!

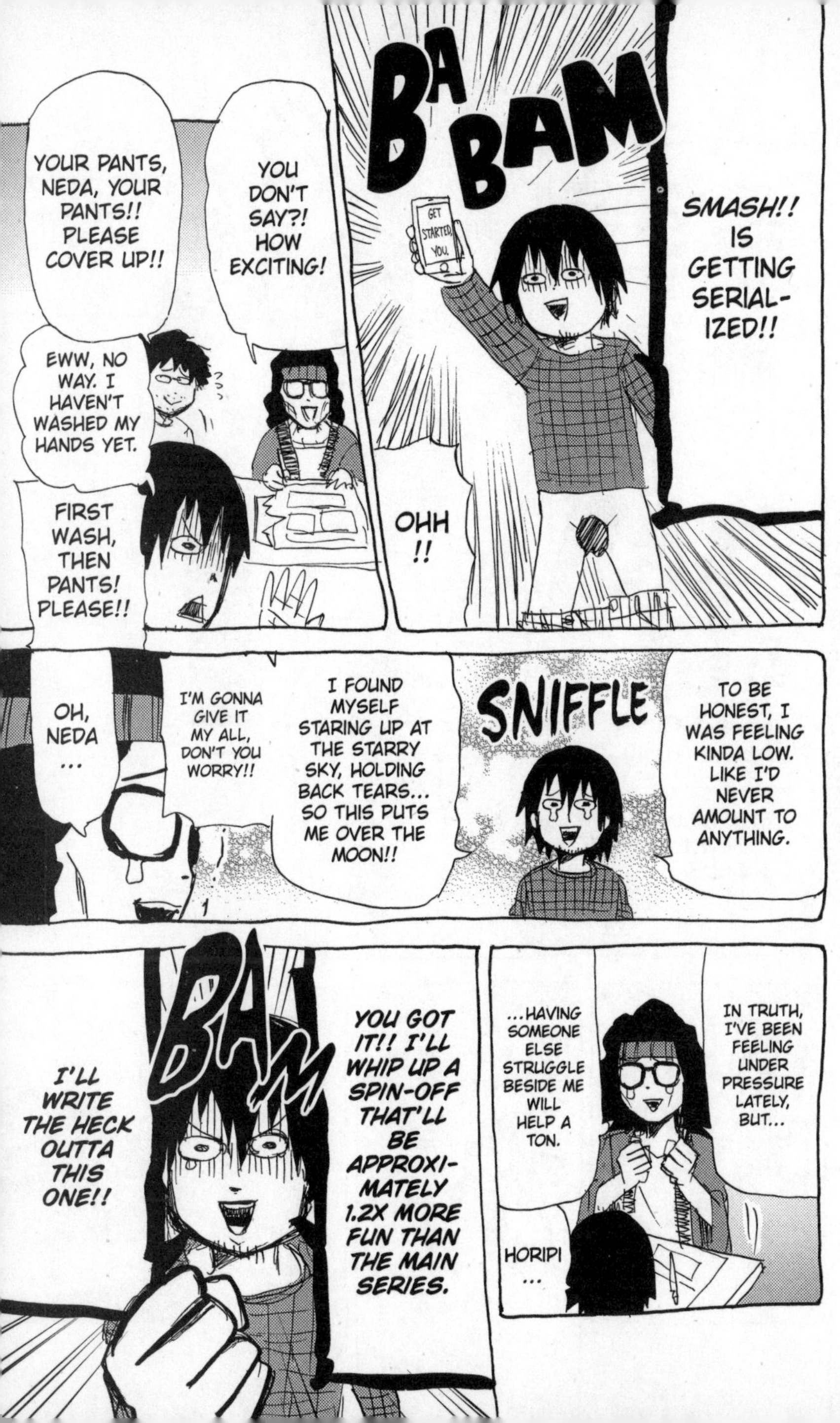

BA BAM
GET STARTED, YOU.
SMASH!! IS GETTING SERIAL-IZED!!
OHH!!
YOU DON'T SAY?! HOW EXCITING!
YOUR PANTS, NEDA, YOUR PANTS!! PLEASE COVER UP!!
EWW, NO WAY. I HAVEN'T WASHED MY HANDS YET.
FIRST WASH, THEN PANTS! PLEASE!!
TO BE HONEST, I WAS FEELING KINDA LOW. LIKE I'D NEVER AMOUNT TO ANYTHING.
SNIFFLE
I FOUND MYSELF STARING UP AT THE STARRY SKY, HOLDING BACK TEARS... SO THIS PUTS ME OVER THE MOON!!
I'M GONNA GIVE IT MY ALL, DON'T YOU WORRY!!
OH, NEDA...
IN TRUTH, I'VE BEEN FEELING UNDER PRESSURE LATELY, BUT...
...HAVING SOMEONE ELSE STRUGGLE BESIDE ME WILL HELP A TON.
HORIPI...
YOU GOT IT!! I'LL WHIP UP A SPIN-OFF THAT'LL BE APPROXI-MATELY 1.2X MORE FUN THAN THE MAIN SERIES.
BAM
I'LL WRITE THE HECK OUTTA THIS ONE!!

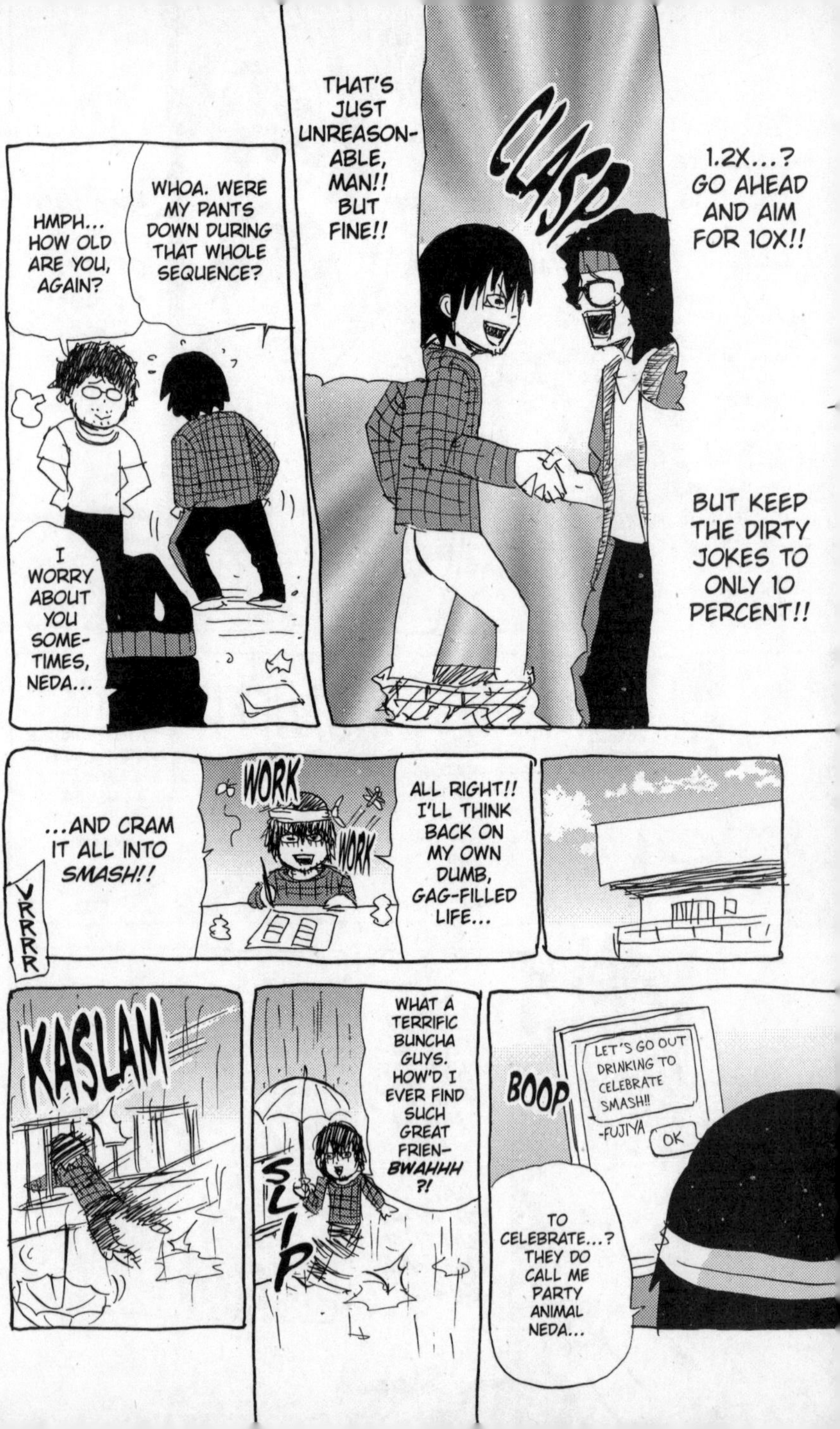
1.2X...? GO AHEAD AND AIM FOR 10X!!
CLASP
THAT'S JUST UNREASON-ABLE, MAN!! BUT FINE!!
BUT KEEP THE DIRTY JOKES TO ONLY 10 PERCENT!!
WHOA. WERE MY PANTS DOWN DURING THAT WHOLE SEQUENCE?
HMPH... HOW OLD ARE YOU, AGAIN?
I WORRY ABOUT YOU SOME-TIMES, NEDA...
ALL RIGHT!! I'LL THINK BACK ON MY OWN DUMB, GAG-FILLED LIFE...
WORK
WORK
...AND CRAM IT ALL INTO *SMASH!!*
VRRRR
LET'S GO OUT DRINKING TO CELEBRATE SMASH!! -FUJIYA
OK
BOOP
TO CELEBRATE...? THEY DO CALL ME PARTY ANIMAL NEDA...
WHAT A TERRIFIC BUNCHA GUYS. HOW'D I EVER FIND SUCH GREAT FRIEN-*BWAHHH?!*
SLIP
KASLAM

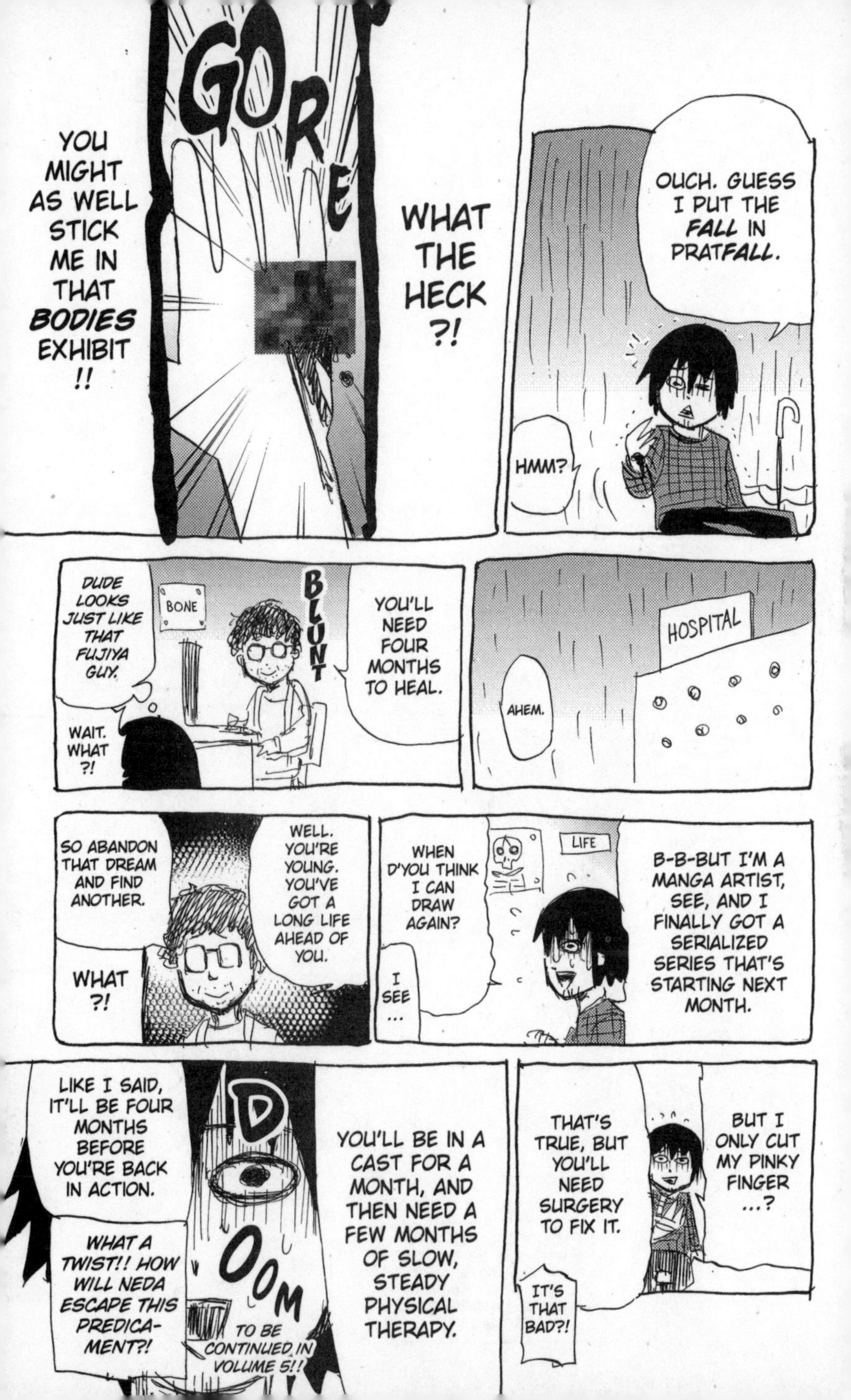
OUCH. GUESS I PUT THE ***FALL*** IN PRAT***FALL***.
HMM?
WHAT THE HECK ?!
GORE
YOU MIGHT AS WELL STICK ME IN THAT ***BODIES*** EXHIBIT !!
HOSPITAL
AHEM.
YOU'LL NEED FOUR MONTHS TO HEAL.
BLUNT
BONE
DUDE LOOKS JUST LIKE THAT FUJIYA GUY.
WAIT. WHAT ?!
B-B-BUT I'M A MANGA ARTIST, SEE, AND I FINALLY GOT A SERIALIZED SERIES THAT'S STARTING NEXT MONTH.
LIFE
WHEN D'YOU THINK I CAN DRAW AGAIN?
I SEE ...
WELL. YOU'RE YOUNG. YOU'VE GOT A LONG LIFE AHEAD OF YOU.
SO ABANDON THAT DREAM AND FIND ANOTHER.
WHAT ?!
BUT I ONLY CUT MY PINKY FINGER ...?
THAT'S TRUE, BUT YOU'LL NEED SURGERY TO FIX IT.
IT'S THAT BAD?!
YOU'LL BE IN A CAST FOR A MONTH, AND THEN NEED A FEW MONTHS OF SLOW, STEADY PHYSICAL THERAPY.
LIKE I SAID, IT'LL BE FOUR MONTHS BEFORE YOU'RE BACK IN ACTION.
DOOM
WHAT A TWIST!! HOW WILL NEDA ESCAPE THIS PREDICA-MENT?!
TO BE CONTINUED IN VOLUME 5!!

OUR PARENTS' ACADEMIA

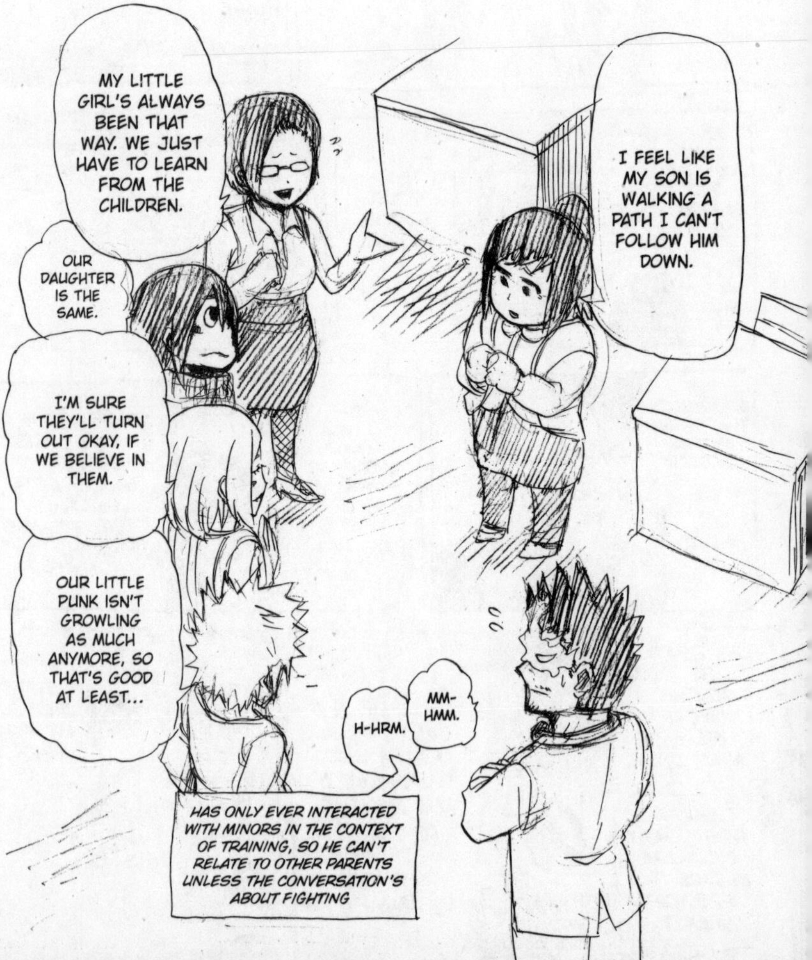
I FEEL LIKE MY SON IS WALKING A PATH I CAN'T FOLLOW HIM DOWN.
MY LITTLE GIRL'S ALWAYS BEEN THAT WAY. WE JUST HAVE TO LEARN FROM THE CHILDREN.
OUR DAUGHTER IS THE SAME.
I'M SURE THEY'LL TURN OUT OKAY, IF WE BELIEVE IN THEM.
OUR LITTLE PUNK ISN'T GROWLING AS MUCH ANYMORE, SO THAT'S GOOD AT LEAST...
MM-HMM.
H-HRM.
HAS ONLY EVER INTERACTED WITH MINORS IN THE CONTEXT OF TRAINING, SO HE CAN'T RELATE TO OTHER PARENTS UNLESS THE CONVERSATION'S ABOUT FIGHTING

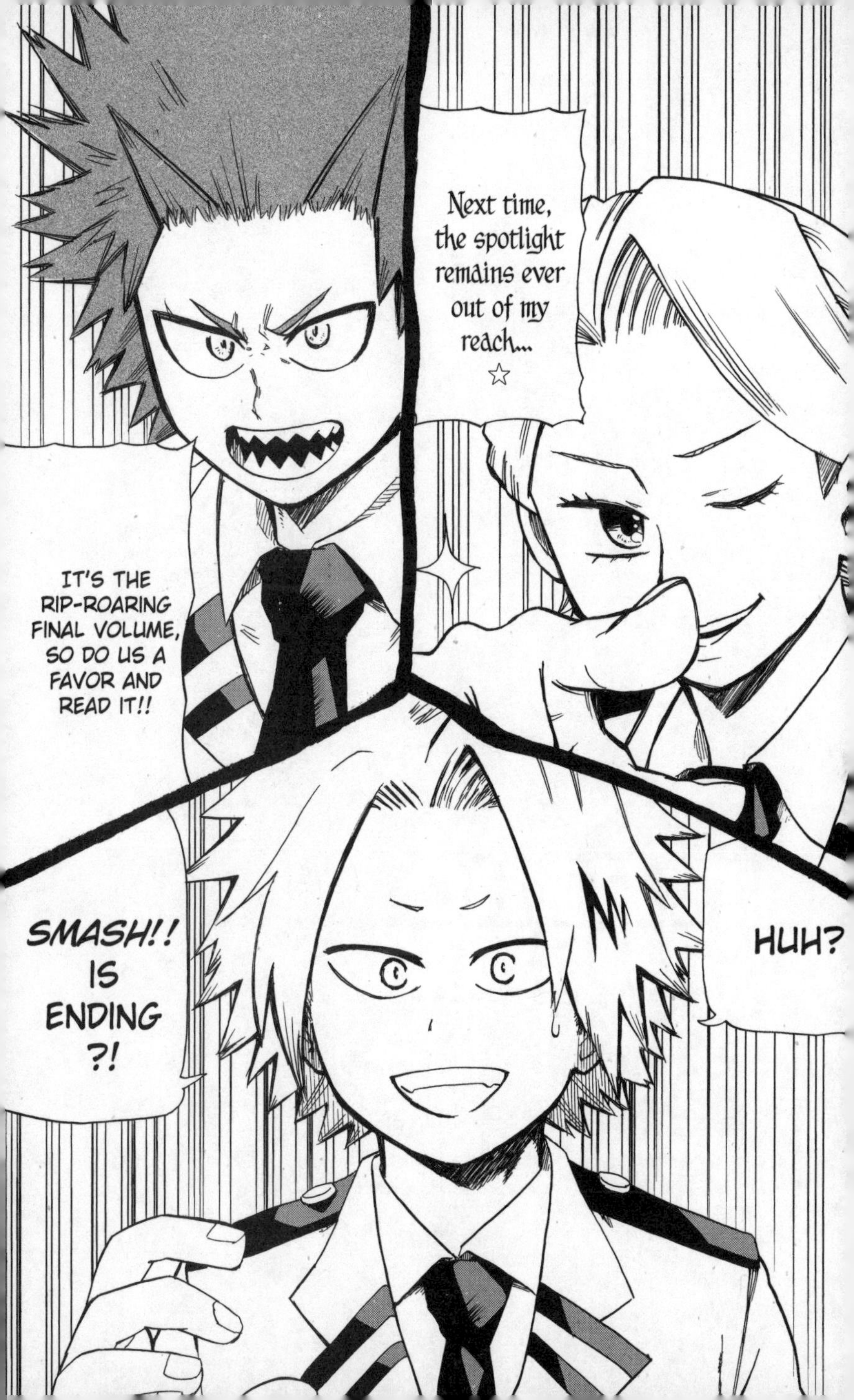
Next time, the spotlight remains ever out of my reach... ☆
IT'S THE RIP-ROARING FINAL VOLUME, SO DO US A FAVOR AND READ IT!!
HUH?
SMASH!! IS ENDING?!

MY HERO ACADEMIA

SCHOOL BRIEFS

ORIGINAL STORY BY KOHEI HORIKOSHI **WRITTEN BY** ANRI YOSHI

Prose short stories featuring the everyday school lives of My Hero Academia's fan-favorite characters!

Dr. STONE

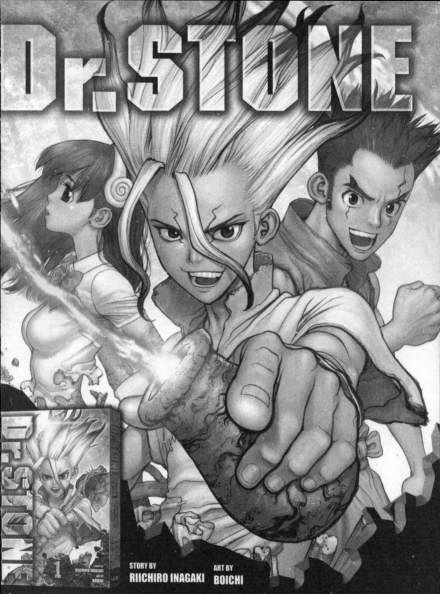

STORY BY
RIICHIRO INAGAKI

ART BY
BOICHI

One fateful day, all of humanity turned to stone. Many millennia later, Taiju frees himself from petrification and finds himself surrounded by statues. The situation looks grim—until he runs into his science-loving friend Senku! Together they plan to restart civilization with the power of science!

DEMON SLAYER

KIMETSU NO YAIBA

Story and Art by

KOYOHARU GOTOUGE

In Taisho-era Japan, kindhearted Tanjiro Kamado makes a living selling charcoal. But his peaceful life is shattered when a demon slaughters his entire family. His little sister Nezuko is the only survivor, but she has been transformed into a demon herself! Tanjiro sets out on a dangerous journey to find a way to return his sister to normal and destroy the demon who ruined his life.

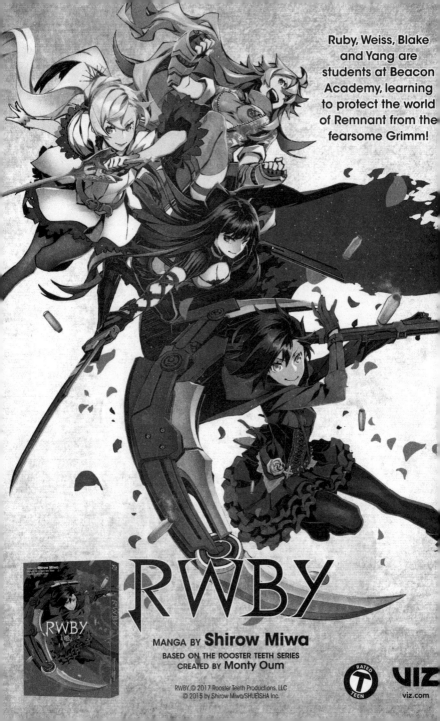

Ruby, Weiss, Blake and Yang are students at Beacon Academy, learning to protect the world of Remnant from the fearsome Grimm!

RWBY

MANGA BY **Shirow Miwa**

BASED ON THE ROOSTER TEETH SERIES
CREATED BY **Monty Oum**

RATED TEEN

VIZ
viz.com

YOU'RE READING THE WRONG WAY!!

My Hero Academia: Smash!! reads right to left, starting in the upper-right corner. Japanese is read right to left, meaning that action, sound effects and word balloon order are completely reversed from English order.

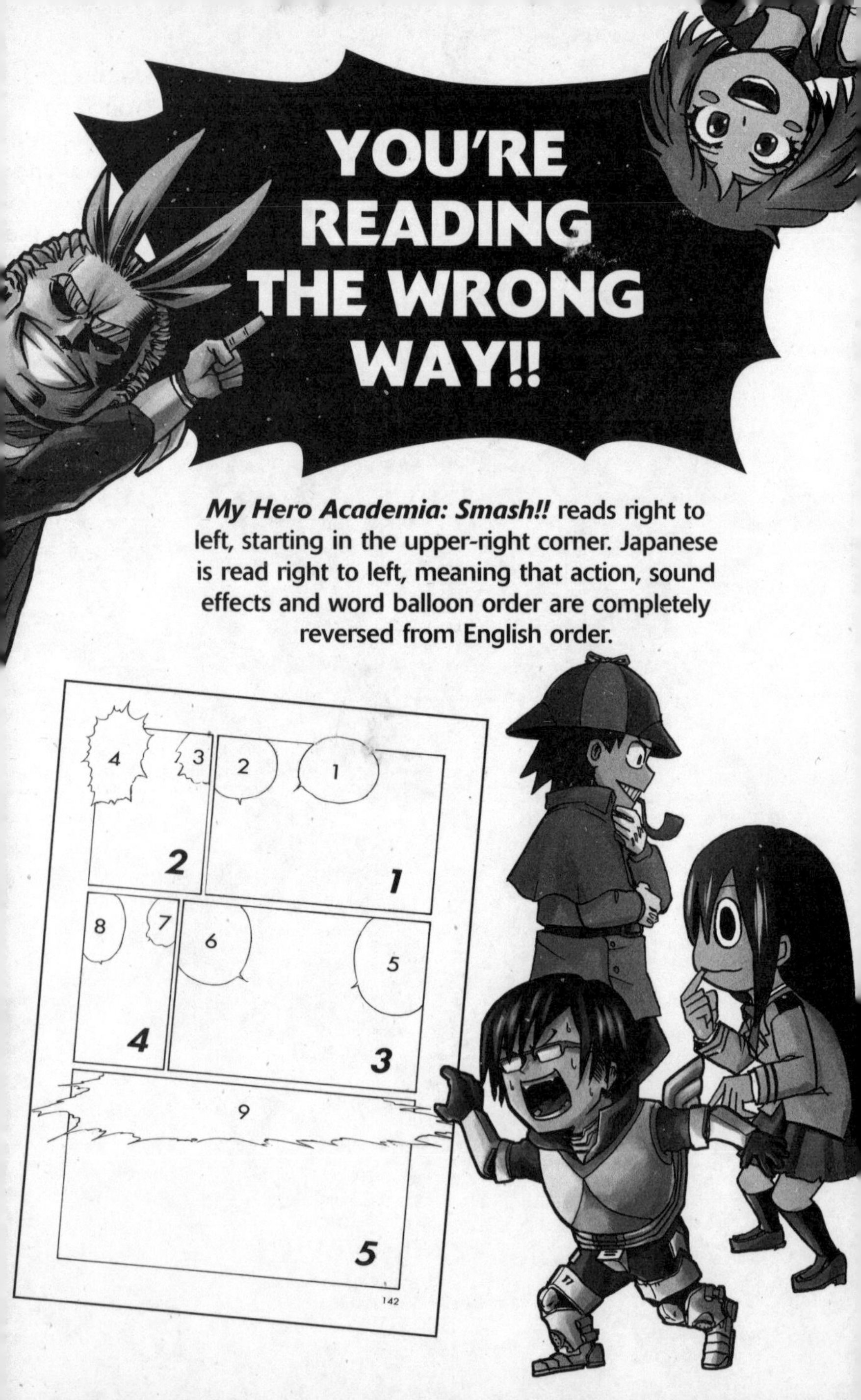
1
2
3
4
5
6
7
8
9
1
2
3
4
5
142